Lecture Notes in Computer Science

Edited by G. Goos, J. Hartmanis, and J. van Lee

Springer
Berlin
Heidelberg
New York
Barcelona
Hong Kong
London
Milan
Paris
Tokyo

Dror G. Feitelson   Larry Rudolph (Eds.)

Job Scheduling Strategies for Parallel Processing

7th International Workshop, JSSPP 2001
Cambridge, MA, USA, June 16, 2001
Revised Papers

Springer

Series Editors

Gerhard Goos, Karlsruhe University, Germany
Juris Hartmanis, Cornell University, NY, USA
Jan van Leeuwen, Utrecht University, The Netherlands

Volume Editors

Dror G. Feitelson
The Hebrew University
School of Computer Science and Engineering
91904 Jerusalem, Israel
E-mail: feit@cs.huji.ac.il

Larry Rudolph
Massachusetts Institute of Technology
Laboratory for Computer Science
Cambridge, MA 02139, USA
E-mail: rudolph@lcs.mit.edu

Cataloging-in-Publication Data applied for

Die Deutsche Bibliothek - CIP-Einheitsaufnahme

Job scheduling strategies for parallel processing : 7th international
workshop ; revised papers / JSSPP 2001, Cambridge, MA, USA, June 16, 2001.
Dror G. Feitelson ; Larry Rudolph (ed.). - Berlin ; Heidelberg ; New York ;
Barcelona ; Hong Kong ; London ; Milan ; Paris ; Tokyo : Springer, 2001
    (Lecture notes in computer science ; Vol. 2221)
    ISBN 3-540-42817-8

CR Subject Classification (1998): D.4, D.1.3, F.2.2, C.1.2, B.2.1, B.6, F.1.2

ISSN 0302-9743
ISBN 3-540-42817-8 Springer-Verlag Berlin Heidelberg New York

Springer-Verlag Berlin Heidelberg New York
a member of BertelsmannSpringer Science+Business Media GmbH

http://www.springer.de

© Springer-Verlag Berlin Heidelberg 2001
Printed in Germany

Typesetting: Camera-ready by author, data conversion by Steingräber Satztechnik GmbH
Printed on acid-free paper   SPIN: 10840923   06/3142   5 4 3 2 1 0

Preface

This volume contains the papers presented at the seventh workshop on Job Scheduling Strategies for Parallel Processing, which was held in conjunction with the SIGMETRICS 2001 Conference in Cambridge, MA, on June 16, 2001. The papers have been through a complete refereeing process, with the full version being read and evaluated by five to seven members of the program committee. We would like to take this opportunity to thank the program committee, Andrea Arpaci-Dusseau, Steve Chapin, Allen Downey, Wolfgang Gentzsch, Allan Gottlieb, Atsushi Hori, Richard Lagerstrom, Virginia Lo, Cathy McCann, Bill Nitzberg, Uwe Schwiegelshohn, Mark Squillante, and John Towns, for an excellent job. Thanks are also due to the authors for their submissions, presentations, and final revisions for this volume. Finally, we would like to thank the MIT Laboratory for Computer Science and the School of Computer Science and Engineering at the Hebrew University for the use of their facilities in the preparation of these proceedings.

This was the seventh annual workshop in this series, which reflects the continued interest in this field. The previous six were held in conjunction with IPPS'95 through IPDPS'00. Their proceedings are available from Springer-Verlag as volumes 949, 1162, 1291, 1459, 1659, and 1911 of the Lecture Notes in Computer Science series. The last three are also available on-line from Springer LINK.

This year saw an emphasis on workloads and their effect, with two invited papers related to heavy tails, and a contributed paper presenting a comprehensive analysis of the workload on a large-scale SMP cluster. We also kept the tradition of having papers that describe real systems, with a much anticipated paper describing the MAUI scheduler. In addition, we saw the maturation of the field as reflected by papers that delved into deeper topics, such as the interaction of scheduling with memory management and communication, the use of SMP clusters, and considerations regarding what metrics to use.

We hope you find these papers interesting and useful.

August 2001

Dror Feitelson
Larry Rudolph

Table of Contents

Performance Evaluation with Heavy Tailed Distributions 1
M.E. Crovella

SRPT Scheduling for Web Servers 11
M. Harchol-Balter, N. Bansal, B. Schroeder, and M. Agrawal

An Efficient and Scalable Coscheduling Technique
for Large Symmetric Multiprocessor Clusters 21
A.B. Yoo and M.A. Jette

Coscheduling under Memory Constraints in a NOW Environment 41
F. Giné, F. Solsona, P. Hernández, and E. Luque

The Influence of Communication on the Performance of Co-allocation 66
A.I.D. Bucur and D.H.J. Epema

Core Algorithms of the Maui Scheduler 87
D. Jackson, Q. Snell, and M. Clement

On the Development of an Efficient Coscheduling System 103
B.B. Zhou and R.P. Brent

Effects of Memory Performance on Parallel Job Scheduling 116
G.E. Suh, L. Rudolph, and S. Devadas

An Integrated Approach to Parallel Scheduling
Using Gang-Scheduling, Backfilling, and Migration 133
Y. Zhang, H. Franke, J.E. Moreira, and A. Sivasubramaniam

Characteristics of a Large Shared Memory Production Workload 159
S.-H. Chiang and M.K. Vernon

Metrics for Parallel Job Scheduling and Their Convergence 188
D.G. Feitelson

Author Index 207

Performance Evaluation
with Heavy Tailed Distributions
(Extended Abstract)*

Mark E. Crovella

Department of Computer Science
Boston University
111 Cummington St.
Boston MA USA 02215
crovella@cs.bu.edu

1 Introduction

Over the last decade an important new direction has developed in the performance evaluation of computer systems: the study of *heavy-tailed* distributions.
Loosely speaking, these are distributions whose tails follow a power-law with low
exponent, in contrast to traditional distributions (*e.g.,* Gaussian, Exponential,
Poisson) whose tails decline exponentially (or faster). In the late '80s and early
'90s experimental evidence began to accumulate that some properties of computer systems and networks showed distributions with very long tails [7,28,29],
and attention turned to heavy-tailed distributions in particular in the mid '90s
[3,9,23,36,44].

To define heavy tails more precisely, let X be a random variable with cumulative distribution function $F(x) = P[X \leq x]$ and its complement $\bar{F}(x) =
1 - F(x) = P[X > x]$. We say here that a distribution $F(x)$ is *heavy tailed* if

$$\bar{F}(x) \sim cx^{-\alpha} \quad 0 < \alpha < 2 \tag{1}$$

for some positive constant c, where $a(x) \sim b(x)$ means $\lim_{x\to\infty} a(x)/b(x) = 1$.
This definition restricts our attention somewhat narrowly to distributions with
strictly polynomial tails; broader classes such as the *subexponential* distributions
[19] can be defined and most of the qualitative remarks we make here apply to
such broader classes.

Heavy tailed distributions behave quite differently from the distributions
more commonly used in performance evaluation (*e.g.,* the Exponential). In particular, when sampling random variables that follow heavy tailed distributions,
the probability of very large observations occurring is non-negligible. In fact,
under our definition, heavy tailed distributions have *infinite variance*, reflect-
ing the extremely high variability that they capture; and when $\alpha \leq 1$, these
distributions have *infinite mean*.

---

* This is a revised version of a paper originally appearing in *Lecture Notes in Computer
Science 1786,* pp. 1–9, March 2000.

D.G. Feitelson and L. Rudolph (Eds.): JSSPP 2001, LNCS 2221, pp. 1–10, 2001.

2   Evidence

The evidence for heavy-tailed distributions in a number of aspects of computer systems is now quite strong. The broadest evidence concerns the sizes of data objects stored in and transferred through computer systems; in particular, there is evidence for heavy tails in the sizes of:

- Files stored on Web servers [3,9];
- Data files transferred through the Internet [9,36];
- Files stored in general-purpose Unix filesystems [25]; and
- I/O traces of filesystem, disk, and tape activity [21,38,39,40]

This evidence suggests that heavy-tailed distributions of data objects are widespread, and these heavy-tailed distributions have been implicated as an underlying cause of *self-similarity* in network traffic [9,30,35,44].

Next, measurements of job service times or process execution times in general-purpose computing environments have been found to exhibit heavy tails [17,23,28].

A third area in which heavy tails have recently been noted is in the distribution of node degree of certain graph structures. Faloutsos *et al.* [14] show that the inter-domain structure of the Internet, considered as a directed graph, shows a heavy-tailed distribution in the outdegree of nodes. These studies have already influenced the way that Internet-like graph topologies are created for use in simulation [32,26]. Another study shows that the same is true (with respect to both indegree and outdegree) for certain sets of World Wide Web pages which form a graph due to their hyperlinked structure [1]; this result has been extended to the Web as a whole in [6].

Finally, a phenomenon related to heavy tails is the so-called *Zipf's Law* [45]. Zipf's Law relates the "popularity" of an object to its location in a list sorted by popularity. More precisely, consider a set of objects (such as Web servers, or Web pages) to which repeated references are made. Over some time interval, count the number of references made to each object, denoted by R. Now sort the objects in order of decreasing number of references made and let an object's place on this list be denoted by n. Then Zipf's Law states that

$$R = cn^{-\beta}$$

for some positive constants c and β. In its original formulation, Zipf's Law set $\beta = 1$ so that popularity (R) and rank (n) are inversely proportional. In practice, various values of β are found, with values often near to or less than 1. Evidence for Zipf's Law in computing systems (especially the Internet) is widespread [2,13,18,33]; a good overview of such results is presented in [5].

3   Implications of Heavy Tails

Unfortunately, although heavy-tailed distributions are prevalent and important in computer systems, their unusual nature presents a number of problems for performance analysis.

The fact that even low-order distributional moments can be infinite means that many traditional system metrics can be undefined. As a simple example, consider the mean queue length in an $M/G/1$ queue, which (by the Pollaczek-Khinchin formula) is proportional to the second moment of service time. Thus, when service times are drawn from a heavy-tailed distribution, many properties of this queue (mean queue length, mean waiting time) are infinite. Observations like this one suggest that performance analysts dealing with heavy tails may need to turn their attention away from means and variances and toward understanding the full distribution of relevant metrics. Most early work in this direction has focused on the shape of the tail of such distributions (*e.g.*, [34]).

Some heavy-tailed distributions apparently have no convenient closed-form Laplace transforms (*e.g.*, the Pareto distribution), and even for those distributions possessing Laplace transforms, simple systems like the the $M/G/1$ must be evaluated numerically, and with considerable care [41].

In practice, random variables that follow heavy tailed distributions are characterized as exhibiting many small observations mixed in with a few large observations. In such datasets, most of the observations are small, but most of the contribution to the sample mean or variance comes from the rare, large observations. This means that those sample statistics that are defined converge very slowly. This is particularly problematic for simulations involving heavy tails, which many be very slow to reach steady state [12].

Finally, because arbitrarily large observations can not be ruled out, issues of scale should enter in to any discussion of heavy tailed models. No real system can experience arbitrarily large events, and generally one must pay attention to the practical upper limit on event size, whether determined by the timescale of interest, the constraints of storage or transmission capacity, or other system-defined limits. On the brighter side, a useful result is that it is often reasonable to substitute finitely-supported distributions for the idealized heavy-tailed distributions in analytic settings, as long as the approximation is accurate over the range of scales of interest [16,20,22].

4   Taking Advantage of Heavy Tails

Despite the challenges they present to performance analysis, heavy tailed distributions also exhibit properties that can be exploited in the design of computer systems. Recent work has begun to explore how to take advantage of the presence of heavy tailed distributions to improve computer systems' performance.

4.1   Two Important Properties

In this regard, there are two properties of heavy tailed distributions that offer particular leverage in the design of computer systems. The first property is related to the fact that heavy tailed distributions show declining hazard rate, and is most concisely captured in terms of conditional expectation:

$$E[X|X > k] \sim k$$

when X is a heavy tailed random variable and k is large enough to be "in the tail." We refer to this as the *expectation paradox*, after [31, p. 343]; it says that if we are making observations of heavy-tailed interarrivals, then the longer we have waited, the longer we should expect to wait. (The expectation is undefined when $\alpha \leq 1$, but the general idea still holds.) This should be contrasted with the case when the underlying distribution has exponential tails or has bounded support above (as in the uniform distribution); in these cases, eventually one always gets to the point where the longer one waits, the less time one should expect to continue waiting.

The second useful property of heavy tailed distributions we will call the *mass-count disparity*. This property can be stated formally as [19]:

$$\lim_{x \to \infty} \frac{P[X_1 + ... + X_n > x]}{P[\max(X_1, ..., X_n) > x]} = 1 \text{ for all } n \geq 2$$

which is the case when the X_i are i.i.d. positive random variables drawn from a heavy-tailed distribution. This property states that when considering collections of observations of a heavy-tailed random variable, the aggregated mass contained in the small observations is negligible compared to the largest observation in determining the likelihood of large values of the sum.

In practice this means that the majority of the mass in a set of observations is concentrated in a very small subset of the observations. This can be visualized as a box into which one has put a few boulders, and then filled the rest of the way with sand. This mass-count disparity means that one must be careful in "optimizing the common case" [27]. The typical *observation* is small; the typical *unit of work* is contained in a large observation.

This disparity can be studied by defining the mass-weighted distribution function:

$$F_w(x) = \frac{\int_{-\infty}^{x} u \, dF(u)}{\int_{-\infty}^{\infty} v \, dF(v)} \tag{2}$$

and comparing $F_w(x)$ with $F(x)$. Varying x over its valid range yields a plot of the fraction of total mass that is contained in the fraction of observations less than x. An example of this comparison is shown in Figure 1. This figure shows $F_w(x)$ vs. $F(x)$ for the Exponential distribution, and for a particular heavy-tailed distribution. The heavy-tailed distribution is chosen to correspond to empirical measurements of file sizes in the World Wide Web [4]; it has $\alpha = 1.0$. Since the denominator in (2) is infinite for heavy tailed distributions with $\alpha \leq 1$, the actual distribution used has been truncated to span six orders of magnitude — which is reasonable for file size distributions (which can range in size from bytes to megabytes).

The figure shows that for the Exponential distribution, the amount of mass contained in small observations is roughly commensurate with the fraction of total observations considered; *i.e.*, the curve is not too far from the line $y = x$. On the other hand, for the heavy tailed distribution, the amount of mass is not at all commensurate with the fraction of observations considered; about 60% of the mass is contained in the upper 1% of the observations! This is consistent

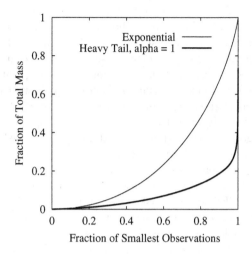

Fig. 1. Total Mass as a Function of Smallest Observations

with results in [37] showing that 50-80% of the bytes in FTP transfers are due to the largest 2% of all transfers.

4.2 Exploiting The Heavy Tail Properties

Once these properties are understood, they can be exploited in a number of ways to improve system performance. This section summarizes some (though not all) recent attempts to do this.

Load Balancing in Distributed Systems In some distributed systems, tasks can be pre-empted and moved from one node to another, which can improve load balance. However, the cost of migration is not trivial and can outweigh performance gains from improved load balance if not used carefully. In [23], the authors show that previous assessments of the potential for pre-emptive migration had mainly used exponential tasks size assumptions and concluded that the potential gains from task migration were small. However, once the task size distribution is understood to be heavy-tailed, two benefits emerge: 1) the mass-count disparity means that relative few tasks need to be migrated to radically improve load balance; and 2) the expectation paradox means that a task's lifetime to date is a good predictor of its expected future lifetime. Taken together, these two benefits form the foundation for a enlightened load balancing policy that can significantly improve the performance of a wide class of distributed systems.

When pre-emption is not an option, understanding of heavy tailed distributions can still inform load balancing policies. The question in these systems is "which queue should an arriving task join?" In the case when service at the nodes is FCFS, and knowledge is available about the size of the arriving task, the best policy is commonly assumed to be joining the queue with the shortest expected delay [43] although this is known to be best only for task size distributions with increasing failure rate. In [24], the authors show a better policy for the case in which task sizes have a heavy-tailed distribution, which they call SITA-E. The idea is to assign an incoming task to a queue based on the incoming task's size. Each queue handles tasks whose sizes lie in a contiguous range, and ranges are chosen so as to equalize load in expectation. This policy is shown to significantly outperform shortest-expect-delay assignment, when $1 < \alpha \leq 2$. The benefits of the policy accrue primarily from the the mass-count disparity in task sizes: grouping like tasks together means that the vast majority of tasks are sent to only a few queues; at these queues, task size variability is dramatically reduced and so FCFS service is very efficient.

Finally, in another paper [8,11], the authors show that in the same setting (distributed system of FCFS servers, task sizes are heavy tailed, and incoming task sizes are known) the *expected slowdown* metric is optimized by policies that do *not* balance load. (Slowdown is defined as a job's waiting time in queue divided by its service demand.) This is possible because of the mass-count disparity; when most tasks are sent to only a few queues, reducing the load at those queues decreases the slowdown experienced at those queues. In this case, most tasks experience decreased slowdown, while the relatively few large tasks experience only slightly increased slowdown. In expectation, slowdown is decreased.

Scheduling in Web Servers In single-node systems, attention has been given to the scheduling issue. Most systems use a variant of timesharing to schedule tasks, possibly incorporating multilevel feedback; this is effective when task sizes are unknown. In [22], the authors argue that Web servers are in a unusual position; they can estimate task size upon task arrival because, for static Web pages, the file size is known at request time. As a result, they argue for the use of shortest-remaining-processing-time (SRPT) scheduling within Web servers. One significant drawback of SRPT is that it improves the response time of small tasks at the expense of large tasks; however the authors argue that this is acceptable when tasks follow heavy-tailed distributions such as are encountered in the Web. The reason is that the mass-count disparity means that under SRPT, although large tasks are interrupted by small tasks, the small tasks represent only a minor fraction of total system load. Thus the great majority of tasks have their response time improved, while the relatively few large tasks are not seriously punished. In [10] the authors describe an actual Web server implemented to use this scheduling policy. The paper shows evidence that the new server exhibits mean response times 4-5 times lower than a popularly deployed server (Apache); and that the performance impacts on large tasks are relatively mild.

Routing and Switching in the Internet In Internet traffic management, a number of improved approaches to routing and switching have been proposed, based on the observation that the lengths of bulk data flows in the Internet exhibit heavy tails.

One promising routing technique is to use switching hardware, by creating *shortcuts* (temporary circuits) for long sequences of packets that share a common source and destination. Shortcuts provide the benefits of fast switch-based routing, at the expense of network and switch overhead for their setup. The authors in [15] argue that Web traffic can be efficiently routed using this technique. Their results rely on the mass-count disparity, showing that the majority of the bytes can be routed by creating shortcuts for only a small fraction of all data flows. They show that in some settings, a setup threshold of 25 packets (the number of same-path packets to observe before creating a switched connection) is sufficient to eliminate 90% of the setup costs while routing more than 50% of the bytes over switched circuits. The choice of threshold implicitly makes use of the expectation paradox: longer thresholds can be used to offset larger setup costs, since longer thresholds identify flows whose expected future length is longer as well.

Another proposed routing technique is *load-sensitive* routing. Load sensitive routing attempts to route traffic around points of congestion in the network; current Internet routing only makes use of link state (up or down). Unfortunately, load-sensitive routing can be expensive and potentially unstable if applied to every routing decision. However, the authors in [42] show that if applied only to the long-lived flows, it can be efficient and considerably more stable. The success of this technique relies on the heavy tailed distribution of Internet flows: the mass-count disparity means that a large fraction of bytes can be routed by rerouting only a small fraction of the flows; and the expectation paradox allows the policy to observe a flow for some period of time to classify it as a long flow.

Acknowledgments

The author is grateful to Mor Harchol-Balter, with whom some of the ideas in this paper were developed and clarified. This work was supported by NSF grants CCR-9501822, CCR-9706685, and by grants from Hewlett-Packard Laboratories.

References

1. Réka Albert, Hawoong Jeong, and Albert-László Barabási. Diameter of the world wide web. *Nature*, 401:130–131, 1999.
2. Virgílio Almeida, Azer Bestavros, Mark Crovella, and Adriana de Oliveira. Characterizing reference locality in the WWW. In *Proceedings of 1996 International Conference on Parallel and Distributed Information Systems (PDIS '96)*, pages 92–103, December 1996.
3. Martin F. Arlitt and Carey L. Williamson. Internet web servers: Workload characterization and performance implications. *IEEE/ACM Transactions on Networking*, 5(5):631–645, 1997.
4. Paul Barford and Mark E. Crovella. Generating representative Web workloads for network and server performance evaluation. In *Proceedings of Performance '98/SIGMETRICS '98*, pages 151–160, July 1998.
5. Lee Breslau, Pei Cao, Li Fan, Graham Phillips, and Scott Shenker. Web caching and zipf-like distributions: Evidence and implications. In *Proceedings of INFOCOM '99*, pages 126–134, 1999.

6. Andrei Broder, Ravi Kumar, Farzin Maghoul, Prabhakar Raghavan, Sridhar Rajagopalan, Raymie Stata, Andrew Tomkins, and Janet Wiener. Graph structure in the web: experiments and models. In *Proceedings the Ninth World Wide Web Conference (WWW9)*, 2000.

7. R. Cáceres, P. B. Danzig, S. Jamin, and D. J. Mitzel. Characteristics of wide-area TCP/IP conversations. *Computer Communication Review*, 21, 1991.

8. M. E. Crovella, M. Harchol-Balter, and C. D. Murta. Task assignment in a distributed system: Improving performance by unbalancing load. Technical Report TR-97-018, Boston University Department of Computer Science, October 31 1997.

9. Mark E. Crovella and Azer Bestavros. Self-similarity in World Wide Web traffic: Evidence and possible causes. *IEEE/ACM Transactions on Networking*, 5(6):835–846, December 1997.

10. Mark E. Crovella, Robert Frangioso, and Mor Harchol-Balter. Connection scheduling in Web servers. In *1999 USENIX Symposium on Internet Technologies and Systems (USITS '99)*, 1999.

11. Mark E. Crovella, Mor Harchol-Balter, and Cristina Duarte Murta. Task assignment in a distributed system: Improving performance by unbalancing load. In *Proceedings of SIGMETRICS '98 (poster paper)*, July 1998.

12. Mark E. Crovella and Lester Lipsky. Simulations with heavy-tailed workloads. In Kihong Park and Walter Willinger, editors, *Self-Similar Network Traffic and Performance Evaluation*. Wiley / Wiley Interscience, New York, 1999.

13. Carlos A. Cunha, Azer Bestavros, and Mark E. Crovella. Characteristics of WWW client-based traces. Technical Report TR-95-010, Boston University Department of Computer Science, April 1995.

14. Michalis Faloutsos, Petros Faloutsos, and Christos Faloutsos. On power-law relationships of the internet topology. In *Proceedings of SIGCOMM '99*, 1999.

15. Anja Feldmann, Jennifer Rexford, and Ramon Caceres. Efficient policies for carrying web traffic over flow-switched networks. *IEEE/ACM Transactions on Networking*, December 1998.

16. Anja Feldmann and Ward Whitt. Fitting mixtures of exponentials to long-tail distributions to analyze network performance models. In *Proceedings of IEEE INFOCOM'97*, pages 1098–1116, April 1997.

17. Sharad Garg, Lester Lipsky, and Maryann Robbert. The effect of power-tail distributions on the behavior of time sharing computer systems. In *1992 ACM Symposium on Applied Computing*, Kansas City, MO, March 1992.

18. Steven Glassman. A caching relay for the World Wide Web. In *Proceedings of the First International World Wide Web Conference*, pages 69–76, 1994.

19. Charles M. Goldie and Claudia Kluppelberg. Subexponential distributions. In Robert J. Adler, Raisa E. Feldman, and Murad S. Taqqu, editors, *A Practical Guide To Heavy Tails*, pages 435–460. Chapman & Hall, New York, 1998.

20. Michael Greiner, Manfred Jobmann, and Lester Lipsky. The importance of power-tail distributions for telecommunication traffic models. *Operations Research*, 41, 1999.

21. S. D. Gribble, G. S. Manku, D. Roselli, E. A. Brewer, T. J. Gibson, and E. L. Miller. Self-similarity in file systems. In *Proceedings of SIGMETRICS '98*, pages 141–150, 1998.

22. M. Harchol-Balter, M. E. Crovella, and S. Park. The case for SRPT scheduling in Web servers. Technical Report MIT-LCS-TR-767, MIT Lab for Computer Science, October 1998.

23. M. Harchol-Balter and A. Downey. Exploiting process lifetime distributions for dynamic load balancing. *ACM Transactions on Computer Systems*, 15(3):253–285, 1997.

24. Mor Harchol-Balter, Mark E. Crovella, and Cristina D. Murta. On choosing a task assignment policy for a distributed server system. *Journal of Parallel and Distributed Computing*, Special Issue on Software Support for Distributed Computing, September 1999.

25. Gordon Irlam. Unix file size survey - 1993. Available at http://www.base.com-/gordoni/ufs93.html, September 1994.

26. Cheng Jin, Qian Chen, and Sugih Jamin. Inet: internet topology generator. Technical Report CSE-TR-433-00, U. Michigan Computer Science, 2000.

27. Butler W. Lampson. Hints for computer system design. *Proceedings of the Ninth SOSP, in Operating Systems Review*, 17(5):33–48, October 1983.

28. W. E. Leland and T. J. Ott. Load-balancing heuristics and process behavior. In *Proceedings of Performance and ACM Sigmetrics*, pages 54–69, 1986.

29. W. E. Leland and D. V. Wilson. High time-resolution measurement and analysis of LAN traffic: Implications for LAN interconnection. In *Proceeedings of IEEE Infocomm '91*, pages 1360–1366, Bal Harbour, FL, 1991.

30. W.E. Leland, M.S. Taqqu, W. Willinger, and D.V. Wilson. On the self-similar nature of Ethernet traffic (extended version). *IEEE/ACM Transactions on Networking*, 2:1–15, 1994.

31. Benoit B. Mandelbrot. *The Fractal Geometry of Nature*. W. H. Freedman and Co., New York, 1983.

32. Alberto Medina, Ibrahim Matta, and John Byers. BRITE: a flexible generator of internet topologies. Technical Report BU-CS-TR-2000-05, Boston University Computer Science, January 2000.

33. Norifumi Nishikawa, Takafumi Hosokawa, Yasuhide Mori, Kenichi Yoshida, and Hiroshi Tsuji. Memory-based architecture for distributed WWW caching proxy. *Computer Networks and ISDN Systems*, 30:205–214, 1998.

34. I. Norros. A storage model with self-similar input. *Queueing Systems*, 16:387–396, 1994.

35. Kihong Park, Gi Tae Kim, and Mark E. Crovella. On the relationship between file sizes, transport protocols, and self-similar network traffic. In *Proceedings of the Fourth International Conference on Network Protocols (ICNP'96)*, pages 171–180, October 1996.

36. Vern Paxson. Empirically-derived analytic models of wide-area tcp connections. *IEEE/ACM Transactions on Networking*, 2(4):316–336, August 1994.

37. Vern Paxson and Sally Floyd. Wide-area traffic: The failure of poisson modeling. *IEEE/ACM Transactions on Networking*, pages 226–244, June 1995.

38. D. Peterson and R. Grossman. Power laws in large shop DASD I/O activity. In *CMG Proceedings*, pages 822–833, December 1995.

39. David L. Peterson. Data center I/O patterns and power laws. In *CMG Proceedings*, December 1996.

40. David L. Peterson and David B. Adams. Fractal patterns in DASD I/O traffic. In *CMG Proceedings*, December 1996.

41. Matthew Roughan, Darryl Veitch, and Michael Rumsewicz. Computing queue-length distributions for power-law queues. In *Proceedings of INFOCOM '98*, pages 356–363, 1998.

42. Anees Shaikh, Jennifer Rexford, and Kang Shin. Load-sensitive routing of long-lived IP flows. In *Proceedings of ACM SIGCOMM '99*, pages 215–226, September 1999.

43. R. W. Weber. On the optimal assignment of customers to parallel servers. *Journal of Applied Probability*, 15:406–413, 1978.
44. Walter Willinger, Murad S. Taqqu, Robert Sherman, and Daniel V. Wilson. Self-similarity through high-variability: Statistical analysis of Ethernet LAN traffic at the source level. *IEEE/ACM Transactions on Networking*, 5(1):71–86, February 1997.
45. G. K. Zipf. *Human Behavior and the Principle of Least-Effort*. Addison-Wesley, Cambridge, MA, 1949.

SRPT Scheduling for Web Servers

Mor Harchol-Balter, Nikhil Bansal, Bianca Schroeder, and Mukesh Agrawal

School of Computer Science, Carnegie Mellon University
Pittsburgh, PA 15213
{harchol, nikhil, bianca, mukesh}@cs.cmu.edu

Abstract. This note briefly summarizes some results from two papers: [4] and [23]. These papers pose the following question:

> *Is it possible to reduce the expected response time of every request at a web server, simply by changing the order in which we schedule the requests?*

In [4] we approach this question analytically via an M/G/1 queue. In [23] we approach the same question via implementation involving an Apache web server running on Linux.

1 Introduction

Motivation and Goals

A client accessing a busy web server can expect a long wait. This delay is comprised of several components: the propagation delay and transmission delay on the path between the client and the server; delays due to queueing at routers; delays caused by TCP due to loss, congestion, and slow start; and finally the delay at the server itself. The aggregate of these delays, i.e. the time from when the client makes a request until the entire file arrives is defined to be the *response time* of the request.

We focus on what we can do to improve the delay at the server. Research has shown that in situations where the server is receiving a high rate of requests, the delays at the server make up a significant portion of the response time [6], [5], [32].

Our work will focus on *static* requests only of the form "Get me a file." Measurements [31] suggest that the request stream at most web servers is dominated by *static* requests. The question of how to service static requests *quickly* is the focus of many companies *e.g.*, Akamai Technologies, and much ongoing research.

Our Idea

Our idea is simple. For static requests, the *size of the request* (i.e. the time required to service the request) is well-approximated by the size of the file, which is well-known to the server. Thus far, no companies or researchers have made use of this information. Traditionally, requests at a web server are scheduled

D.G. Feitelson and L. Rudolph (Eds.): JSSPP 2001, LNCS 2221, pp. 11–20, 2001.

independently of their size. The requests are time-shared, with each request receiving a *fair share* of the web server resources. We call this **FAIR** scheduling (a.k.a. Processor-Sharing scheduling). We propose, instead, *unfair scheduling*, in which priority is given to *short* requests, or those requests which have *short remaining time*, in accordance with the well-known scheduling algorithm Shortest-Remaining-Processing-Time-first (**SRPT**). The expectation is that using SRPT scheduling of requests at the server will reduce the queueing time at the server.

The Controversy

It has long been known that SRPT has the lowest mean response time of any scheduling policy, for any arrival sequence and job sizes [41,46]. Despite this fact, applications have shied away from using this policy for fear that SRPT "starves" big requests [9,47,48,45]. It is often stated that the huge average performance improvements of SRPT over other policies stem from the fact that SRPT unfairly penalizes the large jobs in order to help the small jobs. It is often thought that the performance of small jobs cannot be improved without hurting the large jobs and thus large jobs suffer unfairly under SRPT.

2   Analysis of SRPT Based on [4]

Relevant Previous Work

It has long been known that SRPT minimizes mean response time [41,46]. Rajaraman et al. showed further that the mean slowdown under SRPT is at most twice optimal, for any job sequence [19].

Schrage and Miller first derived the expressions for the response times in an M/G/1/SRPT queue [42]. This was further generalized by Pechinkin *et al.* to disciplines where the remaining times are divided into intervals [36]. The steady-state appearance of the M/G/1/SRPT queue was obtained by Schassberger [40]. The mean response time for a job of size x in an M/G/1/SRPT server is given below:

$$E[T(x)]_{SRPT} = \frac{\lambda(\int_0^x t^2 f(t)dt + x^2(1 - F(x)))}{2(1 - \lambda \int_0^x tf(t)dt)^2} + \int_0^x \frac{dt}{1 - \lambda \int_0^t yf(y)dy}$$

where λ is the average arrival rate and $f(t)$ is the p.d.f. of the job size distribution.

The above formula is difficult to evaluate numerically, due to its complex form (many nested integrals). Hence, the comparison of SRPT to other policies was long neglected. More recently, SRPT has been compared with other policies by plotting the mean response times for specific job size distributions under specific loads [39,37,43]. These include a 7-year long study at University of Aachen under Schreiber et. al. These results are all plots for *specific* job size distributions and loads. Hence it is not clear whether the conclusions based on these plots hold more generally.

It is often cited that SRPT may lead to *starvation* of large jobs [8,47,48,45]. Usually, examples of adversarial request sequences are given to justify this. However, such worst case examples do not reflect the behavior of SRPT on average. The term "starvation" is also used by people to indicate the *unfairness* of SRPT's treatment of long jobs. The argument given is that if a scheduling policy reduces the response time of small jobs, then the response times for the large jobs would have to increase considerably in accordance with conservation laws. This argument is true for scheduling policies which *do not* make use of size, see the famous Kleinrock Conservation Law [28], [29, Page 197].

Very little has been done to evaluate the problem of unfairness analytically. Recently, Bender et al. consider the metric *max slowdown* of a job, as indication of unfairness [8]. They show with an example that SRPT can have an arbitrarily large *max slowdown*. However, *max slowdown* may not be the best metric for unfairness. One large job may have an exceptionally long response time in some case, but it might do well most of the time. A more relevant metric is the *max mean slowdown*.

The question of how heavy-tailed workloads might affect SRPT's performance has not been examined.

Our Model

Throughout paper [4] we assume an M/G/1 queue where G is assumed to be a continuous distribution with finite mean and variance.

It turns out that the job size distribution[1] is important with respect to evaluating SRPT. We will therefore assume a general job size distribution. We will also concentrate on the special case of distributions with the **heavy-tailed property (HT property)**. We define the HT property to say that *the largest 1% of the jobs comprise at least half the load*. This HT property appears in many recent measurements of computing system workloads, including both sequential jobs and parallel jobs [30,24,13,26,38,44]. In particular the sizes of *web files* requested and the sizes of web files stored have been shown to follow a Pareto distribution which possesses the HT property [7,14,16].

Some Results from [4]

In [4], we prove the following results, among others:

- Although it is well-known that SRPT scheduling optimizes mean response time, it is not known how SRPT compares with Processor-Sharing scheduling (a.k.a. FAIR scheduling) with respect to mean slowdown. We prove that SRPT scheduling also outperforms Processor-Sharing (PS) scheduling with respect to mean slowdown for all job size distributions.

---

[1] Note: By "the size of a job" we mean the service requirement of the request. In the case of static web requests, this is proportional to the number of bytes in the request.

- Given that SRPT improves performance over PS both with respect to mean response time and mean slowdown, we next investigate the magnitude of the improvement. We prove that for all job size distributions with the HT property the improvement is very significant under high loads. For example, for load 0.9, SRPT improves over PS with respect to mean slowdown by a factor of at least 4 for all distributions with the HT property. As the load approaches 1, we find that SRPT improves over PS with respect to mean slowdown by a factor of 100 for all distributions with the HT property. In general we prove that for *all* job size distributions as the load approaches one, the mean response time under SRPT improves upon the mean response time under PS by at least a factor of 2 and likewise for mean slowdown.
- The performance improvement of SRPT over PS does *not* usually come at the expense of the large jobs. In fact, we observe via example that for many job size distributions with the HT property every single job, including a job of the maximum possible size, prefers SRPT to PS (unless the load is extremely close to 1).
- While the above result does not hold at all loads, we prove that no matter what the load, at least 99% of the jobs have a lower expected response time under SRPT than under PS, for all job size distributions with the HT property. In fact, these 99% of the jobs do significantly better. We show that these jobs have an average slowdown of at most 4, at any load $\rho < 1$, whereas their performance could be arbitrarily bad under PS as the load approaches 1. Similar, but weaker results are shown for general distributions.
- While the previous result is concerned only with 99% of the jobs, we also prove upper bounds on how much worse any job could fare under SRPT as opposed to PS for general distributions. Our bounds show that jobs never do too much worse under SRPT than under PS. For example, for all job size distributions, the expected response time under SRPT for any job is never more than 3 times that under PS, when the load is 0.8, and never more than 5.5 times that under PS when the load is 0.9. In fact, if the load is less than half, then *for every job size distribution, each job has a lower expected response time and slowdown under SRPT than under PS.*
- The above results show an upper bound on how much worse a job could fare under SRPT as opposed to PS for general job size distributions. We likewise prove lower bounds on the performance of SRPT as compared with PS for general job size distributions.

3   Implementation of SRPT Based on [23]

Relevant Previous Systems Work

There has been much literature devoted to improving the response time of web requests. Some of this literature focuses on reducing *network latency*, e.g. by caching requests ([21], [11], [10]) or improving the HTTP protocol ([18], [34]). Other literature works on reducing the *delays at a server*, e.g. by building more efficient HTTP servers ([20], [35]) or improving the server's OS ([17], [3], [27], [33]).

The solution we propose is different from the above in that we only want to change the order in which requests are scheduled. In the remainder of this section we discuss only work on *priority-based* or *size-based* scheduling of requests.

Almeida et. al. [1] use both a user-level approach and a kernel-level implementation to prioritizing HTTP requests at a web server. The *user-level* approach in [1] involves modifying the Apache web server to include a Scheduler process which determines the order in which requests are fed to the web server. The *kernel-level* approach in [1] simply sets the priority of the process which handles a request in accordance with the priority of the request. Observe that setting the priority of a process only allows very coarse-grained control over the scheduling of the process, as pointed out in the paper. The user-level and kernel-level approaches in this paper are good starting points, but the results show that more fine-grained implementation work is needed. For example, in their experiments, the high-priority requests only benefit by up to 20% and the low priority requests suffer by up to 200%.

Another attempt at priority scheduling of HTTP requests which deals specifically with SRPT scheduling at web servers is our own earlier work [15]. This implementation does not involve any modification of the kernel. We experiment with connection scheduling at the *application level* only. We are able to improve mean response time by a factor of close to 4, for some ranges of load, but the improvement comes at a price: *a drop in throughput by a factor of almost 2*. The problem is that scheduling at the application level does not provide fine enough control over the order in which packets enter the network. In order to obtain enough control over scheduling, we are forced to limit the throughput of requests.

Our Approach

It's not immediately clear what SRPT means in the context of a web server. A web server is not a single-resource system. It is not obvious *which* of the web server's resources need to be scheduled. As one would expect, it turns out that scheduling is only important at the *bottleneck resource*. Frequently this bottleneck resource is the bandwidth on the access link out of the web server. "On a site consisting primarily of *static content, network bandwidth* is the most likely source of a performance bottleneck. Even a fairly modest server can completely saturate a T3 connection or 100Mbps Fast Ethernet connection." [25] (also corroborated by [12], [2]). There's another reason why the bottleneck resource tends to be the bandwidth on the access link out of the web site: Access links to web sites (T3, OC3, etc.) cost thousands of dollars per month, whereas CPU is cheap in comparison. Likewise disk utilization remains low since most files end up in the cache. It is important to note that although we concentrate on the case where the network bandwidth is the bottleneck resource, all the ideas in this paper can also be applied to the case where the CPU is the bottleneck — in which case SRPT scheduling is applied to the CPU.

Since the network is the bottleneck resource, we try to apply the SRPT algorithm at the level of the network. Our idea is to control the order in which the server's socket buffers are drained. Recall that for each (non-persistent) request a connection is established between the client and the web server. Corresponding to each connection, there is a socket buffer on the web server end into which the web server writes the contents of the requested file. Traditionally, the different socket buffers are drained in Round-Robin Order, each getting a fair share of the bandwidth of the outgoing link. We instead propose to give priority to those sockets corresponding to connections for small file requests or where the *remaining data* required by the request is small. Throughout, we use the Linux OS.

Figure 1 shows data flow in standard Linux, which employs FAIR scheduling. Data streaming into each socket buffer is encapsulated into packets which obtain TCP headers and IP headers. Finally, there is a *single*[2] "priority queue" (*transmit queue*), into which *all* streams feed. This single "priority queue," can get as long as 100 packets.

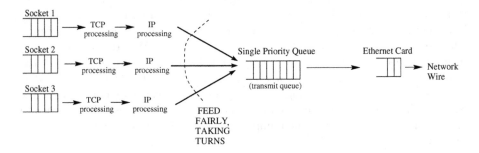

Fig. 1. *Data flow in Standard Linux — FAIR scheduling.*

Figure 2 shows the flow of data in Linux after our modifications: Instead of a single priority queue (transmit queue), there are multiple priority queues. Priority queue i is only allowed to flow if priority queues 0 through $i - 1$ are all empty. We used 6 priority queues in our experiments.

After modifying the Linux kernel, we next had to modify the Apache web server to assign priorities in accordance with SRPT. Our modified Apache determines the size of a request and then sets the priority of the corresponding socket by calling `setsockopt`. As Apache sends the file, the remaining size of the request decreases. When the remaining size falls below the threshold for the current priority class, Apache updates the socket priority.

Lastly, we had to come up with an algorithm for partitioning the requests into priority classes which work well with the heavy-tailed web workload.

---

[2] The queue actually consists of 3 priority queues, a.k.a. bands. By default, however, all packets are queued to the same band.

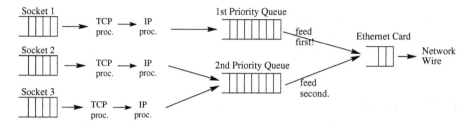

Fig. 2. *Flow of data in Linux with priority queueing (2 priorities shown)*

The combination of (i) the modifications to Linux, (ii) the modifications to the Apache web server, and (iii) the priority algorithm allows us to implement SRPT scheduling. Details on each of these three components are provided in [23].

A very simple experimental architecture is used to run our tests. It involves only two machines each with an Intel Pentium III 700 MHz processor and 256 MB RAM, running Linux 2.2.16, and connected by a 10Mb/sec full-duplex Ethernet connection. The Apache web server is run on one of the machines. The other machine (referred to as the "client machine") hosts 200 or so (simulated) client entities which send requests to the web server.

The client's requests are taken from a 1-day trace from the Soccer World Cup 1998, from the Internet Traffic Archive [22]. The 1-day trace contains 4.5 million HTTP requests, virtually all of which are *static*. The trace exhibits a strong heavy-tailed property with the largest $< 3\%$ of the requests making up $> 50\%$ of the total load.

This request sequence is controlled so that the same experiment can be repeated at many different server loads. The *server load* is the load at the bottleneck device – in this case the network link out of the web server. The load thus represents the fraction of bandwidth used on the network link out of the web server (for example if the requests require 8Mb/sec of bandwidth, and the available bandwidth on the link if 10Mb/sec, then the network load is 0.8).

Some Results from [23]

Our experiments yield the following results:

- SRPT-based scheduling decreases mean response time in our LAN setup by a factor of $3 - 8$ for loads greater than 0.5.
- SRPT-based scheduling helps small requests a lot, while negligibly penalizing large requests. Under a load of 0.8, 80% of the requests improve by a factor of 10 under SRPT-based scheduling. Only the largest 0.1% of requests suffer an increase in mean response time under SRPT-based scheduling (by a factor of only 1.2).
- The variance in the response time is far lower under SRPT as compared with FAIR, in fact two orders of magnitude lower for most requests.

– *There is no negative effect on byte throughput, request throughput, or CPU utilization from using SRPT as compared with FAIR.*

For more details see [23].

4   Conclusion

We have shown both analytically and experimentally that SRPT scheduling of requests is very powerful under workloads with a heavy-tail property, such as web workloads. Under such workloads, 99% of requests see significant improvement in mean response time under SRPT scheduling as compared with the traditionally-used FAIR scheduling. Furthermore, even the very largest requests have lower expected response time under SRPT than under FAIR scheduling in theory. Experimentally, the largest requests may perform negligibly worse under SRPT scheduling as compared with FAIR scheduling. We believe this is simply due to the coarseness of the implementation.

References

1. J. Almeida, M. Dabu, A. Manikutty, and P. Cao. Providing differentiated quality-of-service in Web hosting services. In *Proceedings of the First Workshop on Internet Server Performance*, June 1998.
2. Bruce Maggs at Akamai. Personal communication., 2001.
3. G. Banga, P. Druschel, and J. Mogul. Better operating system features for faster network servers. In *Proc. Workshop on Internet Server Performance*, June 1998.
4. Nikhil Bansal and Mor Harchol-Balter. Analysis of SRPT scheduling: Investigating unfairness. In *Proceeding of ACM Sigmetrics Conference on Measurement and Modeling of Computer Systems (SIGMETRICS '01)*, June 2001.
5. Paul Barford and M. E. Crovella. Measuring web performance in the wide area. *Performance Evaluation Review – Special Issue on Network Traffic Measurement and Workload Characterization*, August 1999.
6. Paul Barford and Mark Crovella. Critical path analysis of tcp transactions. In *SIGCOMM*, 2000.
7. Paul Barford and Mark E. Crovella. Generating representative Web workloads for network and server performance evaluation. In *Proceedings of SIGMETRICS '98*, pages 151–160, July 1998.
8. M. Bender, S. Chakrabarti, and S. Muthukrishnan. Flow and stretch metrics for scheduling continous job streams. In *Proceedings of the 9th Annual ACM-SIAM Symposium on Discrete Algorithms*, 1998.
9. Michael Bender, Soumen Chakrabarti, and S. Muthukrishnan. Flow and stretch metrics for scheduling continuous job streams. In *Proceedings of the 9th Annual ACM-SIAM Symposium on Discrete Algorithms*, 1998.
10. Azer Bestavros, Robert L. Carter, Mark E. Crovella, Carlos R. Cunha, Abdel-salam Heddaya, and Sulaiman A. Mirdad. Application-level document caching in the internet. In *Proceedings of the Second International Workshop on Services in Distributed and Networked Environments (SDNE'95)*, June 1995.

11. H. Braun and K. Claffy. Web traffic characterization: an assessment of the impact of caching documents from NCSA's Web server. In *Proceedings of the Second International WWW Conference*, 1994.
12. Adrian Cockcroft. Watching your web server. The Unix Insider at http://www.unixinsider.com, April 1996.
13. Mark E. Crovella and Azer Bestavros. Self-similarity in World Wide Web traffic: Evidence and possible causes. In *Proceedings of the 1996 ACM SIGMETRICS International Conference on Measurement and Modeling of Computer Systems*, pages 160–169, May 1996.
14. Mark E. Crovella and Azer Bestavros. Self-similarity in World Wide Web traffic: Evidence and possible causes. *IEEE/ACM Transactions on Networking*, 5(6):835–846, December 1997.
15. Mark E. Crovella, Robert Frangioso, and Mor Harchol-Balter. Connection scheduling in web servers. In *USENIX Symposium on Internet Technologies and Systems*, October 1999.
16. Mark E. Crovella, Murad S. Taqqu, and Azer Bestavros. Heavy-tailed probability distributions in the World Wide Web. In *A Practical Guide To Heavy Tails*, pages 3–26. Chapman & Hall, New York, 1998.
17. Peter Druschel and Gaurav Banga. Lazy receiver processing (LRP): A network subsystem architecture for server systems. In *Proceedings of OSDI '96*, October 1996.
18. Fielding, Gettys, Mogul, Frystyk, and Berners-lee. DNS support for load balancing. RFC 2068, April 1997.
19. J.E. Gehrke, S. Muthukrishnan, R. Rajaraman, and A. Shaheen. Scheduling to minimize average stretch online. In *40th Annual symposium on Foundation of Computer Science*, pages 433–422, 1999.
20. The Apache Group. Apache web server. http://www.apache.org.
21. James Gwertzman and Margo Seltzer. The case for geographical push-caching. In *Proceedings of HotOS '94*, May 1994.
22. Internet Town Hall. The internet traffic archives. Available at http://town.hall.org/Archives/pub/ITA/.
23. Mor Harchol-Balter, Nikhil Bansal, Bianca Schroeder, and Mukesh Agrawal. Implementation of SRPT scheduling in web servers. Technical Report CMU-CS-00-170, 2000.
24. Mor Harchol-Balter and Allen Downey. Exploiting process lifetime distributions for dynamic load balancing. In *Proceedings of SIGMETRICS '96*, pages 13–24, 1996.
25. Microsoft TechNet Insights and Answers for IT Professionals. The arts and science of web server tuning with internet information services 5.0. http://www.microsoft.com/technet/, 2001.
26. Gordon Irlam. Unix file size survey - 1993. Available at http://www.base.com/gordoni/ufs93.html, September 1994.
27. M. Kaashoek, D. Engler, D. Wallach, and G. Ganger. Server operating systems. In *SIGOPS European Workshop*, September 1996.
28. L. Kleinrock, R.R. Muntz, and J. Hsu. Tight bounds on average response time for time-shared computer systems. In *Proceedings of the IFIP Congress*, volume 1, pages 124–133, 1971.
29. Leonard Kleinrock. *Queueing Systems*, volume II. Computer Applications. John Wiley & Sons, 1976.
30. W. E. Leland and T. J. Ott. Load-balancing heuristics and process behavior. In *Proceedings of Performance and ACM Sigmetrics*, pages 54–69, 1986.

31. S. Manley and M. Seltzer. Web facts and fantasy. In *Proceedings of the 1997 USITS*, 1997.
32. Evangelos Markatos. Main memory caching of Web documents. In *Proceedings of the Fifth Interntional Conference on the WWW*, 1996.
33. J. Mogul. Operating systems support for busy internet servers. Technical Report WRL-Technical-Note-49, Compaq Western Research Lab, May 1995.
34. V. N. Padmanabhan and J. Mogul. Improving HTTP latency. *Computer Networks and ISDN Systems*, 28:25–35, December 1995.
35. Vivek S. Pai, Peter Druschel, and W. Zwaenepoel. Flash: An efficient and portable web server. In *Proceedings of USENIX 1999*, June 1999.
36. A.V. Pechinkin, A.D. Solovyev, and S.F. Yashkov. A system with servicing discipline whereby the order of remaining length is serviced first. *Tekhnicheskaya Kibernetika*, 17:51–59, 1979.
37. R. Perera. The variance of delay time in queueing system M/G/1 with optimal strategy SRPT. *Archiv fur Elektronik und Uebertragungstechnik*, 47:110–114, 1993.
38. David L. Peterson and David B. Adams. Fractal patterns in DASD I/O traffic. In *CMG Proceedings*, December 1996.
39. J. Roberts and L. Massoulie. Bandwidth sharing and admission control for elastic traffic. In *ITC Specialist Seminar*, 1998.
40. R. Schassberger. The steady-state appearance of the M/G/1 queue under the discipline of shortest remaining processing time. *Advances in Applied Probability*, 22:456–479, 1990.
41. L.E. Schrage. A proof of the optimality of the shortest processing remaining time discipline. *Operations Research*, 16:678–690, 1968.
42. L.E. Schrage and L.W. Miller. The queue M/G/1 with the shortest processing remaining time discipline. *Operations Research*, 14:670–684, 1966.
43. F. Schreiber. Properties and applications of the optimal queueing strategy SRPT - a survey. *Archiv fur Elektronik und Uebertragungstechnik*, 47:372–378, 1993.
44. Bianca Schroeder and Mor Harchol-Balter. Evaluation of task assignment policies for supercomputing servers: The case for load unbalancing and fairness. In *9th IEEE Symposium on High Performance Distributed Computing (HPDC '00)*, August 2000.
45. A. Silberschatz and P. Galvin. *Operating System Concepts, 5th Edition*. John Wiley & Sons, 1998.
46. D.R. Smith. A new proof of the optimality of the shortest remaining processing time discipline. *Operations Research*, 26:197–199, 1976.
47. W. Stallings. *Operating Systems, 2nd Edition*. Prentice Hall, 1995.
48. A.S. Tanenbaum. *Modern Operating Systems*. Prentice Hall, 1992.

An Efficient and Scalable Coscheduling Technique for Large Symmetric Multiprocessor Clusters*

Andy B. Yoo and Morris A. Jette

Lawrence Livermore National Laboratory
Livermore, CA 94551
{ayoo, jette1}@llnl.gov

Abstract. Coscheduling is essential for obtaining good performance in a time-shared symmetric multiprocessor (SMP) cluster environment. The most common technique, gang scheduling, has limitations such as poor scalability and vulnerability to faults mainly due to explicit synchronization between its components. A decentralized approach called dynamic coscheduling (DCS) has been shown to be effective for network of workstations (NOW), but this technique may not be suitable for the workloads on a very large SMP-cluster with thousands of processors. Furthermore, its implementation can be prohibitively expensive for such a large-scale machine. In this paper, we propose a novel coscheduling technique which can achieve coscheduling on very large SMP-clusters in a scalable, efficient, and cost-effective way. In the proposed technique, each local scheduler achieves coscheduling based upon message traffic between the components of parallel jobs. Message trapping is carried out at the user-level, eliminating the need for unsupported hardware or device-level programming. A sending process attaches its status to outgoing messages so local schedulers on remote nodes can make more intelligent scheduling decisions. Once scheduled, processes are guaranteed some minimum period of time to execute. This provides an opportunity to synchronize the parallel job's components across all nodes and achieve good program performance. The results from a performance study reveal that the proposed technique is a promising approach that can reduce response time significantly over uncoordinated time-sharing and batch scheduling.

1   Introduction

The most prevailing machine architecture for large-scale parallel computers in recent years has been the cluster of symmetric multiprocessors (SMPs), which consists of a set of SMP machines interconnected by a high-speed network. Each SMP node is a shared-memory multiprocessor running its own image of an operating system (OS) and often constructed using commodity off-the-shelf (COTS)

---

* This work was performed under the auspices of the U.S. Department of Energy by University of California Lawrence Livermore National Laboratory under contract No. W-7405-Eng-48.

D.G. Feitelson and L. Rudolph (Eds.): JSSPP 2001, LNCS 2221, pp. 21–40, 2001.

components mainly due to economic reasons [1]. Continuous decrease in the price of these commodity parts in conjunction with the good scalability of the cluster architecture has made it feasible to economically build SMP-clusters that have thousands of processors and total physical memory size on the order of Terabytes. The most prominent example of such very large-scale SMP-clusters is the Department of Energy (DOE) Accelerated Strategic Computing Initiative (ASCI) project [5] machines [3,4,6].

Efficiently managing jobs running on parallel machines of this size while meeting various user demands is a critical but challenging task. Most supercomputing centers operating SMP-clusters rely on batch systems such as LoadLeveler [16,26] for job scheduling [31]. We may utilize a system efficiently using these batch systems, but high system utilization usually comes at the expense of poor system responsiveness with a workload dominated by long running jobs, as is typical of many large scale systems [11]. An alternative scheduling technique that improves the system responsiveness while improving fairness and freedom from starvation is *time-sharing*. With time-sharing, we can create virtual machines as desired to provide the desired level of responsiveness.

An important issue in managing message-passing parallel jobs in a time-shared cluster environment is how to coschedule the processes (or tasks) of each running job. Coscheduling here refers to a technique that schedules the set of tasks constituting a parallel job at the same time so that they can run simultaneously across all nodes on which they are allocated. When a parallel job is launched on an SMP-cluster, a set of processes are created on the nodes allotted to the job. These processes of the job usually cooperate with each other by exchanging messages. In most cases, two communicating processes do not proceed until both processes acknowledge the completion of a message transmission. Therefore, the interprocess communication becomes a bottleneck which may prevent the job from making progress if both sending and receiving processes are not scheduled at the time of the message transmission. Without coscheduling, the processes constituting a parallel job suffer high communication latencies due to spin-waiting periods and context switches. The ill effect on system performance of running multiple parallel jobs without coscheduling has been well documented [23]. It is very difficult to coschedule parallel jobs in a time-shared environment using local operating systems running independently on each node alone. A new execution environment is required in which parallel jobs can be coscheduled.

A few research efforts have been made to develop a technique with which the coscheduling can be achieved efficiently for SMP-clusters and networks of workstations (NOW). The simplest approach to coscheduling is a technique called *gang scheduling* [13,14,17,18,19,20]. In gang scheduling, a matrix called gang matrix, which explicitly describes all scheduling information, is used. Each column and each row of a gang matrix represent a processor in the system and a time slice during which the processes in the row are scheduled to run, respectively. The coscheduling is achieved by placing all the processes of a job on the same row of the gang matrix. The gang matrix is usually maintained by a central manager (CM) running on a separate control host. The CM distributes the gang matrix whenever there is a change in schedule. A small daemon process running on each node follows this well-defined schedule to allocate resources to processes on that node. This simple scheduling action guarantees coscheduling of parallel jobs due to the way the gang matrix is constructed. The gang scheduling technique is relatively simple to implement.

A few successful gang scheduling systems have been developed and operational on actual production machines [17,19]. However, gang scheduling has limitations. First, correct coscheduling of jobs entirely depends upon the integrity of the distributed scheduling information. If any of these schedules, which are transmitted through unreliable network, are lost or altered, it is highly likely that the jobs will not be coscheduled. Second, the gang scheduler's central manager is a single point of failure. The last and the most serious drawback of the gang scheduling technique is its poor scalability. As the number of nodes in the system increases, not only the size of the gang matrix but also the number of control messages increases. These control messages convey various information such as the node status, the health of local daemons and the jobs running on each node, and so on. In many cases, the central manager is required to take appropriate actions to process the information delivered by a control message. Due to the excessive load imposed on the central manager, the gang scheduler does not scale well to a very large system.

Another method for achieving coscheduling is a decentralized scheme called *dynamic coscheduling* (DCS) [22,27,28]. In DCS, the coordinated scheduling of processes that constitute a parallel job is performed independently by the local scheduler, with no centralized control. Since there is no fixed schedule to follow in DCS, the local scheduler must rely on certain local events to determine when and which processes to schedule. Among various local events that a local scheduler can use to infer the status of processes running on other nodes, the most effective and commonly-used one is *message arrival*. The rationale here is that when a message is received from a remote node, it is highly likely that the sending process on the remote node is currently scheduled. This implies is that upon receiving a message, the local scheduler should schedule the receiving process immediately, if not already scheduled, to coschedule both the sending and receiving processes.

A few experimental scheduling systems based on this method have been developed [22,27]. All of these prototypes are implemented in an NOW environment, where workstations are interconnected through fast switches like Myrinet [21]. Interprocess communication is carried out using high-performance user-level messaging layers that support user-space to user-space communication [24,29,30] in these systems to reduce communication latency. These implementations rely upon programming the firmware in network interface cards (NIC) so as to communicate scheduling requirements for processes to the operating system. Large SMP clusters are difficult to support under the best of circumstances. The specialized hardware and firmware required by the typical DCS configuration would not normally be supported by the hardware vendor and could be very challenging to support at large scales.

The DCS technique can achieve effective, robust coscheduling of processes constituting a parallel job. However, current DCS implementations available may not be suitable for a large-scale SMP-clusters. Interprocess communications within an SMP typically uses shared-memory for improved performance. Current DCS techniques would need to remove this optimization and route messages through the NIC in order to effect scheduling. Context switching can also induce significant memory management overhead, including both cache refresh and potentially paging. We know of no DCS implementation which addresses memory management issues.

In this paper, we propose and evaluate a novel coscheduling technique for an SMP-cluster. To design a scalable coscheduling technique, we have adopted the DCS approach which allows us to eliminate any form of centralized control. The primary concern of the previous DCS schemes is boosting the priority of a receiving process as quickly as possible on a message arrival to establish immediate coscheduling. To accomplish this, they program the network devices so that an incoming message can be trapped long before the receiving process gets scheduled. We believe that what is more important to improve overall performance is not reacting immediately to incoming messages but keeping the communicating processes coscheduled while they are running[1]. In the proposed scheme, therefore, a process of a parallel job, once scheduled, is guaranteed to remain scheduled for certain period of time assuming that other processes of the job are either already scheduled or getting scheduled through message exchanges.

A mechanism to detect message arrivals is embedded into a message-passing library whose source code is freely available to the public, making the design portable and cost-effective. On a message arrival, the receiving process reports this to a local scheduler which makes appropriate scheduling decisions. Processes that are not scheduled need to be run periodically to trap incoming messages. An adverse effect of this sporadic execution of non-scheduled processes is that they may send messages triggering preemption of other coscheduled processes. This problem is resolved by attaching the status of sending process to each outgoing message.

We implement and evaluate the proposed coscheduling technique on a Compaq Alpha cluster testbed at LLNL. The results from our measurements show that the proposed coscheduling technique can reduce job response time as much as 50% compared with unsynchronized time-sharing. The effect of various system parameters on performance is also analyzed in this study.

The rest of the paper is organized as follows. Section 2 describes the proposed technique and its implementation. Experiment results are reported in Section 3. Finally, Section 4 draws conclusions and presents directions for future research.

---

[1] This view is also shared by another promising decentralized coscheduling scheme called *implicit coscheduling* [2], where the local scheduler allows the currently scheduled process to spin-wait instead of preempting it immediately upon a message arrival as in the DCS coscheduling schemes.

2   Design and Implementation

2.1   Basic Design

The proposed coscheduler for SMP-clusters is based on two design principles.

1. It is essential for achieving coscheduling to make correct decisions on when and which processes on each node to schedule.
2. It is crucial to maximize coscheduled time as a portion of scheduled time for the processes on each node. If preemption occurs too frequently, the parallel job's throughput will suffer from an increase in spin-wait time at synchronization points, cache refresh delays, and potentially paging delays.

A key factor in scalable coscheduler design is decentralization of scheduling mechanism. An ideal scalable coscheduler should not employ any centralized control or data structures, but completely rely upon autonomous local schedulers. Our coscheduling technique also follows such decentralized approach. Without any global information on the status of all the processes in the system, each local scheduler has to determine the status of remote processes and coschedule the local processes with their remote peers. Exchanging control messages that contain process status information among local schedulers is not a scalable solution. An alternative is to use certain implicit local information to infer the status of remote processes. Such implicit information includes response time, message arrival, and scheduling progress [2].

Like all the previous work [2,22,27,28], our coscheduler depends upon message arrival to infer status information of remote processes. The message arrival refers to the receipt of a message from a remote node. When a message is received, this implies the sending process is highly likely to be currently scheduled. Therefore, it is crucial to quickly schedule the receiving process to achieve coscheduling.

In order to implement this idea, we need a mechanism which detects the arrival of a message and reports this to the local scheduler. This message trapping mechanism is performed at user-level in our design to fulfill one of our design goals: cost-effectiveness. The implementation can be easily done by inserting a few lines of code into a small number of application program interfaces (APIs) provided by open-source message-passing libraries like MPICH [15]. This code notifies the local scheduler of message arrival through an interprocess communication (IPC) mechanism. The user-level message trapping mechanism allows us to avoid the purchase of and support of additional hardware or software. In addition, the use of publicly available software makes our design quite portable.

The local scheduler functions include maintaining information such as the process ID (pid) and the status of processes assigned to the node and scheduling appropriate processes for coscheduling. When a process is about to start or terminate execution, the process reports these events to the local scheduler along with its own pid. When notified of these events, the local scheduler adds/removes the pid received to/from the data structure it manages. Similarly, when a message arrives, the receiving process reports this with its pid to the local scheduler, which then responds by performing appropriate scheduling operations. Here the report of message arrival serves as a request to local scheduler to schedule the receiving process.

The group of processes constituting the same parallel job on each node serve as a scheduling unit. That is, whenever a process is scheduled, its peer processes on the same node are simultaneously scheduled. This establishes the coscheduling more quickly. Since the peer processes of a recently scheduled process should eventually be scheduled via message-passing, we can improve concurrency by scheduling the entire group of peer processes together. More importantly, this strategy may increase the number of messages to other unscheduled processes on remote nodes and hence achieve the coscheduling more quickly.

In an attempt to reflect the second design principle, we ensure that all the newly scheduled processes run for a certain period of time without being preempted. This guarantees that each parallel job runs at least for the given time without being preempted by another job. We use a predetermined threshold value for the *guaranteed minimum execution time* (GMET), but the value may be calculated dynamically as well. Receiving a scheduling request from a user process, the local scheduler checks if the currently scheduled processes have run at least for the GMET. If so, a context switch is performed. Otherwise, the request is ignored.

While message arrivals cause user process to send scheduling requests, these scheduling requests can allow the running process to continue to run. This may result in starvation of other jobs. Starvation is prevented by a timer process that periodically sends a context switch request to the local scheduler. The local scheduler, on receiving this request, performs a context switch in a similar fashion to a scheduling request from a user process. In this case, however, the local scheduler selects a new job to run. The local scheduler selects the job which has received the least CPU time as the next one to run improving fairness. The local scheduler keeps track of the CPU time each job has consumed to facilitate this scheduling process. We use a time-slice on the order of seconds in this research, adhering to the second design principle. The rationale behind such a long time-slice is to insure the job establishes coscheduling and executes coscheduled for some minimum time. This also reduces the overhead of cache refresh and paging.

There is a critical issue in conjunction with the user-level message trapping that needs to be addressed. In order for a user process to trap incoming messages, the process itself has to be scheduled. Otherwise, message arrivals will never be detected and reported to the local scheduler. The local scheduler in our design, therefore, periodically schedules all the jobs for a brief period of time to detect any message arrival. A serious side effect of this simple approach is that the local scheduler may receive *false scheduling requests*. A false scheduling request can be sent to the local scheduler when a user process receives a message from a remote process which is scheduled only for the message-trapping purpose. These false scheduling requests may results in wrongful preemption of coscheduled processes and significant performance degradation. We solve this problem by attaching the status of sending process to every outgoing message. With the status of sending process available, the receiving process can easily determine whether a context

Table 1. Summary of newly defined MPI functions.

Function	Request	Event	Local Scheduler Action
MPI_Register	CMDREG	Process Initialization	Register requesting process
MPI_Terminate	CMDOUT	Process Termination	Remove requesting process
MPI_Schedule	CMDSCH	Message Arrival	Schedule requesting process, if allowed

switch would help to achieve coscheduling or not. The design of the coscheduler is shown in Fig. 1.

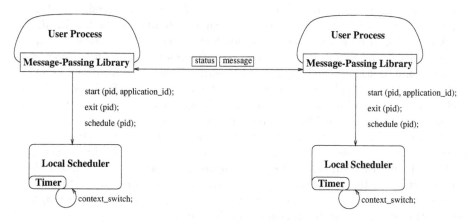

Fig. 1. The design of proposed coscheduler.

2.2   Implementation

The proposed coscheduler described has been implemented and evaluated on an eight-node Compaq Alpha cluster testbed running Tru64 Unix 5.0 at LLNL. Each node has two Compaq Alpha EV6 processor operating at 500 MHz with 1 GB of main memory. The implementation exercise has involved only minor modifications to a user-level message-passing library and the development of two very simple daemon processes. The implementation of this coscheduler is described in detail below.

MPICH Library. We have modified an open-source message-passing library, MPICH [15], to implement the user-level message trapping as well as the process registry operations. The MPICH is a freely-available, high-performance, portable implementation of the popular MPI Message Passing Interface standard. We have chosen the MPICH library mainly due to its popularity and easy access to its source code.

A few new functions are added to the MPICH library in this implementation. These functions notify the local scheduler when certain events occur through IPC. Those requests are accompanied by the pid of sending process. The functions are summarized in Table. 1.

MPI_Register is invoked during the initialization phase of an MPI process. The MPI_Register, when invoked, sends a CMDREG request to local scheduler. An MPI application id is also sent along with the request to notify the local scheduler of which MPI job the process belongs to. The local scheduler creates a small shared-memory region at the time a process is registered through which the process can determine its scheduling status. Similarly, MPI_Terminate is invoked during the finalization phase of the MPI process and sends CMDOUT request to the local scheduler. The terminating process is then removed from the list of processes assigned to the local scheduler. MPI_Schedule sends CMDSCH request along with its pid to local scheduler in an attempt to schedule itself.

A few MPICH functions need to be modified as well to incorporate the capability to handle messages carrying process status information. These functions are net_send, net_recv, and net_recv_timeout. We have modified net_send in such a way that a single byte representing the status of sending process is attached to each outgoing message. The actual length of the message is increased by one byte. The additional byte is prefixed to the message, because the receiving process can specify arbitrary message length. If we postfix the status information to an outgoing message, and a different message length is given in a receiving routine, the information can be lost or even worse, incorrect status information can be extracted by the receiving process. By always sending the status information before actual message body, we can preserve and retrieve correct status information regardless of the message length specified by a user.

With the modifications made to net_recv and net_recv_timeout, the status information is separated from each incoming message, and the actual message is passed to whichever routine invoked these functions. An early scheduling decision, which is whether a context switch is appropriate or not, is made at this level using the status information received. That is, if the sending process is currently scheduled and the receiving process is not, a context switch is desirable. A request for context switch is sent to the local scheduler by calling MPI_Schedule.

Class Scheduler. In our implementation, we use the Compaq Tru64 UNIX priority boost mechanism called *class scheduler* [7] to schedule processes of a parallel job. With the class scheduler, we can define a class of system entities and assign certain percentage of CPU time to the class. The class scheduler ensures that access to the CPUs for each class does not exceed its specified limit. The entities that constitute a class can be users, groups, process groups, pids, or sessions. There may be a number of classes on a system. A database of classes, class members, and the percentage of CPU time for the class is maintained by the class scheduler. The database can be modified while the class scheduler is running, and the changes take effect immediately.

The kernel has very little knowledge of class scheduling. A class, in the kernel, is an element in an array of integers representing clock ticks. A thread that is subject to class scheduling has knowledge of its index in the array. Each time the thread uses CPU time, the number of clock ticks used is subtracted from the array element. When the count reaches zero the thread is either prevented from running altogether or, optionally, receives the lowest scheduling priority possible.

When class scheduling is enabled, a class scheduler daemon is started. The class scheduler daemon wakes up periodically and calculates the total number of clock ticks in the interval. Then, for each class in the database, it divides the total by the percentage allocated to the class and places the result into an array. When finished, the array is written to the kernel.

The class scheduler provides APIs which system developers can use to enable and disable class scheduling, create and destroy a class, add and remove a class member, change the CPU percentage allotment for a class, and so on. Using these APIs, we define a class of pids for each group of processes constituting the same MPI job. We use the application id of the MPI job as the name of the class. Processes of an MPI job can be scheduled at the same time to the class representing those processes. For example, if we allocate 100% of CPU time to a class, only the processes defined in the class will receive CPU time. The local scheduler performs a context switch by swapping the CPU percentage of two classes of processes that are being context-switched.

It was mentioned that all the processes, whether currently scheduled or not, need to receive some CPU time periodically to trap incoming messages at the user-level. One way of doing this is to let the local scheduler periodically allocate 100% of CPU time to each of the classes in the system for a very short time. This is a feasible solution, but it may burden the local scheduler as the number of jobs assigned to the node increases. Therefore, we rely on the class scheduler to achieve the user-level message trapping. In our implementation, 1% of CPU time is allocated to each unscheduled class so that the processes in the class are executed for very short periods of time, and remaining CPU percentage is allocated to a scheduled class. Therefore, if there are n classes in the system, $(n-1)\%$ of CPU time is allocated to $n-1$ classes, and a scheduled class receives $(100 - n + 1)\%$ of CPU time. The class scheduler is configured to strictly adhere to these percentage allocations and time allocated to a class which is not used by that class is not used by other job classes. Whenever a class is created or destroyed, the CPU allotment to the scheduled class is adjusted accordingly.

Daemons. Two daemons, timer and scheduler daemons, are implemented for process scheduling. In our implementation, there are no coordinating activities among the daemons residing on different nodes. Although we may achieve better performance by allowing the daemons to exchange messages for the coordination, we intentionally exclude this option to make our scheme to be scalable. However, we believe that allowing sporadic message exchanges for the coordination among daemons could improve performance.

The task of the timer daemon is to periodically send a request for context switch to scheduler daemon to enforce time-sharing. The timer daemon simply repeats the process of sleeping for a predetermined interval, which works as time-slice, followed by sending the context-switch request to the scheduler daemon.

The scheduler daemon performs key scheduling operations such as managing process and MPI job status and changing the priority of processes. The scheduler daemon is a simple server that acts upon requests from either user process or the timer daemon. Those requests are sent to the scheduler daemon via shared-memory IPC, since the IPC occurs only within a single node and the shared-memory provides the fastest IPC mechanism. A shared-memory region, through which requests are sent, is created when the scheduler daemon starts execution.

The main body of the scheduler daemon consists of a loop in which the daemon waits for a request and then execute certain operations corresponding to the request received. There are five requests defined for the scheduler daemon: CMDREG, CMDOUT, CMDCSW, CMDSCH, and CMDDWN.

The CMDDWN request terminates the scheduler daemon. On receiving this request, the scheduler daemon removes the shared-memory region created for IPC and then exits. CMDREG and CMDOUT requests are associated with the process management operations. An MPI process sends CMDREG to notify that the process is about to start execution. When receiving this request, the scheduler daemon creates an entry in the process table it maintains. An entry in the process table contains information about a process such as its pid and the MPI job that the process belongs to. The table also contains scheduling information about the MPI job assigned to the node. Such information on an MPI job includes the job id, the number of member processes, the time when the job was scheduled and preempted, and a pointer to a shared-memory region from which processes of the job read the job's status. The table is organized in such a way that there is a link between each MPI job and all the processes that constitute the job. When an MPI job is registered for the first time, the scheduler daemon performs two things. First, it creates an entry for the job in the process table. Next, a class is created using the job's application id as the class name. The pid of the requesting process is added to the table and the class created. A newly created class receives 1% of CPU time initially. The CPU time allotment of scheduled class is adjusted accordingly when a new class is created.

CMDOUT, a request issued upon process termination, does the reverse of CMDREG. Receiving CMDOUT request, the scheduler daemon removes the pid of the sending process from the process table and the corresponding class. When the last process terminates, corresponding process table entries and class defined for the terminating job are destroyed, and the CPU time allotment of scheduled class is adjusted.

The CMDCSW request is issued by the timer daemon. Upon receiving this request, the scheduler daemon simply swaps the CPU time allotment of currently scheduled job with that of the next job to be executed. The CMDSCH request also causes a context switch, but it is issued by a user process upon a message arrival. The scheduler daemon, upon receiving this request, first determines whether the context switch is allowed by checking if currently scheduled job has consumed at least the GMET. If so, the requesting job is scheduled by adjusting the CPU time allotment. Otherwise, the request is discarded.

The pseudo codes for the daemons are given below.

Timer Daemon:

```
1. Create a pointer to a  shared-memory region for IPC.
2. loop
      Sleep for n seconds, where n is time-slice length.
      Send CMDCSW to scheduler daemon.
   end loop
```

Scheduler Daemon:

```
1. Create a shared-memory region for IPC.
2. Initialize process table and system queue.
3. loop
     Wait for a request.
     switch (request)
       case CMDDWN:
          Destroy classes, if there are any.
          Remove the shared-memory region.
          Exit.
       case CMDREG:
          if (there is no entry for job corresponding to
                  the requesting process)
          then
            Create an entry in the process table and
              perform initialization for the job.
            Create a new class for the job and assign 1% of
              CPU time to the class.
            Create a shared-memory region for the
              communication of job status.
            if (there are no other job in the system)
            then
              Schedule the newly created job.
            else
              Adjust the CPU time allotment of a scheduled job.
            end if
          end if
          Add the sending process to the process table and
            corresponding class.
       case CMDOUT:
          Remove requesting process from the process table and
            the class the process belongs to.
```

```
    if (the number of processes in an MPI job corresponding
        to the requesting process is zero)
    then
      Destroy the entry and the class defined for the MPI job.
      if (the job is currently scheduled)
      then
        Schedule the next job in the queue, if there is one.
      else
        Adjust the percentage of CPU time allocated to
          a scheduled job.
      endif
    end if
  case CMDCSW:
    Schedule a job that has received the least CPU time by
      adjusting the CPU time allotment.
  case CMDSCH:
    if (currently scheduled job, if exists, has run
        at least for the GMET)
    then
      Schedule the requesting job by adjusting
        the CPU time allotment.
    end if
end switch
```

3 Experimental Results

In this research, we have conducted a performance study on an 8-node Compaq Alpha SMP cluster testbed to evaluate the proposed coscheduler using popular NAS Parallel Benchmarks (NASPB) [8,9,10,25]. Three workloads, each exhibiting different degree of communication intensity, are used to evaluate the performance under various message traffic conditions. Here, the communication intensity of a job is measured by the number of messages exchanged during the course of execution. The first workload consists of randomly selected class A and class B NASPBs and represents a workload with moderate message traffic, under which the communication intensity of jobs varies to a great extent. The second workload is constructed from the three most communication-intense NASPBs (LU, SP, and BT) to represent a workload with heavy message traffic. The third workload consists of only the EP NASPB in which there is little communication between processes. The three workloads are summarized in Table 2. We followed the naming convention used in the NASPB to identify each benchmark. The number of a benchmark within a workload is given in parenthesis. The performance measure of interest in this study is mean job response time.

Fig. 2 compares the performance of the new coscheduling technique with that of uncoordinated time-sharing. The uncoordinated time-sharing (or scheduling)

Table 2. Three workloads used.

Workload	Benchmarks
Workload 1	bt.B.4, ep.B.8 (2), bt.A.4, sp.A.9, mg.A.2, lu.B.4
Workload 2	bt.A.4 (2), lu.A.2 (2), sp.B.9, sp.A.9, sp.A.4, lu.B.2
Workload 3	ep.A.2 (2), ep.A.4 (2), ep.B.8, ep.B.4 (2), ep.A.8

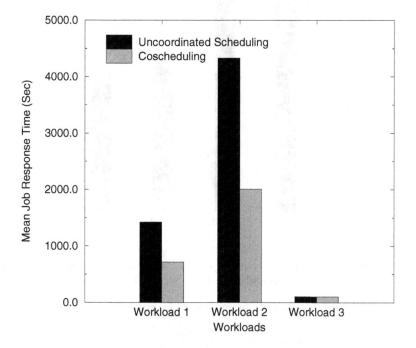

Fig. 2. Comparison of mean job response time for different workloads (Time slice = 15 seconds and GMET = 5 seconds).

here refers to the execution of multiple jobs simultaneously and scheduled solely by the local operating systems on each node. The time slice and GMET used in this experiment are 15 and 5 seconds, respectively. For all three workloads, the new coscheduler shows better or comparable response time behavior compared to the uncoordinated time-sharing. As expected, the best performance is achieved when the message traffic is heavy (Workload 2). Here, the mean job response time is reduced by 50% when the proposed coscheduling technique is used. The measures for mean job response time are almost identical for the Workload 3. This is because the effect of uncoordinated scheduling of the processes constituting a parallel job on performance is not significant when the message traffic is light. These results are a strong indication that the proposed technique is a promising approach to coscheduling, which can efficiently improve the performance of parallel jobs under various message traffic conditions.

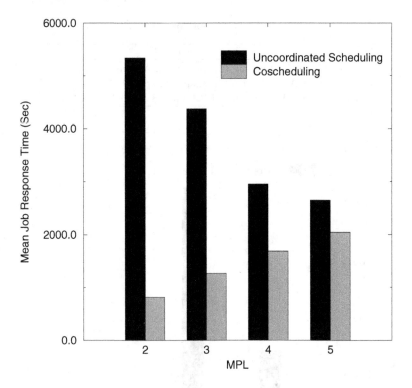

Fig. 3. Comparison of mean job response time for different multiprogramming level (MPL) (Time slice = 15 seconds and GMET = 5 seconds).

Table 3. The workloads used for each MPL.

MPL	Benchmarks
2	sp.A.16, sp.A.9
3	sp.A.16, sp.A.9, lu.A.8
4	sp.A.16, sp.A.9, lu.A.8, cg.A.16, ft.A.8
5	sp.A.16, sp.A.9, lu.A.8, cg.A.16, ft.A.8, ep.A.8

Fig. 3 shows the response-time behavior of the proposed coscheduling technique and uncoordinated time-sharing scheduling for varying multiprogramming level (MPL). The time-slice and the GMET lengths are the same as in Fig. 2. The workloads used in this experiment are summarized in Table 3.

We increase the load to the system by adding a new set of randomly selected NASPBs to existing workload, as MPL increases. In this experiment, only class A benchmarks are considered to minimize the effect of paging overhead. As Fig. 3 indicates, the proposed coscheduling scheme obtains the best performance gain (85 % reduction in response time) when the MPL is 2. This is because without coordinated scheduling, processes of parallel jobs tend to block frequently waiting for their communicating peers to be scheduled, whereas our technique reduces the blocking time considerably through coscheduling of the processes. However, the performance gain decreases as the MPL increases. The reason for this is that as the number of time-shared jobs increases, the waiting time due to blocking is compensated by increased computation and communication interleave, while coscheduling the parallel jobs becomes increasingly difficult. Although the proposed scheme achieves subpar performance with a large MPL, it is expected perform well under normal circumstances in which the MPL is usually kept small in order to minimize the overhead, especially from paging activity [12].

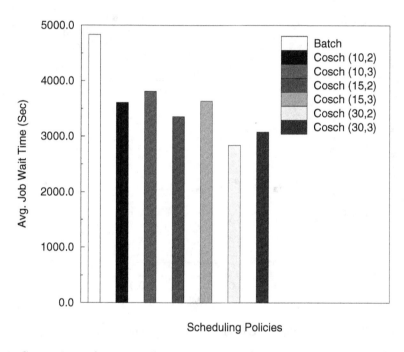

Fig. 4. Comparison of average job wait time under batch and proposed coscheduling technique with different time slice length and MPL (Cosch (time slice, MPL)).

Fig. 4 plots the average job wait time under batch scheduling (without back-filling) and proposed coscheduling technique with varying time slice length and MPL. In this experiment, we submitted 100 NASPBs to the system at once and measured the wait (or queuing) time of each job. The workload consists of 98 class A NASPBs and two class C NASPBs (LU). GMET is set to 2 seconds in this experiment. A separate script starts new jobs in such a way that desired MPL is maintained. Fig. 4 shows that the proposed coscheduling technique reduces the average job wait time by as much as 41% over simple batch scheduling. The poor performance of the batch scheduling is due to what is known as the 'blocking' property of the first come first served (FCFS) scheduling discipline [32]. That is, under the FCFS policy a job has to wait until all preceding jobs finish their execution, and therefore, its wait time is the total of the execution time of all the preceding jobs. On the other hand, the proposed technique, with its time-sharing and coscheduling capability, is not affected by the blocking property and hence performs very well in this experiment. Furthermore, closer examination reveals that the average job wait time increases as the MPL increases. As already discussed in Fig. 3, this is because it becomes increasingly difficult to establish coscheduling as the MPL increases.

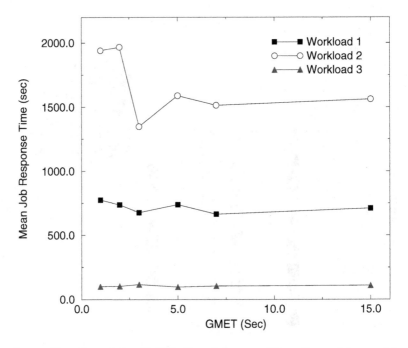

Fig. 5. The effect of the GMET on performance (Time slice = 30 seconds).

Figures 5 and 6 examine the effect of the GMET and the time-slice lengths on performance of the proposed coscheduler, respectively. Fig. 5 shows the response-time behavior of the coscheduler for three workloads described in Table 2 as the length of GMET varies. The time-slice length in this experiment is set to 30 seconds. The results reveal that the GMET length does not affect the performance of the coscheduler for workloads 1 and 3, where the communication intensity is relatively low. On the other hand, the GMET length has significant effect on the system performance for the workload 2 in which the communication intensity is high. If the GMET length is set too small for such a workload with high communication intensity, coscheduling a parallel job is extremely difficult because some of the processes that constitute the parallel job are highly likely to be preempted before the coscheduling is established due to the increased message traffic. If the length of GMET is too large, the coscheduler fails to quickly respond to in-

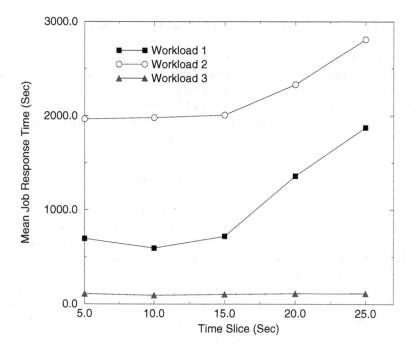

Fig. 6. The effect of time slice on performance (GMET = 5 seconds).

coming context-switch requests from remote processes, and this degrades the performance. However, the performance degradation in this case is not as severe as in the previous case, since the large GMET length still prevents excessive context-switches. This is clearly visible in Fig. 5, where the response-time curve for the workload 2 sharply drops and then increases as the GMET length changes from 2 through 5 seconds. For the GMET lengths greater than 5 seconds, the response-time behavior remains almost unchanged, since most of context-switch requests are discarded with such long GMETs and the performance is strictly governed by the length of the time slice used.

Fig. 6 plots the changes in response time as the time-slice length varies for the three workloads. The GMET length is set to 5 seconds. As expected, the performance of the coscheduler is hardly affected by the time-slice length for workload 3. However, the response time continuously increases for both workloads 1 and 2 with time-slices greater than 15 seconds. This can be explained in conjunction with the results from the previous experiment. Since there is no global control in our design, which could schedule all processes of a parallel job concurrently, a situation in which scheduled processes that constitute different parallel jobs contend for scheduling of their communicating peers occurs quite frequently. If the GMET length is set too large (as in this experiment), the context-switch requests through messages sent to remote nodes are discarded and hence the parallel jobs eventually stall until a context-switch is initiated by one of the timer daemons. Consequently, the waiting time of each job increases as the time-slice length increases.

As shown in Fig. 5 and Fig. 6, the GMET and the time-slice lengths can have significant effect on performance and hence, selecting optimal values for these parameters is critical. However, such optimal values are highly workload-dependent and therefore, careful workload analysis must be conducted. The experiment results also suggest that in general short time-slice and long GMET lengths are favorable to obtaining good system performance.

4   Concluding Remarks and Future Study

Efficiently coscheduling processes of message-passing parallel jobs on a time-shared cluster of computers poses great challenges. In this paper, we propose a new technique for a cluster of SMP machines, which offers a scalable, portable, efficient, and cost-effective solution for achieving coscheduling. The proposed technique uses message arrivals to direct the system towards coscheduling and hence requires no explicit synchronization mechanism. Unlike other coscheduling schemes based on message arrivals, however, incoming messages are processed at the user level to avoid the need for additional hardware and system software. The status of a sending process is attached to each outgoing message so that better scheduling decisions can be made by the recipient. Processes are guaranteed to run at least for a certain period of time once scheduled to ensure that each parallel job makes progress while being coscheduled and that time period is on the order of seconds. This design principle is the key to the success of our coscheduler in obtaining high performance. Experimental results indicate that the proposed technique is a promising and inexpensive approach to efficient coscheduling, which can improve the performance significantly over uncoordinated time-sharing and batch scheduling.

There are a few interesting directions for future research. The performance of our coscheduler is greatly affected by the length of time-slice and GMET. The results from a preliminary analysis reveal that short time-slice and long GMET lengths are beneficial to achieving good system performance. We plan to conduct more rigorous study on the effect of these parameters on performance in the future study. The experiment has been conducted on a rather small cluster. The scalability of the proposed scheme will be measured on a much larger cluster in the future research. In addition, tests of this technique in heterogeneous computing environment could provide the ability to execute even larger problems.

Acknowledgment

The authors would like to thank anonymous referees for their valuable comments that helped us improve the quality of this paper.

References

1. T. E. Anderson, D. E. Culler, and D. A. Patterson. A Case for NOW (Networks of Workstations). *IEEE Micro*, 15(1):54–64, Feb. 1995.
2. A. C. Arpaci-Dusseau, D. E. Culler, and A. M. Mainwaring. Scheduling with Implicit Information in Distributed Systems. In *Proc. ACM SIGMETRICS 1998 Conf. on Measurement and Modeling of Computer Ssystems*, 1998.
3. ASCI Blue Mountain. `http://www.lanl.gov/asci/bluemtn/bluemtn.html`.
4. ASCI Blue Pacific. `http://www.llnl.gov/platforms/bluepac`.
5. ASCI Project. `http://www.llnl.gov/asci`.
6. ASCI Red. `http://www.sandia.gov/ASCI/Red`.
7. Class Scheduler. `http://www.unix.digital.com/faqs/publications/base_doc`.
8. D. H. Bailey et al. The NAS Parallel Benchmarks. *International Journal of Supercomputer Applications*, 5:63–73, 1991.
9. D. H. Bailey et al. The NAS Parallel Benchmarks. Technical Report NASA Technical Memorandom 103863, NASA Ames Research Center, 1993.
10. D. H. Bailey et al. The NAS Parallel Benchmarks 2.0. Technical Report NAS-95-020, NASA Ames Research Center, Dec. 1995.
11. D. H. Bailey et al. Valuation of Ultra-Scale Computing Systems: A White Paper, Dec. 1999.
12. D. G. Feitelson. Memory Usage in the LANL CM-5 Workload. In *Proc. IPPS'97 Workshop on Job Scheduling St rategies for Parallel Processing*, pages 78–94, 1997.
13. D. G. Feitelson and M. Jette. Improved Utilization and Responsiveness with Gang Scheduling. In *Proc. IPPS'97 Workshop on Job Scheduling Strategies for Parallel Processing, Vol. 1291 of Lecture Notes in Computer Science*, pages 238–261. Springer-Verlag, Apr. 1997.
14. H. Franke, P. Pattnaik, and L. Rudolph. Gang Scheduling for Highly Efficient Multiprocessors. In *Proc. Sixth Symp. on the Frontiers of Massively Parallel Processing*, Oct. 1996.
15. W. Gropp and E. Lusk. A High-Performance, Portable Implementation of the MPI Message Passing Interface Standard. *Parallel Computing*, 22:54–64, Feb. 1995.
16. IBM Corporation. *LoadLeveler's User Guide, Release 2.1*.
17. J. E. Moreira et al. A Gang-Scheduling System for ASCI Blue-Pacific. In *Proc. Distributed Computing and Metacomputing (DCM) Workshop, High-Performance Computing and Networking '99*, Apr. 1999.
18. M. Jette. Performance Characteristics of Gang Scheduling in Multiprogrammed Environments. In *Proc. SuperComputing97*, Nov. 1997.
19. M. Jette. Expanding Symmetric Multiprocessor Capability Through Gang Scheduling. In *Proc. IPPS'98 Workshop on Job Scheduling Strategies for Parallel Processing*, Mar. 1998.
20. M. Jette, D. Storch, and E. Yim. Timesharing the Cray T3D. In *Cray User Group*, pages 247–252, Mar. 1996.
21. N. J. Boden et al. Myrinet: A Gigabit-per-second Local Area Network. *IEEE Micro*, 15(1):29–36, Feb. 1995.
22. S. Nagar, A. Banerjee, A. Sivasubramaniam, and C. R. Das. A Closer Look At Coscheduling Approaches for a Network of Workstations. In *Proc. 11th ACM Symp. of Parallel Algorithms and Architectures*, June 1999.
23. J. K. Ousterhout. Scheduling Technique for Concurrent Systems. In *Proc. Int'l Conf. on Distributed Computing Systems*, pages 22–30, 1982.

24. S. Pakin, M. Lauria, and A. Chien. High Performance Messaging on Workstations: Illinois Fast Meessages (FM). In *Proc. Supercomputing '95*, Dec. 1995.
25. S. Saini and D. H. Bailey. NAS Parallel Benchmark (Version 1.0) Results 11-96. Technical Report NAS-96-18, NASA Ames Research Center, Nov. 1996.
26. J. Skovira, W. Chan, H. Zhou, and D. Lifka. The Easy-LoadLeveler API Project. In *Proc. IPPS'96 Workshop on Job Scheduling Strategies for Parallel Processing, Vol. 1162 of Lecture Notes in Computer Science*, pages 41–47. Springer-Verlag, Apr. 1996.
27. P. G. Sobalvarro. *Demand-based Coscheduling of Parallel Jobs on Multiprogrammed Multiprocessors*. PhD thesis, Dept. of Electrical Engineering and Compuer Science, Massachusetts Institutute of Technology, 1997.
28. P. G. Sobalvarro and W. E. Weihl. Demand-based Coscheduling of Parallel Jobs on Multipr ogrammed Multiprocessors. In *Proc. IPPS'95 Workshop on Job Scheduling Strategies for Parallel Processing*, pages 63–75, Apr. 1995.
29. T. von Eicken and A. Basu and V. Buch and W. Vogels. U-Nnet: A User-Level Network Interface for Parallel and Distributed Computing. In *Proc. 15th ACM Symp. on Operating System Principles*, Dec. 1995.
30. T. von Eicken and D. E. Culler and S. C. Goldsten and K. E. Schauser. Active Messages: A Mechanism for Integrated Communication and Computation. In *Proc. 19th Annual Int'l Symp. on Computer Architecture*, Dec. 1995.
31. Top 500 Supercomputer Sites. `http://www.netlib.org/benchmark/top500.html`.
32. B. S. Yoo and C. R. Das. A Fast and Efficient Processor Management Scheme for k-ary n-cubes. *Journal of Parallel and Distributed Computing*, 55(2):192–214, Dec. 1998.

Coscheduling under Memory Constraints in a NOW Environment[*]

Francesc Giné[1], Francesc Solsona[1], Porfidio Hernández[2], and Emilio Luque[2]

[1] Departamento de Informática e Ingeniería Industrial, Universitat de Lleida, Spain.
{sisco,francesc}@eup.udl.es
[2] Departamento de Informática, Universitat Autònoma de Barcelona, Spain.
{p.hernandez,e.luque}@cc.uab.es

Abstract. Networks of Workstations (NOW) have become important and cost-effective parallel platforms for scientific computations. In practice, a NOW system is heterogeneous and non-dedicated. These two unique factors make scheduling policies on multiprocessor/multicomputer systems unsuitable for NOWs. However, the coscheduling principle is still an important basis for parallel process scheduling in these environments. We propose a new coscheduling algorithm for reducing the number of page faults across a non-dedicated cluster by increasing the execution priority of parallel tasks with lower page fault rate. Our method is based on knowledge of events obtained during execution, as communication activity and memory size of every task. The performance of our proposal has been analyzed and compared with other coscheduling implementations by means of simulation.

1 Introduction

The studies in [5] indicate that the workstations in a NOW are normally underloaded. This has invited researchers to develop different techniques in an attempt to adapt the traditional uniprocessor time-shared scheduler to the new situation of mixing local and parallel workloads [1,10]. Basically, there are two methods of making use of these CPU idle cycles, task migration [6,7] and time-slicing scheduling [8,9]. In a NOW, in accordance with the research carried out by Arpaci [10], task migration overheads and the unpredictable behavior of local users may lower the effectiveness of this method.

In a time-slicing environment, two issues must be addressed: how to coordinate the simultaneous execution of the processes of a parallel job, and how to manage the interaction between parallel and local user jobs. One alternative is coscheduling [12,14,22].

Coscheduling ensures that no process will wait for a non-scheduled process for synchronization/communication and will minimize the waiting time at the synchronization points. Thus, coscheduling may be applied to reduce messages waiting time and make good use of the idle CPU cycles when distributed applications are executed in a cluster or NOW system. Coscheduling decisions can

---

[*] This work was supported by the CICYT under contract TIC98-0433

D.G. Feitelson and L. Rudolph (Eds.): JSSPP 2001, LNCS 2221, pp. 41–65, 2001.
© Springer-Verlag Berlin Heidelberg 2001

be made taking implicit runtime information of the jobs into account, basically execution CPU cycles and communication events [12,13,14,15,16,22]. Our framework will be focused on an implicit coscheduling environment, such as scheduling the correspondents -the most recent communicated processes- in the overall system at the same time, taking into account both high message communication frequency and low penalty introduction into the delayed processes. The implicit property is also applied for coscheduling techniques that are not controlled by dedicated nodes or daemons.

However, the performance of a good coscheduling policy can decrease drastically if memory requirements are not kept in mind [2,3,11,18,19,20,21,28,29]. Most of them [2,18,21,20] have proposed different techniques to minimize the impact of the real job memory requirements on the performance of a gang scheduling policy (original coscheduling principle, mostly applied and implemented in MPP's). However, to our knowledge, there is an absence of research into minimizing the impact of the memory constraints in an implicit coscheduling environment. We are interested in proposing implicit coscheduling techniques with memory considerations. That is to coschedule distributed applications taking into account dynamic allocation of memory resources due to the execution of local/distributed jobs by using implicit information (that obtained by observing local events in each cluster node).

In a non-dedicated system, the dynamic behavior of local applications (which consequently also varies its allocated resident memory) or a distributed job mapping policy without memory considerations cannot guarantee that parallel jobs have enough resident memory as would be desirable throughout their execution. In these conditions, the local scheduler must coexist with the operating system's demand-paging virtual memory mechanism. In an uniprocessor system, paging improves memory and CPU utilization by allowing processes to run with only a subset of their code and data to be resident in main memory. However in distributed environments (cluster or NOW), the traditional benefits that paging provides on uniprocessors may decrease depending on various factors, such as for example: the interaction between the CPU scheduling discipline, the synchronization patterns within the application programs, the page reference patterns of these applications [3,28] and so on.

Our main aim is to reduce the number of page faults in a non-dedicated coscheduling system, giving more execution priority to the distributed tasks with lower fault page probability, letting them finish as soon as possible. Thus, on their completion, the released memory will be available for the remaining (local or distributed) applications. Consequently, major opportunities arise for advancing execution for all the remaining tasks.

However, the execution of the distributed tasks must not disturb local task interactivity, so excessive local-task response time should be avoided. It means that a possible starvation problem of this kind of tasks must be taken into account.

In this paper, a new coscheduling environment over a non-dedicated cluster system is proposed. The main aim of this new scheme is to minimize the impact of demand paged virtual memory, with prevention of local-task starvation capabilities. The good performance of this model is demonstrated by simulation.

The rest of the paper is organized as follows. In section 2, the main aim of our work is explained. Next, in section 3, the system model used is defined. A coscheduling algorithm based on this model is presented in section 4. The performance of the proposed coscheduling algorithm is evaluated and compared in section 5. Finally, the conclusions and future work are detailed.

2   Memory Constraints Motivation

Extensive work has been performed in the coscheduling area, but memory consideration effects in cluster computing performance have scarcely been studied. This fact, together with the different works done with coscheduling techniques [16,23,17], gives us a real motivation for an insight into coscheduling of distributed applications with memory constraints.

The execution performance of fine-grained distributed applications -those with high synchronization- could be improved by applying a generic coscheduling technique in cluster computing (section 2.1). However, the coscheduling techniques do not always improve performance. When task memory requirements in any particular cluster node overload the main memory, if virtual memory is supported by the o.s., the page fault mechanism (the swapper) is activated. The swapper interchanges blocks (the secondary memory transfer unit) of pages between the main and secondary memories. The swapper speed is usually at least one order of magnitude lower than the network latency. Thus, high or moderate page fault frequency in one node can drop distributed application performance drastically [3,28,29], overtaking widely in this way coscheduling benefits. In section 2.2, a solution for solving this situation is proposed

2.1   Coscheduling Benefits

How a coscheduling technique increases the performance of distributed applications and the page fault mechanism disturbs its progression is shown by means of the following real example.

Two different environments were evaluated and compared between them, the plain Linux scheduler, (denoted as *LINUX*), and one implicit coscheduling policy, denoted as *COS*, -for further information, see [17]- implemented in a real Linux cluster made up of 4 PC's with the same characteristics (350Mhz Pentium II processor, 128 MB of RAM, 512 KB of cache, Linux o.s. (kernel v. 2.2.14) and PVM 3.4.0). *COS* policy is based on giving more scheduling priority to tasks with more message sending and receiving frequency. The well known NAS [30] parallel benchmarks *MG* is used in this trial. Also, two synthetic local tasks have been executed jointly with the MG benchmark in each node.

Fig. 1(a) shows the good performance of the *COS* policy in relation to *LINUX* one in the execution of the MG benchmark when the main memory is not overloaded. As it was expected, COS policy gives priority the execution of the MG benchmark due to its intensive communication.

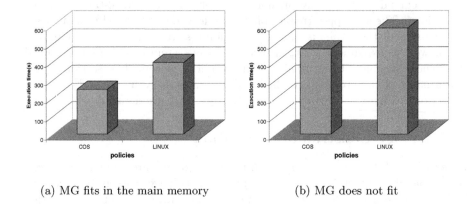

(a) MG fits in the main memory   (b) MG does not fit

Fig. 1. Execution times (in seconds) for MG application.

Fig. 1(b) shows the execution time of the MG benchmark when it does not fit in its resident memory set because memory requirements of local tasks have been increased. As it can be seen on this figure, the page faulting mechanism (one or two orders of magnitude slower than the network latency) will corrupt the performance of distributed applications. This adverse effect is increased in applications with intensive communication because every page fault causes cascading delays on other nodes, thus decreasing the overall system performance. This fact points to the idea that memory requirements should be taken into account on the coscheduling processes with the aim of reducing the probability of page faults. This is certainly the main aim of this article.

2.2   Motivation

The following example (see Fig. 2) will help us to explain how the reduction of page fault rate is achieved and as, a consequence, the global performance is improved.

Let two intensive message-passing distributed applications, J_1 and J_2 and a cluster C made up of three homogeneous machines, N_1, N_2 and N_3 with a main memory size of M units. Each distributed application is composed of three tasks, each one is mapped in a different machine. Moreover, one local task is executed in every node. It is assumed that tasks memory requirements do not fit in the main memory of such node. The memory requirements of distributed tasks J_1, J_2 and local task (LOCAL) are denoted as m_1, m_2 and m_L, respectively. Figure 2 shows the contents of the swap memory (at the top) and main memory (in the middle) for node N_3 through the time. At the bottom, a two dimensional timing diagram representing the accumulative CPU time (in the Y axis) and the total executing time (executing plus waiting time, in the X axis) is also shown.

It can be seen that without any memory control policy, (Fig. 2 (a)) the local task is finished after 300 units, whereas distributed tasks J_1 and J_2 finish

Node N₃ behavior

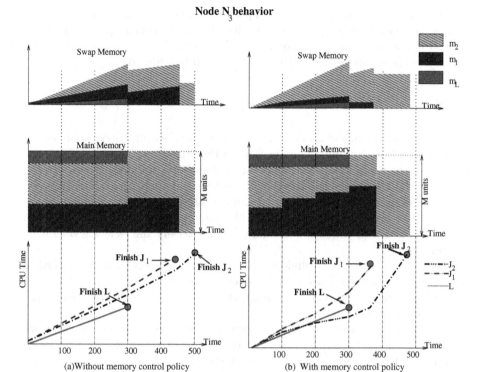

Fig. 2. Coscheduling under memory constraints.

after 450 units and 500 units, respectively. Figure 2 (b) shows the execution times obtained by applying a memory control policy consisting of giving more execution priority to the distributed task with the lowest page fault rate. That, in turn, means that the main memory space allocated to task J_1 -it has lower page number into the swap than J_2- is increased with time until it has all its address space residents in main memory, at the expense of memory space reduction for task J_2. Thus, task J_1 finishes its execution sooner than in case (a) (at time 350). When J_1 finishes execution, it frees its assigned memory and so the memory available for task J_2 is considerably increased, leading to a speedy execution of such task.

From the comparison of both techniques (fig. 2(a) and (b)), we can conclude that, by applying a memory policy control, the execution times for both distributed tasks, J_1 and J_2, have been reduced whereas local task one (task L) has been maintained. It is worth pointing out that although the progression of task J_2 during the first three periods is slower in case (b), when J_1 is finished, the J_2 CPU execution rate rises significantly because all the resources (CPU and memory) are available.

Note that this memory control policy should be applied with priority to distributed tasks with high synchronization requirements because, as synchronization grows more frequently, the impact of delaying any one node by a page fault is increased drastically. It suggests that the above memory policy should be applied in combination with a coscheduling technique based on communication activity. Section 4 explains how this coordination is achieved.

3   System Model

In this section, our model for cluster systems is explained. It provides for the execution of various distributed applications at the same time. This model assumes that all the nodes in a non-dedicated cluster (or NOW) are under the control of our coscheduling scheme and also that the distributed applications are composed by a suite of tasks which are allocated and executed in the nodes making up the cluster. Also, every local coscheduler will take autonomous decisions based on local information provided for the majority of existing time-sharing operating systems.

The model description is divided into two basic sub-models, basic coscheduling and memory model. This way, the model will be more easily understood and a clearer separation between the basic underlying system requirements and the memory ones is performed.

In developing the model, various assumptions are made. Some of them are chosen with the aim of simplifying the model as much as possible. We are interested in developing a model that could be implemented further in a time-sharing o.s. Linux [25], due to its free property, fits in our purpose. Therefore, some assumptions are made taking Linux properties into account.

3.1   Basic Coscheduling Model

The model represents a cluster system for executing both distributed and local applications, so some preliminary assumptions must be performed. If different applications must be run in the cluster jointly, the underlying o.s. must be time-sharing. In a time-sharing cluster node, a task may be in different states (ready to run or simply ready, blocked, etc).

In this environment, tasks cannot communicate with their correspondents release the CPU before the expiration of their Time Slice and chance to the blocked state. It is assumed that incoming (out-going) messages to (from) a cluster node are buffered in a Receiving Message Queue, RMQ (Sending Message Queue, SMQ). This is a non-arbitrary assumption. For example, Unix-like systems [4], with the standard *de facto* TCP(UDP)/IP protocol, maintain (with particular differences) some sort of these buffers.

Let a cluster $C = \{N_k\}$, $k = 1...n$ and a task l, denoted as $task_l$, of node k (N_k). Every task belongs to a parallel/local job, denoted as *Job*. Next, some basic notation (and used in the remainder of this article) is summarized as follows:

- $RQ[k]$: pointer to the task on the position k of the Ready Queue (RQ). Special cases are k = 0 (*top*) and $k = \infty$ (*bottom*) of RQ. "*Top*" task is the currently executing task in the CPU and *"bottom"* is the latest one to be executed.

- $task_l.c\_mes$: number of current receiving-sending messages for $task_l$. It is defined as follows:

$$task_l.c\_mes = task_l.rec + task_l.send, \tag{1}$$

where $task_l.rec$ is the number of receiving messages for $task_l$ in the RMQ queue and $task_l.send$ is the number of sending messages for $task_l$ in the SMQ queue.

- $task_l.mes$: Past receiving-sending message number for $task_l$. This is defined as follows:

$$task_l.mes = P * task_l.mes + (1 - P) * task_l.c\_mes, \tag{2}$$

where P is the percentage assigned to the past messages ($task_l.mes$) and $(1 - P)$ is the percentage assigned to the current messages ($task_l.c\_mes$). This field will be used to distinguish between local tasks ($task_l.mes = 0$) and distributed tasks ($task_l.mes \neq 0$). Based on experimental results [17], a $P = 0.3$ has been chosen.

- $task_l.de$: number of times that task l has been overtaken in the RQ by another task due to a coscheduling cause, since the last time such a task reached the RQ. This field will be used to avoid the starvation of the local and distributed tasks.

Note that some of this information is not explicitly maintained by the operating system, but can be easily obtained. For example, in a Linux o.s., $task_l$ will be represented by the *task_struct* structure (the Linux PCB, Process Control Block). The *de* field is not provided by the Linux o.s. but it could be added to the *task_struct* structure.

3.2   Memory Model

The Memory Management Unit (MMU) of each node is based on pages with an operating system which provides demand-paging virtual memory.

If the referenced page by a task is not in its *resident set* (allocated pages in the main memory), a page fault will occur. This fault will suspend the task until the missing page is loaded in the resident set. Next, such a task will be reawakened and moved to the RQ. Meanwhile another task could be dispatched for execution into the CPU.

The page replacement algorithm is applied to all the pages of the memory regardless of which process "owns" them (global replacement policy). Thus, the task resident size may vary randomly. Every node, taking into account some existing operating system trends, uses *the Last Recently Used (LRU) replacement algorithm,* in which the chosen page for replacement is the one that has not been referenced for a longest time. One example is the Linux o.s. that runs *the clock algorithm* [25] (a *LRU* approximation algorithm).

Some studies [24,3] have shown the relation between the task page fault rate with respect to its resident set size and memory pattern access (*locality*). Locality is normally related to procedures, functions or some other kind of program-code association. The *working set* of a task [24], denoted as *task.wrk*, is a technique for obtaining an approximation to the locality. A task working set at time t with parameter τ is defined as the set of pages touched by the task during the last τ time units $(t\text{-}\tau,t)$. Large τ values can overlap various localities. On the other hand, low values for τ, may produce poor locality approximations [3].

We propose to calculate the page fault probability for each task. This way, it will be possible to determine which tasks have their working set resident in main memory. Low (high) page fault probability for a task will mean that its respective resident set fits (does not fit) its associated working set very well.

The proposed algorithm with memory constraints (see next section) will use the following notation (all of them use the memory concepts explained above):

- $task_l.vir\_mem$: virtual memory size for task l.
- $task_l.res\_mem$: resident memory size for task l.
- $task_l.nrpg\_fault$: accumulative page fault number for task l.
- $task_l.fault$: page fault probability for task l. It is computed as follows:

$$task_l.fault = \begin{cases} 0 & \text{if } task_l.wrk < task_l.res\_mem \\ \frac{task_l.res\_mem}{task_l.wrk} & \text{if } task_l.wrk \geq task_l.res\_mem \end{cases} \quad (3)$$

- $N_k.M$: main memory size of the node k. Given that a homogeneous cluster is assumed, this parameter will be denoted simply as M.
- $N_k.mem$: memory requirements into node k. It is computed as follows:

$$N_k.mem = \sum_l task_l.vir\_mem \quad (4)$$

It is important to note that all the above fields are generally provided by the Linux operating system. For example, $task_l.res\_mem$, $task_l.vir\_mem$ and $task_l.nrpg\_fault$ are maintained in the *task_struct* structure, whereas M is a global system parameter. Although Linux does not provide the working set of every task directly, it can be easily obtained from kernel space.

4 CSM: Coscheduling Algorithm under Memory Constraints

In this section, a local coscheduling algorithm with memory constraints, denoted as CSM (see Algorithm 1) is proposed and discussed. Next, how CSM achieves the global coordination through the cluster is explained.

4.1 CSM Algorithm

The CSM algorithm must decide which task is going to run next, according to three different goals:

1. In a NOW, parallel applications must coexist with the operating system's demand-paged virtual memory. Paging is typically considered [18,21] to be too expensive due to its overhead and adverse effect on communication and synchronization. So, one of the aims will be to minimize the number of page faults throughout the cluster.
2. The coscheduling of the communication-synchronization processes. No processes will wait for a non-scheduled process (correspondents) for synchronization/communication and the waiting time at the synchronization points will be minimized.
3. The performance of the local jobs. CSM algorithm should avoid the starvation of the local processes, minimizing the overhead produced by the execution of parallel jobs.

Algorithm 1 is implemented inside a generic routine (called *insert_RQ*). This is the routine chosen to implement our coscheduling algorithm because all the ready-to-run tasks must pass it before being scheduled. The *INITIALIZATION* section is the place where the different initializations (these may be global variables) are done. Note that an original *insert_RQ* routine should only contain one line of the form *(RQ[∞] := task_h)*, which should insert $task_h$ at the bottom of the RQ.

If the RQ is empty (line 3), $task_h$ is inserted on the top, otherwise the algorithm works to find the position of the RQ where the task should be inserted in accordance with the starvation condition, communication rates and the page fault probabilities.

CSM is applied mainly to distributed tasks (those with $task_h.mes \neq 0$). It has no effect on the local tasks (generally tasks without remote communication, $task_h.mes = 0$), which are inserted at the bottom of the RQ ($RQ[∞] := task_h$ in line 4).

The only way that CSM algorithm can know which task is currently executing in another node is taking the reception of the messages into account. For this reason, if the task to be inserted on the RQ has any incoming message in the RMQ queue ($task_h.rec \neq 0$) and the main memory in such node is overloaded ($N_k.mem > M$), the inserted task is led to the *top* of the RQ ($RQ[0]$). Thus, CSM applies a *dynamic technique* [15] to ensure that fine-grained distributed applications are coscheduled. In this technique, the more scheduling priority is assigned to tasks the more the receiving frequency is.

For the rest of the cases, the *SCHED_COND* function together with the *STARV_COND* one will establish the task ordering in the RQ.

From line 15 to 21, the scheduling function is established according to memory constraints. If the memory requirements of all the resident tasks in such node ($N_k.mem$) exceed the main memory size (M), the *SCHED_COND* will depend on the page fault probability of the distributed tasks ($RQ[i].fault > task_h.fault$, line 17). This mode will be denoted as CSM mode. So, CSM gives more priority to the tasks with less probability of making a page fault. Taking into account the page replacement algorithm defined in the previous section, the pages associated with tasks with less chance of being scheduled will get old early. So, every time a page fault happens, the older pages will be replaced by the missing page. It means that with time, more memory resources will be allocated to tasks distributed with a lower page fault rate. In terms of locality, the local scheduler will settle for the resident set of such distributed tasks as can fit its locality.

Otherwise, when memory requirements of all the tasks fit in main memory, another implicit coscheduling technique is applied. The condition shown in line 19 ($RQ[i].mes < task_h.mcs$) is based on the *predictive technique*, [14,23]. In predictive coscheduling, in contrast to the dynamic coscheduling, both sending and receiving frequencies are taken into account. The reason for doing it this way is that perhaps distributed tasks performing only receiving messages have no necessity to be coscheduled. This is also true for sending processes. We think that processes performing both sending and receiving have higher potential coscheduling than those performing only sending or receiving.

The *STARV_COND* function, defined from line 22 to 26, avoids both the starvation of local tasks and distributed ones. For this reason, the inserting $task_h$ overtakes only the tasks whose *delay* field ($RQ[i].de$) is not higher than a constant named *MNOL* (Maximum Number of Overtakes) for local tasks or *MNOD* for distributed ones. The task field *de* is used to count the number of overtakes (by distributed tasks) since the last time the task reached the RQ. In line 9, this field is increased. The default value for *MNOL* is 2, as higher values may decrease the response time (or interactive performance) of local tasks excessively. Thus, starvation of local tasks (normally of the interactive kind and not communicating tasks) is avoided. It's worthwhile to point the necessity of evaluating also the field *de* for distributed tasks in order to avoid the starvation of a parallel job with a high page fault rate. For instance, if it wasn't taken into account, a continuous stream of parallel jobs with small memory requirements could provoke that a parallel job with a high page fault rate was always pushed to the end of the RQ. The value of *MNOD* constant will be evaluated experimentally.

How CSM algorithm maintains the coordination between the local decisions take in every node through the cluster is explained in the next section.

4.2   Global Coordination

As it has been explained above, CSM takes decisions locally. Also, depending on the characteristics of its resident tasks, it can work in different modes (Dynamic, Predictive or CSM) as it can be seen from the flow graph of figure 3. To simplify, the STARV_COND has been assumed the same for both, distributed and local tasks ($MNO = MNOL = MNOD$).

Thus, global coordination (through all the cluster) of the tasks making up distributed applications is performed in an independent manner in each cluster node, and depends on the three different execution modes:

1. Predictive mode: it establishes the task progression with high communication rates in nodes where main memory is not exhausted.
2. Dynamic mode: when the main memory is exhausted, CSM gives priority to the reception of messages in order to achieve the coscheduling between distributed tasks with high communication rates.

---

1 **procedure insert_RQ** ($task_h$:task)

2 *INITIALIZATION*

3 if($RQ[0] = NULL$) $RQ[0] := task_h$;

4 else if ($task_h.mes = 0$) $RQ[\infty] := task_h$; //Local task

5 else if(($task_h.rec \neq 0$) and ($N_k.mem > M$)) $RQ[0] := task_h$; //Dynamic mode

6 else

7   $i := \infty$;

8   while(STARV_COND(i) and SCHED_COND($i,task_h$))

9     $RQ[i].de ++$;

10     $i - -$;

11   endwhile;

12   $RQ[i] := task_h$;

13 endif;

14 **endprocedure**

15 **function SCHED_COND** (i:int, $task_h$:task)   return boolean

16 if($N_k.mem > M$)

17   return($RQ[i].fault > task_h.fault$); //CSM mode

18 else

19   return($RQ[i].mes < task_h.mes$); //Predictive mode

20 endif;

21 **endfunction**

22 **function STARV_COND** (i:int)   return boolean

23 **cons** $MNOL, MNOD$; //MNO≡ Maximum   Nr.   Overtakes   (L:Local, D:Distributed);

24 if($RQ[i].mes = 0$) return ($RQ[i].de < MNOL$);

25 else return ($RQ[i].de < MNOD$);

26 **endfunction**

Algorithm 1. CSM algorithm

Procedure insert_RQ(task)

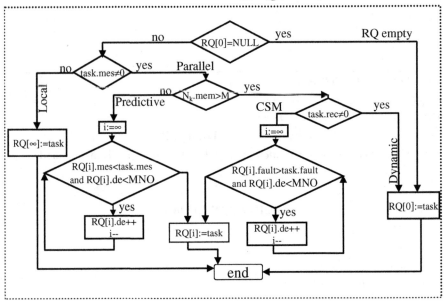

Fig. 3. Flow graph associated to the CSM algorithm.

3. CSM mode: this mode, jointly with the Dynamic one, works out in nodes where the main memory is exhausted. It schedules first tasks with lower page fault rate. This behavior favors tasks with locality fitting in its resident set. So jobs with smaller memory requirements will get priority implicitly with regard to jobs with bigger ones. Thus, in this situation, CSM behaves as a Small Job First policy

The above explained behavior could damage the performance of parallel jobs with little synchronization and high memory requirements. This is because CSM algorithm gives priority to the execution of jobs with small memory require-ments in nodes whose main memory has been exhausted. CSM, by means of the starvation condition, avoids this situation. In the same way, distributed jobs with small memory requirements have associated a low execution time [2]. As a consequence, the memory released by these small jobs will be available for the remaining (local or distributed) applications sooner and then, they will be able to speed up its execution.

It's worthwhile to point out that decision taken by every local CSM scheduler depends on the ones made in the overall nodes of the cluster system. That is to say, a readjustment between the node modes in the overall system will be produced continuously.

There is an special case which requires particular attention. Suppose that CSM in one node gives priority to a task which belongs to a particular dis-

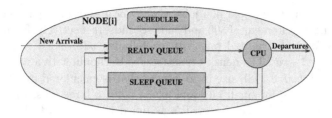

Fig. 4. Simulation of a node.

tributed application, while CSM in another node gives priority to a task which belongs to another distributed application. In this situation, the slowdown introduced in the implicated distributed application should be minimized by the starvation condition and the implemented dynamic mode, which maintains the synchronization between tasks in different nodes.

Finally, note that the CSM behavior would lead to a FIFO coscheduling policy when all the distributed applications had similar memory requirements.

5   Experimentation

In this section, some simulation results are presented that compare the performance of the CSM policy, described in section 4, with other coscheduling algorithms. First, the simulation environment and the metrics used are explained. Then, the results obtained in the simulations are described and commented on.

5.1   Simulation and Metrics

Every node of the cluster has been simulated as shown in fig. 4. In this model, based on [26], when a task quantum is expired, the task is removed from the CPU and is reinserted in the RQ whenever the task has not finished all its requesting time. If a task does not expire its quantum due to a communication primitive or a page fault requesting service, it will be inserted in the SLEEP QUEUE. The local SCHEDULER will fix the order of the tasks in the RQ according to four different policies, a *round-robin policy* (RR), *a predictive coscheduling policy* (PRED), *a dynamic coscheduling policy* (DYN) and *a coscheduling policy with memory constraints* (CSM). The PRED policy will correspond to the predictive mode of algorithm 1, whereas CSM policy will be the complete algorithm 1. DYN policy will correspond to the dynamic mode (line 5) described in section 4 without the memory constraints.

The chosen global simulation parameters are the following:

- Total processing requirement (*Job.tc*): the total processing requirement is chosen from a hyper-exponential distribution with mean $\overline{tc}$. It models the high variability that is expected in parallel super-computing environments [27]. It is assumed that jobs can belong to three different classes - local tasks, small and large parallel jobs. *Small/local* and *large* jobs have a mean processing requirement of 300 and 3600 seconds, respectively. Each generated job is a *large* distributed one with probability *pdt*, and a *small* one with probability 1 - *pdt*. The density function is a Bernoulli with a *pdt* probability.

- Job size (*Job.size*): job size is an integer that is calculated by 2^k within the range $[1, ..., n/8]$ for small jobs and $[n/4, ..., n]$ for large jobs, where n is the number of nodes in the cluster. It's assumed that a local task is a job with a *Job.size* = 1. By default, a value of n=32 is chosen. A static mapping of one distributed task per node is assumed. The mapping policy is based on obtaining an uniform memory load ($N_k.mem$) around the cluster.
- Mean inter-arrival time (*mit*): mean time for arriving distributed (local) tasks to the cluster (node). The chosen density function is a Poisson with mean = *mit*. The value for the *mit* parameter (for a predetermined average memory load of the cluster) has been calculated by means of the following equation:

$$mean\_load = \frac{mean\_size \times \overline{tc} \times (\sum_k N_k.mem)}{mit \times n^2 \times M} \quad (5)$$

where n denotes the number of nodes in the cluster, M the main memory size of a node and *mean_size* the mean job size, respectively. Note that a *mem_load* < 1 means a mean memory requirements per node smaller than the main memory size (M), whereas a *mem_load* > 1 denotes a mean memory requirements per node bigger than the main memory size (M). The *mean_size* is defined as follows:

$$mean\_size = \frac{\sum_k Job_k.size}{K} \quad (6)$$

where K is the number of executed jobs on the cluster.

- Memory size of the tasks ($task_l.vir\_mem$): an uniform distribution has been chosen for assigning a variable memory size (in page size units, the page size = 4KB) to each task in the range: $[1,...,mest]$ for local, $[mest,...,2*mest]$ for small and $[2*mest,...,4*mest]$ for large tasks (*mest*=8Kpages). Initially, the number of pages in the task resident set ($task_l.res\_mem$) will be computed according to the following equation:

$$task_l.res\_mem = \begin{cases} task_l.vir\_mem & \text{if } N_k.mem < M \\ \frac{(task_l.vir\_mem) \times M}{N_k.mem} & \text{if } N_k.mem \geq M \end{cases} \quad (7)$$

where $N_k.mem$ is defined according to the equation 4. However, during the simulation $task_l.res\_mem$ will be readjusted according to the scheduling frequency of a task and the page replacement algorithm explained in section 3.

- Mean service time (time slice): mean time in serving tasks (by the CPU). The chosen density function is an exponential with mean = 100ms.

- Message frequency ($task_l.mes$): the own message receiving-sending frequency is generated for each distributed task. The time between successive arrivals (sending) is simulated by means of an exponential distribution with mean=$mfreq$.
- Working set ($task_l.wrk$): in the 1970s, several empirical studies independently revealed important properties of program behavior [24]. These studies showed that programs tend to consist of *phases* which clearly dominate the fraction of total memory references and *transitions,* which account for a considerable fraction of the program's page fault. The working set size during every *phase* is computed by means of a normal distribution with mean=$0.5 * task_l.vir\_mem$ for local tasks and a mean=$0.8 * task_l.vir\_mem$ for distributed tasks, according to the experimental results shown in [3]. The length of every phase will be calculated by means of an exponential distribution with mean=$0, 1 * (task_l.tc)$. Thus, a new working set will be established after every phase.
- Page fault probability ($task_l.fault$): every time that a task is scheduled in the CPU, a new page reference belonging to the working set of such task is generated. The density function is uniformly discrete. In the case that the referenced page was not in its associated memory resident set, a new page fault would be generated. The page fault probability will be computed according to equation 3.

- Page fault latency: although the page fault latency can vary considerably depending on the cause of a page fault, in order to simplify it, a constant latency of 20 ms is assumed.
- Physical memory size (M): by default, a value of 32K pages is chosen.

The performance of CSM policy with respect to another coscheduling techniques (RR, DYN and PRED) will be validated by means of three different metrics:

- Mean page fault number: it is defined as follows:

$$mean\_pg\_fault = \frac{\sum_k N_k.(\frac{\sum_l task_l.nrpg\_fault}{load})}{n} \qquad (8)$$

where n is the number of nodes of the cluster, $task_l.nrpg\_fault$ is the number of page faults and *load* is the number of executed tasks into node k.
- Correlation: this parameter shows how good is the coordination between decision taking by CSM algorithm in different nodes. It is defined as follows:

$$Correlation = 100 - \frac{\sum_k (\frac{Job_k.tr_{fast} - Job_k.tr_{slow}}{Job_k.tc})}{K'} \times 100 \qquad (9)$$

where K' is the number of parallel jobs executed into the cluster, $Job_k.tr_{fast}$ and $Job_k.tr_{slow}$ are the faster and slower response time of a task belonging to the job k, respectively. Note that according to the implemented mapping policy every node has at most one task belonging to a specific job.

– Slowdown: It is defined as follows:

$$Slowdown = \frac{\sum_k Job_k.tr}{\sum_k Job_k.tc} \qquad (10)$$

where $Job_k.tr$ and $Job_k.tc$ are the response time and execution time of the job k. For instance, let us suppose that 1000 jobs were executed in an experiment. The mean response time of these 1000 jobs was 50 minutes, and their mean execution time on processors was 25 minutes. Then, the Slowdown metric would be 2.

To sum up, the main goal of the CSM algorithm is to minimize the *mean_pg_fault* and *Slowdown* metrics and maximize the *Correlation* metric.

5.2   Evaluation of the CSM Performance

With the aim of verifying the good behavior of our simulator, a static workload made up of two *large* parallel jobs -J_1 and J_2- and two *local* tasks -L_1 and L_2- in every node of our cluster has been simulated. Traces of the evolution of the memory resident size ($task_l.res\_mem$) -at the top of fig. 5- and the progression of accumulative CPU time along the return time (CPU plus waiting time) -at the bottom of fig. 5- has been obtained with PRED and CSM algorithms for every task of one specific node (N_1). In this experiment, the communication frequency of both parallel jobs was initialized with the same value, attention being focused on the influence of memory constraints over the performance of the distributed tasks.

By analyzing the evolution of the CPU time obtained with PRED algorithm (fig. 5(c)), we see how distributed applications are considerably favored with respect to the local ones, as was expected. It must be taken into account that predictive algorithm gives more execution priority to tasks with higher communication frequency. The analysis of its memory resident size (fig. 5(a)) reflects how distributed tasks increase its memory resources and CPU accumulative time as soon as the execution of local tasks is finished.

Figure 5(b) and (d) reflects the behavior of CSM algorithm on node N_1. At first sight, it can be seen that the execution priority and the memory resources allocated to task J_1 are much bigger than those in task J_2. In fact, when task J_1 starts its execution, the overall memory requirements of such node are below 100%, and therefore all the initial memory resources requirements for J_1 are satisfied. When J_2 begins its execution, 10s after that J_1, the memory requirements in such node exceed 100% of the main memory and J_2 cannot fit its working set in its resident set. Therefore, as CSM gives more execution priority to tasks with lower page fault probability, J_1 advances execution faster than J_2. When J_1 execution finishes (after 5400s) - 3072s before PRED case -, the J_2 accumulated CPU time rises sharply and proportionally to its memory resident size. For this reason, J_2 under CSM execution control has also a response time slightly better than with PRED case.

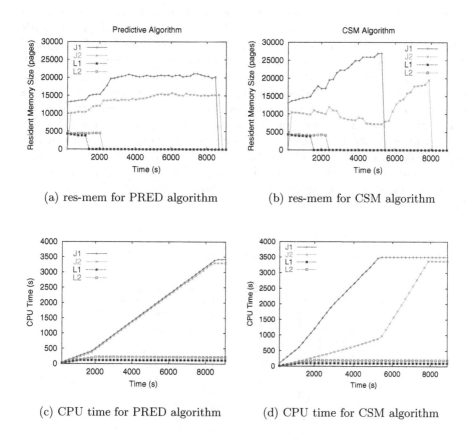

(a) res-mem for PRED algorithm   (b) res-mem for CSM algorithm

(c) CPU time for PRED algorithm   (d) CPU time for CSM algorithm

Fig. 5. PRED vs CSM behavior on node N_1.

A dynamic workload has been used in next trials to verify the good performance of CSM algorithm. With this aim, three different environments has been simulated with a *mem_load* parameter equal to 0.7, 1.0 and 1.5, respectively. Every result shown in this section represents the average of 10 experiments, each of which runs 1000 jobs. This way, how CSM works under different memory constraints is analyzed in detail.

Analysis with low memory requirements. *Small* distributed jobs with *pdt* probability and *local* tasks with $(1 - pdt)$ probability have been generated in this experimentation. Thus, a *mem_load* parameter equal to 0.7 corresponds with an average *load* per node equal to 2.8 tasks. In this subsection, the behavior of CSM algorithm is compared to the RR and dynamic (DYN) coscheduling algorithm. Note that under low memory requirements CSM algorithm works under the predictive mode explained in section 4.

Fig. 6 shows the level of correlation obtained with the three coscheduling policies. DYN and CSM policies reach a high correlation (over 80%), whereas RR reaches a low correlation. While DYN is independent of the *pdt* probability and so of the kind of task (parallel or local), RR and CSM algorithms decrease with respect to *pdt* probability. RR correlation decreases with the rise of *pdt* because more parallel tasks are blocked waiting for a communication event, whereas CSM correlation decreases because in every node it can gives priority to a task belonging to different parallel jobs. For instance, while in node N_k job J_i could get top priority because it has the higher receive-sending message frequency, in the node N_{k+i}, another job J_j could get top priority over J_i for the same reason. Note that this situation is more plausible when more parallel jobs are executing concurrently in the cluster -*pdt* near 1-. However, CSM obtains the best correlation for all *pdt* values.

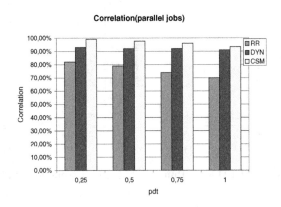

Fig. 6. Correlation metric: CSM vs DYN and RR Algorithm.

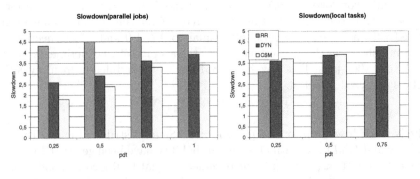

(a) Slowdown for parallel jobs   (b) Slowdown for local tasks

Fig. 7. Slowdown metric: CSM vs DYN and RR Algorithm.

Fig. 7 (a) shows the obtained *Slowdown* metric for parallel jobs with respect the *pdt* probability. The good performance obtained for the CSM mode demonstrates its effectiveness in making use of the coscheduling potential. This is due to the fact that the CSM technique takes both the current received-sending messages and the past messages into account whereas dynamic only works with the current received messages. This implies that more coscheduling chances are given in the CSM model. The high slowdown introduced by RR mode is a consequence of the low correlation reached by this technique.

Fig. 7 (b) shows the slowdown metric for local tasks. As it was expected, DYN and CSM techniques introduce a little more overhead than RR technique. It's worthwhile to point that CSM and DYN policies obtain similar results with this metric. The reason is that the number of delayed tasks is similar, and thus the introduced overhead is also equal. The dynamic policy increases executing priority of the distributed tasks fewer times than the CSM. However, when a distributed task increases its priority under DYN policy, it overtakes many more tasks than the CSM does (always moved on top of the RQ), and the consequence is that both methods introduce the same overhead.

In [23] a detailed comparison of the predictive technique, used by CSM algorithm, with another coscheduling techniques by means of simulation can be found, whereas [17] shows a real implementation of the predictive coscheduling over Linux o.s. together with a detailed experimental analysis of its good performance.

Analysis with medium memory requirements. In this experiment a *mem_load* equal to 1 has been chosen. This trial reflects the situation where memory requirements in some node can overload its main memory size due, for instance, to the activity of the local owner of such node. Thus, the three metrics (mean_pg_fault, correlation and slowdown) will be evaluated with respect to the message frequency for every implemented coscheduling policy: RR, PRED and CSM. In this trial, the three kinds of tasks (local, small and large) have been generated with a *pdt* value of 0.5. Taking these parameters into account, the simulated environment corresponds with an average *load* per node equal to 3.2.

Firstly, the influence of the MNOD constant (Maximum number of Overtakes for Distributed tasks) over the performance of distributed tasks has been evaluated. Fig. 8 shows the slowdown obtained applying CSM algorithm for small parallel jobs (fig. 8(a)) and large ones (fig. 8(b)) under different values of communication frequency and MNOD constant. Note how a MNOD constant greater than the average load per node does not have any sense because a task can not overcome more tasks than average load required in such node. As it was expected, the slowdown for large jobs decreases with respect to the value of the MNOD constant. On the other hand, the performance of small tasks increases with the value of MNOD due to the fact that tasks with lower page fault rate have more opportunities for overcoming such distributed tasks with higher page fault rate. In both graphs, the slowdown decreases with respect communication frequency because CSM gives priority to the RQ top of such tasks with any

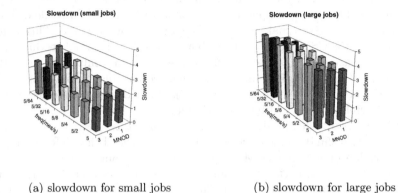

(a) slowdown for small jobs   (b) slowdown for large jobs

Fig. 8. Variation of the slowdown metric with respect communication frequency and MNOD constant (mean_load=1).

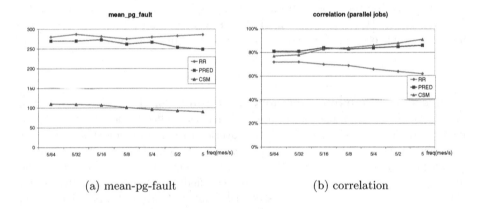

(a) mean-pg-fault   (b) correlation

Fig. 9. mean_pg_fault and correlation metric (mean_load=1).

waiting receive-send message and thus CSM favors intensive communication task execution. Taking these results into account, a $MNOD = 2$ has been chosen in this experimentation.

Fig. 9(a) and (b) shows the mean_pg_fault and correlation metric, respectively. The behavior of the mean_pg_fault reflects as CSM reaches totally its purpose of diminishing the number of page faults. The comparison of this parameter between RR and PRED algorithms reflects that both makes a similar number of pages faults. The analysis of the correlation metric (fig. 9(b)) shows that CSM reaches the best result for intensive communication jobs whereas PRED correlation overcomes CSM correlation for non-intensive communication tasks. This is because CSM coordination under medium/high memory constraints is based on

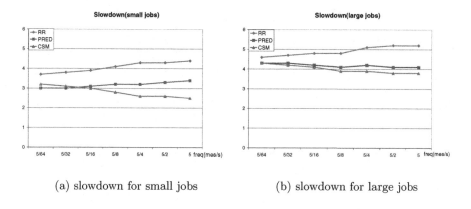

(a) slowdown for small jobs   (b) slowdown for large jobs

Fig. 10. Slowdown for parallel jobs (mean_load=1).

the current received messages whereas PRED takes an average receive-sending messages into account. As it was expected, RR reaches the worst coordination between nodes.

Fig. 10(a) and (b) shows the slowdown metric for small and large distributed jobs, respectively. For small jobs and as it was reflected in the correlation metric, CSM obtains the best results for higher communication frequencies whereas for lower communication frequencies, CSM and PRED obtain similar results. On the other hand, the performance of large jobs for the three coscheduling techniques is significantly worse. Large jobs performance feels more the effects of page faults and for this reason the slowdown is greater than for small ones. CSM and PRED techniques show a similar performance for large jobs. Although CSM, as it is reflected in fig. 9 (a), has a lower number of page faults than in other modes and so, it should be reflected in the gain of this algorithm, the mechanism of priority of this algorithm damages the performance of large jobs. Thus, CSM should take into account an agreement between the *MOND* value and the priority given for lower page faults rate tasks.

Analysis with high memory requirements. In this experiment, a *mem_load* equal to 1.5, a *pdt* = 0.5 and a *MNOD* = 3 constant have been chosen. This trial reflects the situation, where memory requirements in the majority of nodes overload its main memory size. This simulated environment corresponds with an average *load* per node equal to 4.1.

Fig. 11 (a) and (b) shows the *mean_pg_fault* and *correlation* metric, respectively. The *mean_pg_fault* metric evolution reaffirms the good behavior of CSM algorithm pointed in the previous trial (mem_load=1) together with the poor results obtained by PRED and RR algorithms. The analysis of the *correlation* metric reveals how the negative impact of the page faults is increased for intensive communication tasks. As a consequence of the low page fault rate reached

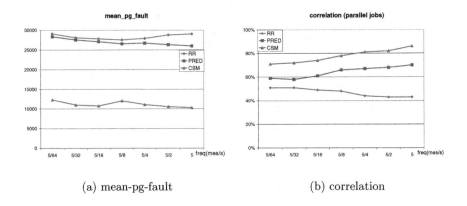

(a) mean-pg-fault   (b) correlation

Fig. 11. mean_pg_fault and correlation metric (mean_load=1.5).

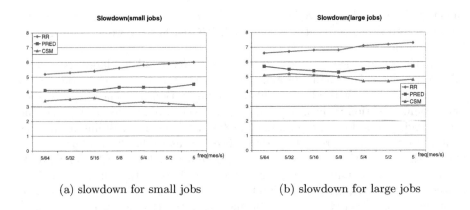

(a) slowdown for small jobs   (b) slowdown for large jobs

Fig. 12. Slowdown for parallel jobs (mean_load=1.5).

by CSM together with the coordination mechanisms implemented in such algorithm (see section 4.2), it obtains the best coordination between remote nodes for high memory requirements.

Figure 12 shows the slowdown metric for small jobs (a) and large parallel jobs (b), respectively. CSM reaches the best performance for small jobs as a consequence of its good obtained mean_pg_fault *and* correlation metric. This good trend is also reflected for large parallel jobs. Although CSM, as it was explained in section 4.2, favors the execution of the smallest jobs against the large ones, the interaction between low page faults rates and the *MNOD* constant implemented in CSM for avoiding the starvation of such kind of tasks, lead to the good behavior of CSM for large parallel jobs with respect to RR and PRED techniques.

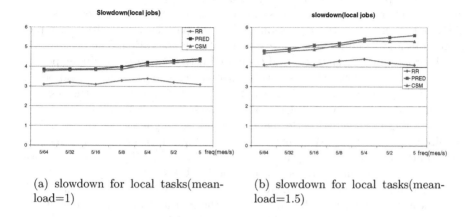

(a) slowdown for local tasks(mean-load=1)

(b) slowdown for local tasks(mean-load=1.5)

Fig. 13. Slowdown for local tasks.

Slowdown of local tasks under memory constraints. The local tasks slowdown obtained in both simulated environments above analyzed ($mem\_load = 1$ and 1.5) is shown in fig. 13 (a) and fig. 13 (b), respectively. In general, RR mode obtains the best results, although CSM and PRED results are very close to the RR ones. This is because of the influence of the implemented mechanism to avoid the starvation of local tasks. The delay introduced in the $mean\_load = 1$ case is not very high -in all the cases is lower than 4.5- and so the response time (the most important parameter for measuring interactivity) of the local tasks will be acceptable. Note that this difference will depend on the value assigned to the *MNOL* constant and the characteristics of the distributed tasks, as for example the communication frequency and memory requirements. It is worthwhile to point out that both coscheduling techniques (PRED and CSM) introduce the same overhead for local tasks, as both use the same mechanism to avoid local task starvation. As it was expected, when the $mean\_load$ is increased (see fig. 13 (b)) the slowdown obtained is worse. One aspect that is not reflected in this figure because our simulator does not take it into account, is the influence of the context switches over the local task performance. In this case, we think that the local tasks performance with CSM algorithm would slightly improve with respect to the other modes because the reduction of page faults obtained with this technique would provoke lower context switches and, as a consequence, an improvement of the performance.

6   Conclusions and Future Work

Demand-paged virtual memory attempts to optimize both CPU and physical memory use. The tradeoffs, which are well known for uniprocessors, are not nearly so clear for NOW environments.

In this paper, a new coscheduling algorithm, abbreviated as CSM, for reducing the number of page faults across a non-dedicated cluster has been presented. CSM policy increases the execution priority of parallel tasks with lower page fault rates and simultaneously, it avoids local-task starvation. The performance of this proposal has been tested and compared with another coscheduling policies by means of simulation. The results obtained have demonstrated its good behavior, reducing the *Slowdown* of distributed tasks and maintaining the response time of local tasks with respect to another coscheduling policy.

According to the good performance of the CSM algorithm, future work will be directed towards investigating new coscheduling algorithms under memory constraints and implementing these in real PVM and/or MPI environments over time-sharing operating systems (such as the LINUX o.s.).

A new improvement to be introduced into our coscheduling system, would be to adjust the length of the quantum to the real necessity of the distributed tasks. This means that for parallel tasks with high CPU time requests, relatively coarse grain time sharing is probably necessary to provide good service to these jobs while not penalizing smaller jobs. So, our purpose would be to increase the length of quantum progressively by an amount proportional to context switching overhead. This way, our algorithm would amortize the context switch overhead associated to processes with large CPU requirements.

References

1. D.G. Feitelson, L. Rudolph, U. Schwiegelshohn, K.C. Sevcik and P. Wong. "Theory and Practice in Parallel Job Scheduling". *In Job Scheduling Strategies for Parallel Processing*, D.G. Feitelson and L. Rudolph (eds), Lecture Notes in Computer Science, Vol. 1291, 1997.
2. S. Setia, M.S. Squillante and V.K. Naik. "The Impact of Job Memory Requirements on Gang-Scheduling Performance". *In Performance Evaluation Review*, March 1999.
3. D. Burger, R. Hyder, B. Miller and D. Wood. "Paging Tradeoffs in Distributed Shared-Memory Multiprocessors". *Journal of Supercomputing,* vol. 10, pp.87-104, 1996.
4. M. Bach. "The Design of the UNIX Operating System". *Prentice-Hall International Editions,* 1986.
5. T. Anderson, D. Culler, D. Patterson and the Now team." A case for NOW (Networks of Workstations)". *IEEE Micro,* 1995.
6. M. Litzkow, M. Livny and M. Mutka." Condor - A Hunter of Idle Workstations". 8th Int'l *Conference of Distributed Computing Systems,* 1988.
7. S. Russ, J. Robinson, B. Flachs and B. Heckel. "The Hector Distributed Run-Time Environment". *IEEE trans. on Parallel and Distributed Systems,* Vol.9 (11). 1988.
8. A.C. Dusseau, R.H. Arpaci and D.E. Culler. "Effective Distributed Scheduling of Parallel Workloads". *ACM SIGMETRICS'96,* 1996.
9. M. Crovella et al. "Multiprogramming on Multiprocessors". *3rd IEEE Symposium on Parallel and Distributed Processing,* 1994.
10. R.H. Arpaci, A.C. Dusseau, A.M. Vahdat, L.T. Liu, T.E. Anderson and D.A. Patterson. "The Interaction of Parallel and Sequential Workloads on a Network of Workstations". *ACM SIGMETRICS'95,* 1995.

11. D.G. Feitelson. "Memory Usage in the LANL CM-5 Workload". In *Job Scheduling Strategies for Parallel Processing*, Lecture Notes in Computer Science, vol. 1291, pp. 78-84, 1997.
12. J.K. Ousterhout. "Scheduling Techniques for Concurrent Systems." In *3rd. Intl. Conf. Distributed Computing Systems*, pp.22-30, 1982.
13. F. Petrini and W. Feng. "Buffered Coscheduling: A New Methodology for Multitasking Parallel Jobs on Distributed Systems". *International Parallel & Distributed Processing Symposium*, Cancun, 2000.
14. P.G. Sobalvarro and W.E. Weihl. "Demand-based Coscheduling of Parallel Jobs on Multiprogrammed Multiprocessors". *IPPS'95 Workshop on Job Scheduling Strategies for Parallel Processing*, 1995.
15. P.G. Sobalvarro, S. Pakin, W.E. Weihl and A.A. Chien. "Dynamic Coscheduling on Workstation Clusters". *IPPS'98 Workshop on Job Scheduling Strategies for Parallel Processing*, 1998.
16. F. Solsona, F. Giné, P. Hernández and E. Luque. "Implementing Explicit and Implicit Coscheduling in a PVM Environment". *6th International Euro-Par Conference (Europar'2000)*, Lecture Notes in Computer Science, vol. 1900, 2000.
17. F. Solsona, F. Giné, P. Hernández and E. Luque. "Predictive Coscheduling Implementation in a non-dedicated Linux Cluster". *To appear in 7th International Euro-Par Conference (Europar'2001)*, August 2001.
18. S. Setia. "The Interaction between Memory Allocation and Adaptive Partitioning in Message Passing Multicomputers". In *IPPS Job Scheduling Workshop*, Apr. 1995.
19. E. Parsons and K. Sevcik. "Coordinated Allocation of Memory and Processors in Multiprocessors". In Proc. ACM Sigmetrics/Performance'96, pp. 57-67, May 1996.
20. W. Leinberger, G. Karypis and V. Kumar. "Gang Scheduling for Distributed Memory Systems". *6th International Euro-Par Conference (Europar'2000)*, Lecture Notes in Computer Science, vol. 1900, 2000.
21. A. Batat and D. G. Feitelson. "Gang Scheduling with Memory Considerations". *Intl. Parallel and Distributed Processing Symposium*, pp. 109-114, May 2000.
22. A.C. Arpaci-Dusseau, D.E. Culler and A.M. Mainwaring. "Scheduling with Implicit Information in Distributed Systems". *ACM SIGMETRICS'98*, 1998.
23. F. Solsona, F. Giné, P. Hernández and E. Luque. "CMC: A Coscheduling Model for non-Dedicated Cluster Computing". *IPDPS'2001*, April 2001.
24. P.J. Denning. "Working Sets Past and Present". *IEEE Transactions on Software Engineering*, vol. SE-6, No 1, January 1980.
25. M. Beck et al. "LINUX Kernel Internals". *Addison-Wesley*, 1996.
26. L. Kleinrock. "Queuing Systems". *John Wiley and Sons*, 1976.
27. D. Feitelson and B. Nitzberg. "Job Characteristics of a Production Parallel Scientific Workload on the NASA Ames IPSC/860". In *Proceedings of the IPPS'95 Workshop on Job Scheduling Strategies for Parallel Processing*, pp. 215-227, April 1997.
28. K.Y. Wang and D.C. Marinescu. "Correlation of the Paging Activity of Individual Node Programs in the SPMD Execution Model". In *28th Hawaii Intl. Conf. System Sciences*, vol. I, pp. 61-71, Jan 1995.
29. V.G.J. Peris, M.S. Squillante and V.K. Naik. "Analysis of the Impact of Memory in Distributed Parallel Processing Systems". In *Proceedings of ACM SIGMETRICS Conference*, pp. 158-170, May 1993.
30. Parkbench Committee. Parkbench 2.0. http://www.netlib.org/parkbench, 1996.

The Influence of Communication
on the Performance of Co-allocation

A.I.D. Bucur and D.H.J. Epema

Parallel and Distributed Systems Group
Faculty of Information Technology and Systems
Delft University of Technology, P.O. Box 356,
2600 AJ Delft, The Netherlands
anca@pds.twi.tudelft.nl, epema@pds.twi.tudelft.nl

Abstract. In systems consisting of multiple clusters of processors interconnected by relatively slow connections such as our Distributed ASCI[1] Supercomputer (DAS), jobs may request co-allocation, i.e., the simultaneous allocation of processors in different clusters. The performance of co-allocation may be severely impacted by the slow intercluster connections, and by the types of job requests. We distinguish different job request types ranging from ordered requests that specify the numbers of processors needed in each of the clusters, to flexible requests that only specify a total. We simulate multicluster systems with the FCFS policy—and with two policies for placing a flexible request, one tries to balance cluster loads and one tries to fill clusters completely—to determine the response times under workloads consisting of a single or of different request types for different communication speeds across the intercluster connections. In addition to a synthetic workload, we also consider a workload derived from measurements of a real application on the DAS. We find that the communication speed difference has a severe impact on response times, that a relatively small amount of capacity is lost due to communication, and that for a mix of request types, the performance is determined not only by the separate behaviours of the different types of requests, but also by the way in which they interact.

1 Introduction

Over the last decade, most of the research on scheduling in parallel computer systems has been dedicated to homogeneous multiprocessors and single-cluster systems. Much less attention has been devoted to multicluster systems consisting of single clusters with fast internal communication interconnected by relatively slow links, although many such systems are in use. One such system is the Distributed ASCI Supercomputer (DAS) [7], which was designed and deployed by the Dutch Advanced School for Computing and Imaging (ASCI) in the Netherlands. In such systems, jobs may ask for, or, due to the numbers of processors in the separate clusters and the number of processors requested,

---

[1] In this paper, ASCI refers to the Advanced School for Computing and Imaging in the Netherlands, which came into existence before, and is unrelated to, the US Accelerated Strategic Computing Initiative.

D.G. Feitelson and L. Rudolph (Eds.): JSSPP 2001, LNCS 2221, pp. 66–86, 2001.

need co-allocation, i.e., the simultaneous allocation of processors in more than one cluster. In this paper, we assess the performance of co-allocation in a model of multicluster systems based on the DAS, with a special emphasis on the effect of the differences in communication speeds between intracluster and intercluster links, for different (combinations of) job structures, and for a workload based on actual measurements on the DAS.

Because of the potentially large computational power they offer at a low cost, multiclusters are an attractive option. Possibly widely distributed groups of users, each with exclusive access to their own clusters of processors, may join forces in order to share the multicluster consisting of the total of the original single clusters. However, together with this advantage of a more powerful system at a lower cost, this solution also has the potential disadvantage of increased execution times of jobs co-allocated across multiple clusters, and a decreased system utilization as a consequence, due to the slow communication among the clusters.

The possibility of creating multiclusters fits in with the recent interest in computational and data GRIDs [12,17], in which it is envisioned that applications can access resources—hardware resources such as processors, memory, and special instruments, but also data resources—in many different locations at the same time to accomplish their goal. In addition to many other problems that need to be solved in order to realize this vision, such as security issues and resource discovery, these GRIDs need schedulers that work across the boundaries of the domains governed by single resource managers to achieve co-allocation. Such schedulers have been called metaschedulers and superschedulers. Globus [13] is one of the software systems incorporating a co-allocation component.

In our model we specify the structure of the jobs, and the way jobs communicate this structure to the scheduler. Many scheduling strategies have been developed for parallel systems in an attempt to improve their performance, such as gang scheduling and dynamic jobs. However, a simple and yet often used and very practical strategy is to allow only rigid jobs, scheduled by pure space sharing, which means that jobs require fixed numbers of processors, and are executed on them exclusively until their completion. Therefore, we also only consider rigid jobs scheduled by pure space sharing. However, we do allow different request types in that jobs have the option to specify only the total number of processors they need, or also the numbers of processors in each of the clusters in the multicluster system. We assess the performance of FCFS scheduling depending on the amount of communication and on the ratio between the speeds of intracluster and intercluster links, for workloads consisting of a single or of a mix of different request types. The performance is evaluated in terms of the average response time as a function of the utilization.

This paper is a follow-up to our previous paper [19], in which we focused on different scheduling policies—in addition to FCFS we also considered some forms of backfilling—and on the system capacity lost due to none of the (first few) jobs in the queue fitting on the processors left idle by the jobs in execution; communication was not considered. Here we do include communication, we also perform simulations based on actual measurements of a real application on the DAS, we include a new type of requests—flexible requests which the scheduler is allowed to split up in any way across the clusters—and two different ways of scheduling these, we also consider workloads consisting of a mix of request types, and we assume a more realistic distribution of the sizes of jobs.

2   The Model

In this section we describe our model of multicluster systems. This model is based on the Distributed ASCI Supercomputer, the performance of which we intend to evaluate depending on the structure of the jobs, on the amount and pattern of communication, and on the scheduling decisions.

2.1   The Distributed ASCI Supercomputer

The DAS [6,7] is a wide-area distributed computer system consisting of four clusters of workstations located at four Dutch universities. One of the clusters contains 128 nodes, the other three contain 24 nodes each. All the nodes are identical Pentium Pro processors. The clusters are interconnected by ATM links for wide-area communications, while for local communication inside the clusters Myrinet LANs are used. The operating system employed is RedHat Linux. The system was designed by the Advanced School for Computing and Imaging (ASCI, in the Netherlands) and is used for research on parallel and distributed computing. On single DAS clusters a local scheduler called prun is used; it allows users to request a number of processors bounded by the cluster's size, for a time interval which does not exceed an imposed limit.

We have created an interface between prun and Globus, and we have installed the Globus toolkit [13] on the DAS system. However, there is also a way around using Globus for submitting multicluster jobs to the DAS, which was used for the measurements in Sect. 4. So far, co-allocation has not been used enough on the DAS to let us obtain statistics on the sizes of the jobs' components.

2.2   The Structure of the System

We model a multicluster distributed system consisting of C clusters of processors, cluster i having N_i processors, $i = 1, \ldots, C$. We assume that all processors have the same service rate. As to the communication and the communication network, we assume that any two processors can communicate with each other, and that the communication between the tasks of a parallel application is synchronous, so that a task doing a send operation can only continue when it knows the receiving task has received the message. All intracluster communication links are assumed to be of the same capacity, as are all the intercluster links. Since LAN links are faster than WAN links, we assume the speed of intracluster links to be significantly higher than the speed of intercluster links. This implies that the amount of time needed for sending a message between two processors within a cluster is smaller than the time required to send the same message between two processors from different clusters. The two parameters related to communication in our model are the total time needed to complete a single synchronous send operation between processors in the same and in different clusters.

By a job we understand a parallel application requiring some number of processors. A job can simultaneously ask for processors in more than one cluster (co-allocation). We will call a task the part of an application that runs on a single processor. Tasks can communicate by exchanging messages over the network. Jobs are rigid, meaning that the numbers of processors requested by and allocated to a job are fixed, and cannot be changed during their execution. Job requests can have different degrees of flexibility in the way they allow their components to be spread over the clusters (see Sect. 2.3). All tasks of a job start and end at the same time, which implies that all the processors allocated to a job are being simultaneously occupied and released. We also assume that jobs only request processors and we do not include in the model other types of resources.

The system has a single central scheduler, with one global queue. For both interarrival times and service times we use exponential distributions.

In our simulations we make the simplification that all the clusters have an equal number N of processors. In order to assess the performance loss due to the wide-area links, we also compare the performance of a multicluster system with C clusters with a single-cluster system with CN processors.

2.3   The Structure of Job Requests

Jobs that require co-allocation have to specify the number and the sizes of their components, i.e., of the sets of tasks that have to go to the separate clusters. The distribution D we use for the sizes of these job components is defined as follows: D takes values on some interval $[n_1, n_2]$, with $0 < n_1 \leq n_2 \leq N$, and the probability of having job component size i is $p_i = q^i/Q$ if i is not a power of 2 and $p_i = 3q^i/Q$ if i is a power of 2, with Q such that the sum of the probabilities equals 1, and with $q = 0.95$. This distribution favours small sizes, and sizes that are powers of two, which has been found to be a realistic choice [8].

We will consider four cases for the structure of jobs, which are differentiated by the flexibility of their requests:

1. An *ordered request* is represented by a tuple of C values $(r_1, r_2, \ldots, r_C)$, each generated from distribution D. The positions of the request components in the tuple specify the clusters from which the processors must be allocated. This is the most restrictive of the request types considered.
2. An *unordered request* is again specified by a tuple of C values $(r_1, r_2, \ldots, r_C)$, each of them obtained from D, but now by these values, the job only specifies the numbers of nodes it needs in separate clusters, and not the precise clusters where the nodes must be allocated. Because it leaves the scheduler the freedom to choose the clusters on which to place each of the C components, this request type is more flexible than the previous one.
3. A *flexible request* is represented by a single number obtained as a sum of C values $r_1, r_2, \ldots, r_C$, each of them obtained from the distribution D. With this request the job specifies only the total number of processors it requires; it leaves to the scheduler the decision about how to spread the tasks over the clusters.
4. For *total requests*, there is a single cluster with size CN, and a request only specifies the single number of processors it requires. An instance of this case is characterized

by a cluster number C. The distribution of the numbers of processors required by jobs is again the sum of C copies of the distribution D. We include this case in order to compare the multicluster cases above with a single-cluster case in which the total job sizes have the same distribution.

As long as we do not take into account the characteristics of the applications (e.g. the amount of communication between processors), the case of total requests amounts to the same as the case of flexible requests in multiclusters. The speed difference between intercluster and intracluster links makes the two cases distinct also from the performance point of view. The way we determine the job component sizes in ordered and unordered requests and the total job sizes for flexible and total requests, makes the the results for the four cases comparable.

Ordered requests are used in practice when a user has enough information about the complete system to take full advantage of the characteristics of the different clusters. For example, the data available at the different clusters may dictate a specific way of splitting up an application. Unordered requests (especially when grouping request components on the same cluster would be allowed) are modeled by applications like FFT, where tasks in the same job component share data and need intensive communication, while tasks from different components exchange little or no information. The flexible requests are the best from the system's point of view because their lack of restrictions concerning the placement of their tasks gives the scheduler the possibility to improve the overall performance of the system.

2.4   The Communication Pattern

The communication between the tasks of single jobs is an important part of our model, one of our aims being to study the influence of the amount of communication on the performance of the system for the different request types, and its sensitivity to the ratio between the intercluster and intracluster speeds. As a model for the structure of jobs we consider a general parallel application that can be solved by an iterative method (it can be anything from a Poisson problem solved by an iterative method to an implementation of surface rendering using the Marching Cubes technique). Such applications have in common that the space of the problem is divided among the processes making up the application, with each of them performing the algorithm on its subdomain, alternating computation and communication steps. The communication is necessary for example to exchange border information or to compute a global error as a stopping criterion. The communication steps realize also the synchronization between the processes.

For the simulations in Sect. 3, we will assume that each task does a fixed number of iterations. Each iteration consists of a communication step in which a message of a fixed size is sent to every other task, and a computation step. We assume that a task sends its messages successively and synchronously, which means that it waits until its first message has been received before it sends the second, etc., and that in the mean time, it receives all messages sent to it by the other tasks. When all these messages have been sent and received, the tasks do their computation step. Although the sizes of the messages are equal, the time costs will not be the same, depending on whether the sender and the receiver are in the same cluster or not. Since we assume that jobs release all their processors at once, the slowest task will determine the job duration.

The simulations in Sect. 4.2 are based on measurements of the execution of a real application on the DAS. This application has a structure that deviates somewhat from the general structure outlined above. Details on this application can be found in Sect. 4.1.

2.5   The Scheduling Decisions

In all our simulations the First Come First Served (FCFS) policy is used. FCFS is the simplest scheduling scheme, processors being allocated to the job at the head of the queue. When this job does not fit, the scheduler is not allowed to choose another job further down in the queue. This restriction has a negative influence on the maximal processor utilization, since processors may have to stay idle even when one or more jobs in the queue do fit. For ordered and total requests it is clear when a job fits or not, and there is basically only one way of allocating processors.

In order to determine whether an unordered request fits, one can first order the job component sizes, and then try to schedule the components in decreasing order of their sizes. Whatever way of placement is used, if placing the job components in this order does not succeed, no other order will. Possible ways of placement include First Fit (fix an order of the clusters and pick the first one on which a job component fits), Best Fit (pick the cluster with the smallest number of idle processors on which the component fits), or Worst Fit (pick the cluster with largest number of idle processors). In our simulations, we employ Worst Fit. If we consider the influence each placement has on the jobs following in the queue, Worst Fit can be expected to give better results than the other placement methods when combined with the FCFS policy, because it leaves in each cluster as much room as possible for subsequent jobs.

For flexible requests the scheduling algorithm first determines whether there are enough idle processors in the whole system to serve the job at the head of the queue. If so, the clusters on which the job will be scheduled are again chosen in a Worst Fit manner by taking the smallest set of clusters with enough idle processors. (One can simply order the clusters according to their numbers of idle processors, in decreasing order, and add a cluster at a time until enough idle processors are obtained.) The reason for this selection of clusters is that because of the higher cost of intercluster communication it is preferable to schedule the job on as few clusters as possible. The only decision still to be taken is how to spread the request over the selected clusters. We implemented two ways of doing so, both starting to use clusters in the decreasing order of their number of idle processors. The first method, called *cluster-filling*, completely fills the least loaded clusters until all the tasks are distributed; the second, *load-balancing*, distributes the request over the clusters in such a way as to balance the load.

Cluster-filling has the potential advantage of a smaller number of intercluster links among the tasks in a job, and so of a smaller communication overhead, while load-balancing potentially improves the performance of the system when the workload includes more types of requests. As an example, consider a flexible request of 18 processors coming in an empty system consisting of four clusters with 8 processors each. When load-balancing is used, there are 216 intercluster messages in a single all-pairs message exchange among the job's tasks, and only 192 for cluster-filling (see Fig. 3). When all the requests in the system are flexible, balancing the load does not change the maximal utilization, but when combined with ordered requests for example, the advantage of having comparable loads and avoiding completely filling some clusters while leaving some others emptier is obvious. Using cluster-filling for flexible requests would be very obstructionist towards both ordered and unordered requests, and would result in a higher capacity loss.

3   Co-allocation in the Presence of Communication

In order to estimate the performance of multicluster systems such as the DAS, for different types of requests in the presence of communication, we modeled the corresponding queuing systems and studied their behaviour using simulations.

The simulation programs were implemented using the CSIM simulation package [5]. Simulations were performed for a single-cluster system with 32 processors and for a multicluster system with 4 clusters of 8 nodes each. The job component sizes were generated from the distribution presented in Sect. 2.3. The sizes of the total requests in the single-cluster system with 32 processors we use for comparison, are the sum of 4 numbers obtained from the same distribution. In Sect. 3.4 we also use for the job components a uniform distribution on the interval $[1, 4]$.

In all the simulations reported in this section, the mean of the service time is equal to 1, and the inter-arrival time is varied in order to determine the response time as a function of the utilization of the system. We consider the performance to be better when either for the same utilization, the average response time is smaller, or when the maximum utilization is larger. The simulations for this section were done for tasks performing only a single iteration consisting of a communication step followed by a computation step, because it is the ratio of communication to computation that matters. The (deterministic) amount of time needed for the synchronous communication between two tasks in the same cluster is set to 0.001.

3.1   The Influence of the Ratio between Intercluster and Intracluster Communication Speed

Even more than the total amount of communication, the ratio between the speeds of intercluster and intracluster links, included in our model as the ratio between the time intervals necessary for sending the same message inside a cluster and between two processors from different clusters, is an interesting factor to consider because of its different influence on each of the distinct types of requests. Below we evaluate the influence of this ratio on the performance of our model for the different request types.

Figure 1 compares the average response time for the four types of requests, for communication ratios of 10, 50, and 100. It turns out that for ordered, unordered and flexible requests, the increase of the ratio between intercluster and intracluster communication deteriorates the performance, increasing the response time and decreasing the maximal utilization. The performance seems to be affected more for ordered and unordered requests than for flexible ones. This suggests that in those cases the average amount of intercluster communication per job is higher. The variation of the communication ratio does not affect the results for total requests since in single clusters there is only intracluster communication and they can be used as a reference in the graphs.

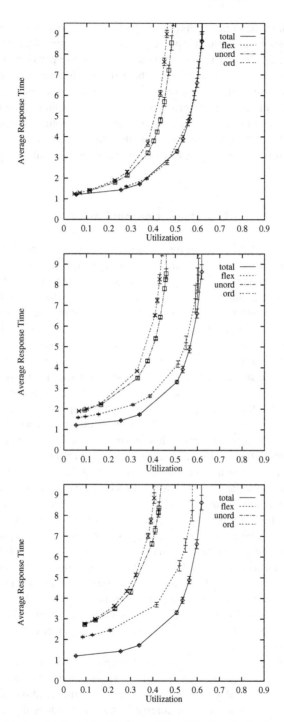

Fig. 1. The average response time as a function of the utilization for the four request types and for communication speed ratios of 10 (top), 50 (middle), 100 (bottom)

In Fig. 2 we show the same results (except for total requests), but ordered in a different way: now we depict the performance per request type for different communication speed ratios in the same graph. It can be noticed that the change in performance is significant for all utilizations. For low utilizations, where in the absence of communication all the request types have similar response times, taking as a reference the curve of total requests, now we can see a large increase of the average response time for all the other request types. The results indicate that the communication ratio decreases the maximal utilization as well, but the deterioration is smaller than in the case of the response time. An approximation for the extra capacity loss due to communication is presented in the following section.

3.2   The Extra Capacity Loss Due to Communication

In both single-cluster and multicluster systems, it may of course happen that some processors are idle while there are waiting jobs in the queue. For single clusters this happens only when the number of idle processors is smaller than the number of processors requested by the job at the head of the queue. The same is true for jobs with flexible requests in multiple clusters. For the more restrictive types of requests this phenomenon occurs more often, and a larger fraction of the processors may stay idle because even if the total number of idle processors covers the number of processors requested by the job, it may happen that their division over the clusters does not satisfy the requirements of the job. If ρ_m is the average utilization of the system such that the system is unstable at utilizations ρ with $\rho > \rho_m$ and stable for $\rho < \rho_m$, we have $\rho_m < 1$. The quantity $L = 1 - \rho_m$ is called the capacity loss of the system. Capacity loss and the utilization of high-performance computer systems has been a major concern [14]. In [19], we presented an approximation of capacity loss in single clusters, and some simulations for capacity loss in multiclusters, in the absence of communication.

In the presence of communication there is an additional component L_c of the capacity loss, which is due to the fact that jobs are not preempted during communication steps. If the queue is not empty during such a step, one or more jobs at the head of the queue might have fit on the system if we did preempt jobs when they start communicating. Such jobs might have taken part or all of the processors freed by the preempted job, in which case we talk about *internal capacity loss*, denoted by L_i. There is also an external capacity loss L_e resulting from the fact that if the processors would be released during communication, another job at the head of the queue could be scheduled, which would take the processors freed by the communicating job, but also some other processors which are idle otherwise. The idle processes which would be occupied if the job involved in communication gave up its processors generate this additional external component to the capacity loss.

Table 1 contains the estimated values for the capacity loss due to communication L_c for different communication ratios and for all four types of requests. They are obtained by subtracting the maximal utilization in the presence of communication from the maximal utilization for a system without communication. We can conclude that the capacity loss increases with the ratio between intercluster and intracluster communication speed and it is higher for the job request types which generate more communication (a larger number

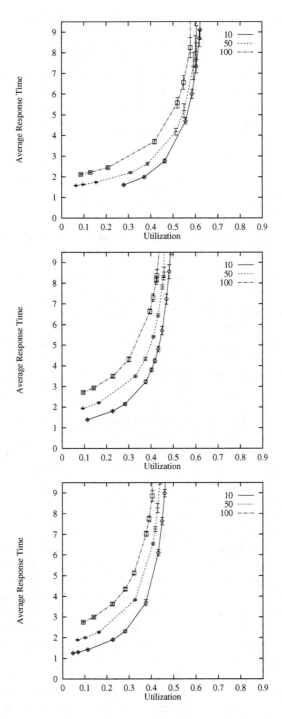

Fig. 2. The average response time as a function of the utilization for three communication speed ratios, for flexible (top), unordered (middle) and ordered (bottom) requests

Table 1. The extra capacity loss due to communication for the four request types

request	communication ratio		
type	10	50	100
ord.	0.00553	0.02075	0.03100
unord.	0.00393	0.01581	0.02415
flex.	0.00013	0.00034	0.00050
total	0.00006	0.00006	0.00006

of intercluster messages). For total requests in single clusters the extra capacity loss is small since all the communication is fast intracluster one.

3.3   A Comparison between Balancing the Load and Filling the Clusters

As we stated before, both ways of dealing with flexible requests choose the minimal number of clusters on which the request can be scheduled using Worst Fit. They differ however in the way the jobs are spread over this minimal number of clusters.

The placement which fills the least loaded clusters is aiming to reduce the number of intercluster messages taking into account that this type of communication is more costly than the intracluster one. The placement which balances the load accepts to have a larger number of intercluster messages but leaves as much room as possible in the clusters for other jobs. If there are only flexible requests in the system, filling the clusters does not affect the performance and there is no benefit from balancing the load, but if besides flexible requests the system also schedules more restrictive ones, such as ordered or unordered requests, keeping an equilibrium between the loads of the cluster becomes essential. Ordered and unordered requests specify the number of processors they need in distinct clusters and if one of those clusters is full such a job will not be scheduled even if the total number of free processors in the system is large enough. This would determine an extra capacity loss that can be avoided by an even loading of the clusters.

In our case, since jobs are rigid, even when only flexible requests are present in the system, load-balancing brings a better performance then cluster-filling. Figure 5 shows the evolution of the response time function of the utilization of the system for both techniques, for communication speed ratios of 50 and 100. Although in the system are only flexible requests, for both ratios load-balancing proves to be better. This can be explained by the fact that in the case of rigid jobs it is not the average duration of tasks which matters but the longest task because a job will only finish when its last task ends. Although cluster-filling has a smaller average for the communication time, having fewer intercluster messages per job, this communication time is not evenly spread between the tasks. This is why, on average, cluster-filling generates jobs with a higher time average spent with communication.

As an example, consider that an empty system with four clusters of eight processors each receives a flexible request asking for 18 processors. Figure 3 shows the decisions for each technique. The average communication time is in favour of cluster-filling with only 192 intercluster messages which gives an average of 10.7 intercluster messages per task compared to 12 for load-balancing. However, if we look at the longest task in both

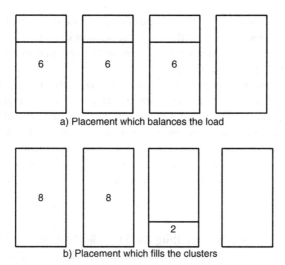

a) Placement which balances the load

b) Placement which fills the clusters

Fig. 3. A numerical example comparing load-balancing and cluster-filling

cases, which sets the amount of time spent with communication by the job, it has only 12 intercluster messages when using load-balancing, compared to 16 intercluster messages in the other case.

3.4 Performance Evaluation for a Mix of Job Request Types

Real systems have to be able to schedule multiple request types and not just a single type. The overall performance of the system is determined by the way the scheduler deals with all types of requests, in such a way as to give acceptable performance to all of them and to improve the total performance. It is a fact that the different request types in the system influence each other. Results obtained for a system with just one type of job requests are not always valid also for a system where more types of requests are being submitted. In order to obtain a more general model we study a multicluster system where both flexible and ordered requests are present. To show how much the scheduling decisions for jobs with one type of request can influence the results for jobs with other requirements we compare the performance of the system when for flexible requests is chosen the way of placement which balances the load to the one when tasks are distributed to the clusters in such a way as to completely fill the least loaded ones.

We study the performance of the system for different ratios between flexible and ordered jobs. The communication ratio in all the simulations in this section is 50.

The Influence of the Ratio between Ordered and Flexible Requests. Figure 4 shows the average response time as a function of the utilization of the system for different ratios of ordered and flexible requests. In the first graph the flexible requests were spread over the clusters in such a way as to fill the clusters, in the second one the load was balanced. The results show that the average response time grows with the increase in the percentage of ordered jobs, indifferent of the manner in which the flexible jobs are spread over the clusters. The maximal utilization of the system decreases when there is a higher percentage of ordered jobs.

At low utilizations the increase of the response time with the percentage of ordered jobs is low but it gradually grows when the utilization becomes larger. For less than 10% ordered jobs, the load is still dominated by the flexible jobs and that is why the deterioration of the performance is small. When the percentage of ordered and flexible requests is the same, the average response time is already significantly larger than for a system with just flexible requests, especially at high utilizations. When 90% or more of the job requests are ordered, in both cases the performance is determined by the ordered requests.

Load-Balancing versus Cluster-Filling for Flexible Requests. In this section we evaluate the two ways of placement used for flexible requests in the more general case of a system with mixed requests. As Fig. 5 indicates, for up to 50% ordered jobs the system behaves better when flexible requests are placed in such a way as to balance the load. This better performance is due mostly to the better response time obtained by the flexible jobs. Because the jobs are large enough not to permit in average the presence in the system of more than two jobs simultaneously, there is little or no benefit for the ordered jobs from the fact that the load is balanced.

There are more factors which can influence the performance of the system. Both types of placement for flexible requests tend to deteriorate the performance of ordered requests by the fact that they look for the minimum number of clusters where such a job fits. The maximal utilization and the response time could be improved by trying to spread the flexible jobs over all the clusters. However, that change would cause a deterioration of the performance for flexible requests by increasing the cost of communication. For smaller jobs using load-balancing can improve the performance of the system by leaving more room for ordered jobs and allowing them to obtain the needed resources sooner. Figure 6 depicts the variation of the response time for a job mix of 50% ordered requests and 50% flexible requests, where the components of the job requests are obtained from a uniform distribution on the interval $[1, 4]$. In this case the performance is visibly better when load-balancing is used for flexible requests.

These results indicate that the scheduling decisions must be a compromise convenient for all types of jobs present in the system.

4   Simulations Based on a Real Application

We extracted a more complex communication pattern from an application implementing a parallel iterative algorithm to solve the Poisson equation with a red-black Gauss-Seidel scheme. We ran the application on the DAS system and measured the durations of the different steps of the algorithm, subsequently placing these values in our simulation model for ordered and total requests, and assessing the performance of the system in terms of average response time as a function of the utilization, for this specific application.

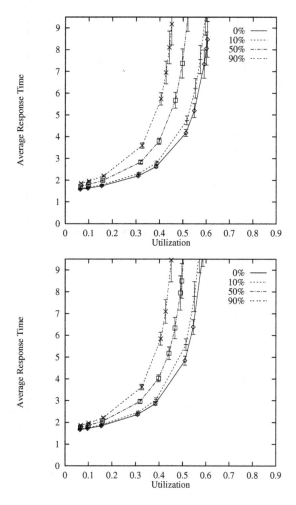

Fig. 4. The performance of a system with mixed requests for different percentages of flexible and ordered requests, with load-balancing (top) and cluster-filling (bottom)

4.1 Description of the Application

The application searches for a solution in two dimensions; the computational domain is the unit square, split into a grid of points with a constant step. The number of points in the grid constitute the size of the grid. At each iteration (computation step) each grid point has its value updated as a function of its previous value and the values of its neighbours. The grid is split into "black" and "red" points, and first all points of one colour are visited followed by the ones of the other colour. With such an approach the values of the grid points are updated only twice during a sweep over all points.

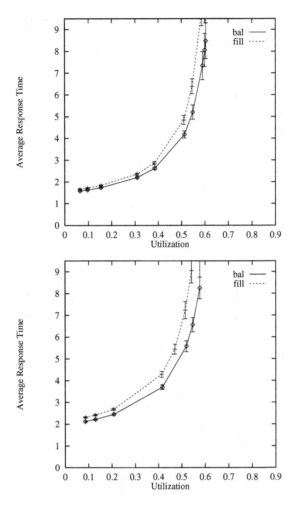

Fig. 5. Performance comparison between load-balancing and and cluster-filling for flexible requests, for communication ratios of 50 (top) and 100 (bottom)

The domain of the problem is split into rectangles among the participating processes. Each process gets a contiguous part of the domain containing a number of grid points and does its own computation. However, processes must communicate in order to exchange the values of the grid points on the borders and to compute a global stopping criterion. The amount of communication, so also the communication time, is influenced by the way processes split up the domain, the number of participating processors, the size of the grid, and the initial data. In our example we chose to maintain constant the grid size and the initial data. When running the application on a multicluster system, the way processes are distributed over clusters influences the communication time, since sending an intercluster message takes significantly longer than sending an intracluster one. For

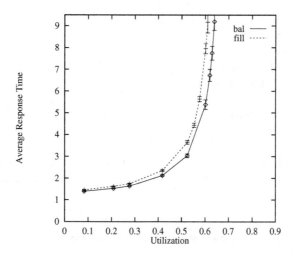

Fig. 6. The performance of a system with mixed requests for equal percentages of flexible and ordered request, with components obtained from an uniform distribution on $[1, 4]$

the same grid size and the same initial data, we ran the application on the DAS, for different numbers of processes and for different divisions on lines and columns:

8 processes - 4x2, 8x1
16 processes - 2x8, 4x4

All the rules for rigid jobs and pure space sharing are obeyed: each process is scheduled on a distinct processor where it runs until completion, and all the processors granted to the application are simultaneously acquired and released. Since the domain is evenly split among the participating processes, the amount of computation, communication, and the number of iterations are dependent on the number of processors used to perform the algorithm. The application is implemented in MPI and has the following structure:

```
if (proc_index == 0)
{
  read the initial data;
 /* number of points in the data
  domain, number of nodes, sources */
  broadcast data to all the processes;
}
/* start computation */
do
    {
      update half of the points
            (e.g. black points);
      update the other half of the
            points (e.g. red points);
```

```
      exchange borders with the
            neighbours;
      compute local-error;
      distribute local-error;
      compute global-error;
   }
   until global-error <= limit;
write results;
```

We ran the application on a single cluster for all the cases mentioned above, and deter-mined the duration of the job and the number of iterations needed to reach convergence. The results are presented in Table 2.

Table 2. Results of the measurements

Config	Nr Iterations	Elapsed Time Update (ms)	Exchange Borders Single-Cluster (ms)	Exchange Borders Multicluster (ms)
4x2	2436	0.953-0.972	0.408-0.450	5.9-7.3
8x1	2418	0.970-0.994	0.260-0.315	–
4x4	2132	0.480-0.515	0.350-0.425	6.3-7.7
8x2	2466	0.470-0.525	0.337-0.487	–

For the cases 4x2 and 4x4, we also ran the application on four clusters of the DAS, scheduling an equal number of processes on each cluster. More detailed measurements for the different steps of the algorithm were done, to be used in simulations: the duration of the computation steps, the time needed for exchanging borders in both single cluster and multicluster cases, and the time cost of diffusing local errors and computing the global error. The two *update* steps were measured together and considered as a single computation step. Being a single comparison instruction, the *compute local-error* step was ignored. The last two steps were also measured together, being performed as a single MPI routine. Comparing the results from the multicluster with the single cluster case we can notice as expected that the communication time is larger when messages are sent over the intercluster links. Since the duration of the communication in general is influenced also by the way the job is spread over the clusters, and there are many other ways of spreading the tasks, we do not assume that the data extracted concerning the communication steps is valid also in other configurations. However, the duration of the computation steps does not depend on the way tasks are distributed over nodes, but only on the size of the problem domain, the number of participating nodes and the way they divide the problem domain. Since the exchange of borders produces an important part of the communication amount, and intercluster communication takes longer, we can expect that the extra-time due to communication increases with the number of borders shared by processors from different clusters.

4.2 Simulation Results

The way of co-allocation provided on the DAS corresponds to the case of ordered requests from our simulations. We used this application structure and the data collected from the DAS in the simulations, replacing the distribution D of job component sizes chosen before with the two job sizes considered above: (2,2,2,2) and (4,4,4,4) and assessed the performance of the system (response time as a function of the system utilization) for ordered requests. Because the job components are equal, identical performance results would be obtained for unordered requests. Simulations were also performed for the single cluster, using the data collected for job sizes 8 and 16 (cases 4x2 and 4x4 respectively). The results of the simulations are presented in Fig. 7. Since for the multicluster simulations the components of the requests are equal and they sum up to the two values of requests used for the single cluster case, and the total size of the multicluster is equal to the size of the single cluster, the two cases would have identical performance in the absence of communication. This implies that the worse performance displayed by the ordered requests compared to total requests is caused by the slow intercluster communication and not by the rigidity of the ordered requests.

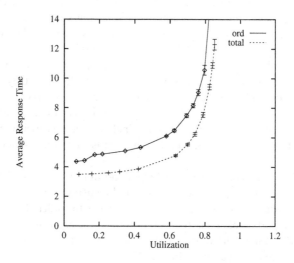

Fig. 7. The average response time as a function of the utilization for ordered requests compared to total requests, with data obtained from an application implementing a parallel iterative algorithm

Only the main loop of the algorithm was simulated, the initialization and the I/O part of the algorithm being ignored. It can be noticed that the chosen algorithm has a very regular and localized communication structure (each process communicates with all his neighbours and just with them) and requires strong synchronization. Its structure is typical for parallel iterative algorithms. It is very suited to be submitted as a flexible request being advantageous to schedule such a job on the smallest number of clusters possible and minimizing the number of intercluster borders (borders shared by processors from different clusters). Because of its synchrony, the performance of a job performing such an algorithm is determined by its slowest task.

5   Related Work

The problem of scheduling rigid jobs by pure space sharing in a multiprocessor system has been studied extensively; for instance, see [1]. Whereas we approach the problem of the maximal utilization from a more theoretical perspective, in [14] a study of the utilizations as observed in existing supercomputing installations is presented. Experience with a large range of machines over more than a decade shows that employing FCFS results in a $40\% - 60\%$ utilization, that more sophisticated policies such as backfilling give an improvement of about 15 percentage points, and that reducing the maximal job size allowed increases utilization.

In [4], the influence of splitting the processors of multiprogrammed, shared-memory NUMA multiprocessors into groups on the performance of the system is studied. It is assumed that a job starts as a single process, and that it may grow by creating additional processes. The best strategy for initial placement was found to be Worst Fit, because it leaves the largest room for the growth of jobs inside a pool. In [18], a general discussion of some problems occurring in designing meta-schedulers is presented, along with a performance comparison of two such designs. In the first, parts of the systems making up the metacomputing system are dedicated to metajobs, i.e., jobs that need resources under the control of different schedulers. In the second, no resources are dedicated to metajobs, and reservations for such jobs are only made when they are submitted. Overall, the latter design yields better results, for instance, in terms of utilization. In [2], an algorithm for co-allocating a fixed set of applications is simulated. All applications together are represented by a single DAG that includes the precedence constraints and resource conflicts among all of their tasks. The aim is to find a co-allocation yielding the minimum makespan.

In [16], two multidimensional bin-packing algorithms, in which both bins and items are represented by d-dimensional vectors, are studied using simulations. This problem resembles the scheduling problem studied in this paper for ordered jobs without communication. An important element in the algorithms is the extensive search of the list of items for a suitable candidate to place next, which is not realistic in our setting as we don't want to deviate too much from FCFS.

Finally, let us briefly mention some of the other research that is being performed in the context of the DAS project, a general overview of which can be found in [7]. Whereas the research presented in this paper is at the operating systems level, the other research on the DAS is done at the level of the run-time system [15] and of the applications [3]. In [15], a library is presented with 'wide-area optimal' versions of the collective communication primitives of MPICH, a widely used version of MPI. It was shown that substantial performance improvements over MPICH are obtained for communication in wide-area systems. In [3], several techniques for optimizing algorithms on a multi-level communication structure (LAN clusters connected by a WAN, such as the DAS) were implemented and analyzed. The optimizations either reduced intercluster traffic or masked the effect of intercluster communications and caused a significant performance improvement. The authors concluded that many medium-grain parallel applications can be optimized to run well on a multilevel, wide-area system.

6 Conclusions

We modeled multicluster systems such as our DAS system, where rigid jobs are scheduled by pure space sharing, and studied its performance in the presence of communication in terms of the average response time as a function of the utilization. We distinguished four types of requests: total, flexible, unordered and ordered, and simulated workloads consisting of only a single type of requests, and of mixes of flexible and ordered requests. For flexible requests we compared the results for two ways of placement on the clusters for the case when only flexible requests are present in the system, and also for the case when they are combined with ordered requests.

Our results show that the performance of multicluster systems deteriorates with the increase of the ratio of the speeds of intercluster and intracluster communication. In addition, it turns out that the performance for flexible requests is much closer to that for total requests than to that of either ordered or unordered requests.

In both single-cluster and multicluster systems, communication introduces some extra capacity loss. This capacity loss is larger for multicluster systems and also grows with the increase of the communication speed ratio. It is also dependent on the total amount of communication, being larger for ordered and unordered requests where more intercluster messages are sent, than for flexible requests. Reducing the amount of intercluster communication may help provided that the number of intercluster messages is evenly spread among jobs. If the algorithm is modified in such a way as to have a lower average for the communication time, but some tasks of the job communicate more than before, the performance is decreased instead of being improved. Under a workload consisting of a mix of requests types, the performance is determined not only by the separate behaviours of the different types of jobs, but also by the way in which they interact. The scheduling decisions for each of them must be taken considering also the effects they have on other job types, and are a compromise among the requirements of the distinct request types.

Future work will include simulations and measurements using traces from the DAS instead of theoretical distributions, different numbers of clusters, clusters with distinct sizes, and requests with variable number of components. We also intend to extend our model of a multicluster allowing the simultaneous presence in the system of jobs requiring co-allocation and jobs asking for nodes from just one cluster. We would like to look at different communication patterns from real applications and compare their performance in the presence of co-allocation. The model with mixed requests can also be detailed in the hope to find scheduling decisions which can better satisfy the different request types.

References

1. K.Aida, H.Kasahara and S.Narita. Job Scheduling Scheme for Pure Space Sharing Among Rigid Jobs. In Job Scheduling Strategies for Parallel Processing, Lecture Notes in Computer Science 1459, pages 98-121. Springer-Verlag, 1998.

2. A.H. Alhusaini, V.K. Prasanna, and C.S. Raghavendra, A Framework for Mapping with Resource Co-Allocation in Heterogeneous Computing Systems, Proc. 9th Heterogeneous Computing Workshop (HCW2000), C.S. Raghavendra (ed.), pp. 273-286, 2000.
3. Bal, H.E., Plaat, A., Bakker, M.G., Dozy, P., Hofman, R.F.H.: Optimizing Parallel Applications for Wide-Area Clusters. Proceedings of the 12th International Parallel Processing Symposium (1998) 784–790
4. Brecht, T.B.: An Experimental Evaluation of Processor Pool-Based Scheduling for Shared-Memory NUMA multiprocessors. Job Scheduling Strategies for Parallel Processing, Lecture Notes in Computer Science **1291** Springer-Verlag (1997) 139–165
5. The CSIM18 Simulation Engine, User's Guide. Mesquite Software, Inc.
6. The Distributed ASCI Supercomputer; http://www.cs.vu.nl/das/
7. Bal, H.E., et al.: The Distributed ASCI Supercomputer Project. ACM Operating Systems Review **34(4)** (2000) 76–96
8. Feitelson, D.G., Rudolph, L.: Toward Convergence in Job Schedulers for Parallel Supercomputers. Job Scheduling Strategies for Parallel Processing, Lecture Notes in Computer Science **1162** Springer-Verlag (1996) 1–26
9. Feitelson, D.G., Rudolph, L.: Theory and Practice in Parallel Job Scheduling Job Scheduling Strategies for Parallel Processing, Lecture Notes in Computer Science **1291** Springer-Verlag (1997) 1–34
10. Feitelson, D.G., Jette, M.A.: Improved Utilization and Responsiveness with Gang Scheduling. Job Scheduling Strategies for Parallel Processing, Lecture Notes in Computer Science **1291** Springer-Verlag (1997) 238–261
11. Feitelson, D.G.: Packing Schemes for Gang Scheduling. Job Scheduling Strategies for Parallel Processing, Lecture Notes in Computer Science **1162** Springer-Verlag (1996) 89–110
12. The Global Grid Forum; http://www.gridforum.org
13. Globus; http://www.globus.org
14. Patton Jones, J., Nitzberg, B.: Scheduling for Parallel Supercomputing: A Historical Perspective of Achievable Utilization. Job Scheduling Strategies for Parallel Processing, Lecture Notes in Computer Science **1659** Springer-Verlag (1999) 1–16
15. Kielmann, T., Hofman, R.F.H., Bal, H.E., Plaat, A., Bhoedjang, R.A.F.: MagPIe: MPI's Collective Communication Operations for Clustered Wide Area Systems. ACM SIGPLAN Symposium on Principles and Practice of Parallel Programming (1999) 131–140
16. Leinberger, W., Karypis, G., Kumar, V.: Milti-Capacity Bin Packing Algorithms with Applications to Job Scheduling under Multiple Constraints. Proc. 1999 Int'l Conference on Parallel Processing (1999) 404–412
17. Foster, I., Kesselman, C. (eds): The Grid: Blueprint for a New Computing Infrastructure. Morgan Kaufmann (1999)
18. Snell, Q., Clement, M., Jackson, D., Gregory, C.: The Performance Impact of Advance Reservation Meta-Scheduling. Job Scheduling Strategies for Parallel Processing, Lecture Notes in Computer Science **1911** Springer-Verlag (2000) 137–153
19. Bucur, A.I.D., Epema, D.H.J: The Influence of the Structure and Sizes of Jobs on the Performance of Co-Allocation. Job Scheduling Strategies for Parallel Processing, Lecture Notes in Computer Science **1911** Springer-Verlag (2000) 154–173

Core Algorithms of the Maui Scheduler

David Jackson, Quinn Snell, and Mark Clement

Brigham Young University, Provo, Utah 84602
jacksond@supercluster.org, {snell, clement}@cs.byu.edu

Abstract. The Maui scheduler has received wide acceptance in the HPC community as a highly configurable and effective batch scheduler. It is currently in use on hundreds of SP, O2K, and Linux cluster systems throughout the world including a high percentage of the largest and most cutting edge research sites. While the algorithms used within Maui have proven themselves effective, nothing has been published to date documenting these algorithms nor the configurable aspects they support. This paper focuses on three areas of Maui scheduling, specifically, backfill, job prioritization, and fairshare. It briefly discusses the goals of each component, the issues and corresponding design decisions, and the algorithms enabling the Maui policies. It also covers the configurable aspects of each algorithm and the impact of various parameter selections.

1 Introduction

The Maui scheduler [1] has received wide acceptance in the HPC community as an highly configurable and effective batch scheduler. It is currently in use on hundreds of IBM SP-2, SGI Origin 2000, and Linux cluster systems throughout the world including a high percentage of the largest and most cutting edge research sites. While Maui was initially known for its advance reservation and backfill scheduling capabilities, it also possesses many additional optimizations and job management features. There are many aspects of the scheduling decision which must be addressed. This paper documents the underlying algorithms associated with the Maui scheduler. While Maui originated as a project designed to purely maximize system utilization, it rapidly evolved into a tool with a goal of maximizing scheduling performance while supporting an extensive array of policy tools. The words *performance* and *policy* go a long way to complicating this problem.

2 Overview

Maui, like other batch schedulers [2,3,4], determines when and where submitted jobs should be run. Jobs are selected and started in such a way as to not only enforce a site's mission goals, but also to intelligently improve resource usage and minimize average job turnaround time. Mission goals are expressed via a combination of policies which constrain how jobs will be started. A number of base concepts require review to set the groundwork for a detailed discussion of the algorithms.

D.G. Feitelson and L. Rudolph (Eds.): JSSPP 2001, LNCS 2221, pp. 87–102, 2001.

2.1   Scheduling Iteration

Like most schedulers, Maui schedules on a iterative basis, scheduling, followed by a period of sleeping or processing external commands. Maui will start a new iteration when one or more of the following conditions is met:

- a job or resource state-change (i.e. job termination, node failure) event occurs
- a reservation boundary event occurs
- the scheduler is instructed to resume scheduling via an external command
- a configurable timer expires

2.2   Job Class

Maui supports the concept of a job class, also known as a job queue. Each class may have an associated set of constraints determining what types of jobs can be submitted to it. These constraints can limit the size or length of the job and can be associated with certain default job attributes, such as memory required per job. Constraints can also be set on a *per-class* basis specifying which users, groups, etc., can submit to the class. Further, each class can optionally be set up to only be allowed access to a particular subset of nodes. Within Maui, all jobs are associated with a class. If no class is specified, a default class is assigned to the job.

2.3   QoS

Maui also supports the concept of quality of service (QoS) levels. These QoS levels may be configured to allow many types of special privileges including adjusted job priorities, improved queue time and expansion factor targets, access to additional resources, or exemptions from certain policies. Each QoS level is assigned an access control list (ACL) to determine which users, groups, accounts, or job classes may access the associated privileges. In cases where a job may possess access to multiple QoS levels, the user submitting the job may specify the desired QoS. All jobs within Maui are associated with a QoS level. If no QoS is specified, a default QoS is assigned.

2.4   Job Credentials

Each batch job submitted to Maui is associated with a number of key attributes or credentials describing job ownership. These credentials include the standard user and group ID of the submitting user. However, they also include an optional account, or project, ID for use in conjunction with allocation management systems. Additionally, as mentioned above, each job is also associated with a job class and QoS credential.

2.5   Throttling Policies

Maui's scheduling behavior can be constrained by way of throttling policies, policies which limit the total quantity of resources available to a given credential at any given moment. The resources constrained include things such as processors, jobs, nodes, and memory. For example, a site may choose to set a throttling policy limiting the maximum number of jobs running simultaneously per user to 3 and set another policy limiting the group, staff, to only using a total of 32 processors at a time. Maui allows both *hard* and *soft* throttling policy limits to be set. Soft limits are more constraining than hard limits. Each iteration, Maui attempts to schedule all possible jobs according to soft policy constraints. If idle resources remain, Maui will re-evaluate its queue and attempt to run jobs which meet the less constraining hard policies.

3   Scheduling Iterations

On each scheduling iteration, Maui obtains fresh resource manager information, updates its own state information, and schedules selected jobs. These activities are broken down into the following general steps:

1. Obtain updated resource manager information. Calls are issued to the resource manager to get up-to-date detailed information about node and job state, configuration, etc.
2. Update statistics. Historical statistics and usage information for running jobs are updated. Statistics records for completed jobs are also generated.
3. Refresh reservations. Maui adjusts existing reservations incorporating updated node availability information by adding and removing nodes as appropriate. Changes in node availability may also cause various reservations to slide forward or backward in time if the reservation timeframe is not locked down. Maui may also create or remove reservations in accordance with configured reservation time constraints during this phase. Finally, idle jobs which possess reservations providing immediate access to resources are started in this phase.
4. Select jobs meeting minimum scheduling criteria. A list is generated which contains all jobs which can be feasibly scheduled. Criteria such as job state, job holds, availability of configured resources, etc. are taken into account in generating this list. Each job's compliance with various throttling policies is also evaluated with violating jobs eliminated from the feasible job list.
5. Prioritize feasible jobs. The list of feasible jobs is prioritized according to various job attributes, scheduling performance targets, required resources, and historical usage information.
6. Schedule jobs in priority order. Jobs which meet *soft* throttling policy constraints are selected and then started sequentially in a highest-priority-first order. When the current highest priority idle job is unable to start due to a lack of resource availability, the existing reservation space is analyzed and

the earliest available time at which this job can run is determined. A reservation for this job is then created. Maui continues processing jobs in priority order, starting the jobs it can and creating reservations for those it can't until it has made reservations for the top N jobs where N is a site configurable parameter.

7. Soft policy backfill. With the priority FIFO phase complete, Maui determines the current available *backfill windows* and attempts to best fill these holes with the remaining jobs which pass all soft throttling policy constraints. The configured backfill algorithm and metric is applied when filling these windows.

8. Hard policy backfill. If resources remain after the previous backfill phase, Maui selects jobs which meet the less constraining *hard* throttling policies and again attempts to schedule this expanded set of jobs according to the configured backfill algorithm and metric.

4   Backfill

Backfill is a scheduling optimization which allows a scheduler to make better use of available resources by running jobs out of order. When Maui schedules, it prioritizes the jobs in the queue according to a number of factors and then orders the jobs into a highest-priority-first sorted list. It starts the jobs one by one stepping through the priority list until it reaches a job which it cannot start. Because all jobs and reservations possess a start time and a wallclock limit, Maui can determine the completion time of all jobs in the queue. Consequently, Maui can also determine the earliest the needed resources will become available for the highest priority job to start.

Backfill operates based on this earliest-job-start information. Because Maui knows the earliest the highest priority job can start, and which resources it will need at that time, it can also determine which jobs can be started without delaying this job. Enabling backfill allows the scheduler to start other, lower-priority jobs so long as they do not delay the highest priority job. If Backfill is enabled, Maui, protects the highest priority job's start time by creating a job reservation to reserve the needed resources at the appropriate time. Maui then can start any job which will not interfere with this reservation.

Backfill offers significant scheduler performance improvement. Both anecdotal evidence and simulation based results indicate that in a typical large system, enabling backfill will increase system utilization by around 20% and improve average job turnaround time by an even greater amount. Because of the way it works, essentially filling in holes in node space, backfill tends to favor smaller and shorter running jobs more than larger and longer running ones. It is common to see over 90% of these small and short jobs backfilled as is recorded in the one year CHPC workload trace [5]. Consequently, sites will see marked improvement in the level of service delivered to the small, short jobs and only moderate to no improvement for the larger, long ones.

Suspicions arise regarding the use of backfill. Common sense indicates that in all systems there must be a tradeoff. In scheduling systems this tradeoff generally involves trading system utilization for fairness, or system utilization for turnaround time. However, tradeoffs are not always required. While it is true that tradeoffs are generally mandatory in a highly efficient system, in a less efficient one, you can actually get something for nothing. Backfill takes advantage of inefficiencies in batch scheduling actually improving system utilization and job turnaround time and even improving some forms of fairness such balancing average expansion factor distribution along a job duration scale.

4.1 Backfill Drawbacks

While backfill scheduling is advantageous, minor drawbacks do exist. First, the ability of backfill scheduling to select jobs out of order tends to dilute the impact of the job prioritization algorithm in determining which jobs are most important. It does not eliminate this impact, but does noticeably decrease it.

Another problem, widely ignored in the HPC realm, is that in spite of reservations to protect a job's start time, backfill scheduling can actually delay a subset of backlogged jobs. The term delay is actually inaccurate. While the start time of a job with a reservation will never slide back in time, backfill can prevent it from sliding forward in time as much as it could have otherwise, resulting in a *psuedo-delay*. This behavior arises through the influence of inaccuracies in job run time estimates and resulting wallclock limits. When a user submits a job, he makes an estimate of how long the job will take to run. He then pads this estimate to make certain that the job will have adequate time to complete in spite of issues such as being assigned to slow compute resources, unexpectedly long data staging, or simply unexpectedly slow computation. Because of this padding, or because of poor initial estimates, wallclock limits have been historically poor, averaging approximately 20 to 40% across a wide spectrum of systems. Feitelson reported similar findings [6] and the online traces at supercluster.org for the Center for High Performance Computing at the University of Utah and the Maui High Performance Computing Center show wallclock accuracies of 29.4% and 33.5% respectively.

This problem is exhibited in a simple scenario shown in Figure 1 involving a six-node system with a running job on 4 nodes, job A, which estimates its completion time will be in 3 hours. Two jobs are then queued, job B, requiring five nodes, cannot start until job A completes while job C requires only two nodes and three hours of walltime. A standard backfill algorithm would reserve resources for job B and then start job C. Now, lets assume the wallclock estimate of job A is off and it actually completes one hour early. Job B still cannot run because job C is now using one of its needed nodes. Because backfill started job C out of order, the start of the higher priority job B was actually delayed from its *potential* start time by one hour.

This is not a significant problem and is outweighed by the positive effects of backfill. Studies have shown that across a number of systems, only a small percentage of jobs are truly delayed. Figure 2 is representative of these results. To obtain this information, a large job trace from the Maui High Performance Computing Center was run with and without backfill enabled. The differences

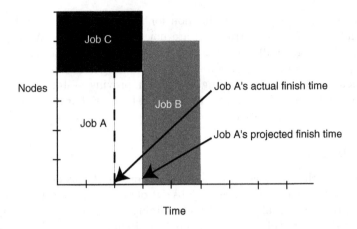

Fig. 1. Wallclock accuracy induced backfill delays.

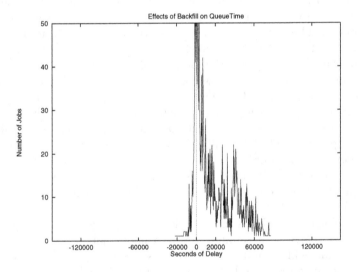

Fig. 2. Actual queue-time delay resulting from backfill based on inaccurate walltime estimates.

in individual queue times were calculated and plotted. Roughly 10% of the jobs experience a greater queue time with backfill enabled. These results are further examined in forthcoming studies. The percentage of delayed jobs is reduced by two primary factors. First, backfill results in general improvements in system utilization and job turnaround time for all jobs, not just those that are actually backfilled. This is because even jobs which are not backfilled are often blocked from running by other jobs which do get backfilled. When the blocking job is started early, the blocked job also gets to start earlier. Its a classic case of *a rising tide lifts all ships* and virtually every job benefits. The second relevant factor is that wall clock limit inaccuracies are widespread. The 2D bin packing view of an HPC system where the start time of each job can be effectively calculated out to infinity is grossly misleading. The real world situation is far more sticky with jobs constantly completing at unexpected times resulting in a constant reshuffling of job reservations. Maui performs these reservation adjustments in a priority order allowing the highest priority jobs access to the newly available resources first, thus providing a mechanism to favor priority jobs with every early job completion encountered. This priority based evaluation consequently provides priority jobs the best chance of improving their start time. Thus, priority based reservation adjustment counters, as far as possible, the wallclock accuracy psuedo-delays.

Given the pros and cons, it appears clear for most sites that backfill is definitely worth it. Its drawbacks are rare and minor while its benefits are widespread and significant.

4.2   Backfill Algorithm

The algorithm behind Maui backfill scheduling is mostly straightforward although there are a number of issues and parameters to be aware of. First of all, Maui makes two backfill scheduling passes. For each pass, Maui selects a list of jobs which are eligible for backfill according to the user specified throttling policy limits described earlier. On the first pass, only those jobs which meet the constraints of the *soft* policies are considered and scheduled. The second pass expands this list of jobs to include those which meet the less constraining *hard* fairness throttling policies.

A second key concept regarding Maui backfill is the concept of backfill windows. Figure 3 shows a simple batch environment containing two running jobs and a reservation for a third job. The present time is represented by the leftmost end of the box with the future moving to the right. The light gray boxes represent currently idle nodes which are eligible for backfill. To determine backfill windows, Maui analyzes the idle nodes essentially looking for largest node-time rectangles. In the case represented by figure 2, it determines that there are two backfill windows. The first window contains only one node and has no time limit because this node is not blocked by any reservation. The second window, Window 2, consists of 3 nodes which are available for two hours because some of the nodes are blocked by a reservation. It is important to note that these backfill windows partially overlap yielding larger windows and thus increasing backfill scheduling opportunities.

Once the backfill windows have been determined, Maui begins to traverse them. By default, these windows are traversed widest window first but this can be configured to allow a longest window first approach to be employed. As each backfill window is evaluated, Maui applies the backfill algorithm specified by the BACKFILLPOLICY parameter, be it FIRSTFIT, BESTFIT, etc.

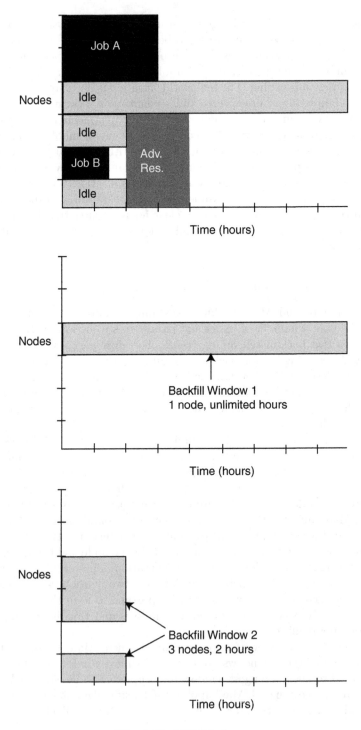

Fig. 3. Backfill Windows.

Assuming the BESTFIT algorithm is applied, the following steps are taken.

1. The list of feasible backfill jobs is filtered, selecting only those which will actually fit in the current backfill window.
2. The *degree-of-fit* of each job is determined based on the SCHEDULINGCRITERIA parameter (i.e., processors, seconds, processor-seconds, etc.) (i.e., if processors is selected, the job which requests the most processors will have the best fit)
3. The job with the best fit is started and the backfill window size adjusted.
4. While backfill jobs and idle resources remain, repeat step 1.

Other backfill policies behave in a similar manner with more details available in the Maui documentation.

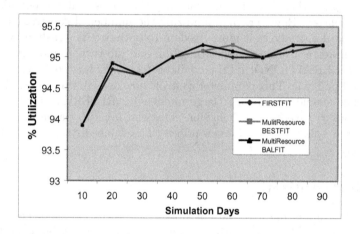

Fig. 4. Comparison of various backfill algorithms.

Figure 4 shows a comparison of backfill algorithms. This graph was generated using the emulation capabilities within the Maui scheduler which have be demonstrated in [7,8,9]. Notice that over the life of the simulation, the resulting utilization for all three algorithms track each other closely; so closely that it doesn't seem to matter which algorithm is chosen. When Maui starts up, priority jobs are scheduled. A backfill round then follows which places all possible jobs on the remaining resources until the space is insufficient to allow any backfill job to run. After this first iteration, Maui can only backfill when a new job is submitted (i.e., it may be small enough to run on available idle resources) or when a running job completes freeing additional resources for scheduling. Scheduling iteration granularity is generally so small that most often only a single job completes or enters the queue in a single iteration. Often, a large percentage of the freed resources are dedicated to a FIFO priority job and are not available for backfill. The reduced set of free resources is rarely adequate to run more than one backfill job. These conditions often result in the backfill algorithms making the same job selection for backfill. In the cases where more than one job could be run, the algorithms often selected the jobs in different order, but were constrained by resource availability to start the same set of jobs. The cases that allowed more than two jobs to be backfilled within a single iteration allowed the algorithms to differentiate themselves. However, these cases were so infrequent statistically as to have no significant impact on the overall statistics. The algorithms could be reevaluated with very large scheduling intervals to increase job turnover. However, it would not reflect real world conditions as the current results do.

There is one important note. By default, Maui reserves only the highest priority job resulting in a very liberal and aggressive backfill. This reservation guarantees that backfilled jobs will not delay the highest and only the highest priority job. This reservation behavior fails to provide any resource protection for priority jobs other than the first, meaning these jobs could potentially be significantly delayed. However, by minimizing the number of constraints imposed on the scheduler, it allows it more freedom to optimize its schedule, potentially resulting in better overall system utilization and job turnaround time. The parameter RESERVATIONDEPTH is available to control how conservative/liberal the backfill policy is. This parameter controls how deep down the priority queue reservations should be made. A large number for RESERVATIONDEPTH results in conservative backfill behavior. Sites can use this parameter to obtain their desired balance level between priority based job distribution and system utilization.

5   Job Prioritization

Job prioritization is an often overlooked aspect of batch job management. While trivially simple FIFO job prioritization algorithms can satisfy basic needs, much in the way of site policy can be expressed via flexible job prioritization. This allows the site to avoid resorting to an endless array of queues and being affected by the potential resource fragmentation drawbacks associated with them. The Maui prioritization mechanism takes into account 6 main categories of information which are listed in Table 1.

Priority components can be weighted and combined with other scheduling mechanisms to deliver higher overall system utilization, balanced job queue time expansion factors, and prevent job starvation. Priority adjustments are also often used as a mechanism of obtaining quality of service targets for a subset of jobs and for favoring short term resource distribution patterns along job credential and job requirement boundaries.

5.1   Priority Algorithm

Because there are so many factors incorporated into the scheduling decision, with a corresponding number of metrics, (i.e., minutes queued and processors requested) a hierarchy of priority weights is required to allow priority tuning at a sensible level. The high-level priority calculation for job J is as follows:

Table 1. Maui Priority Components

Priority Component	Evaluation Metrics	Use
Service	Current queue time and expansion factor	Allows favoring jobs with lowest current scheduling performance (promotes balanced delivery of job queuetime and expansion factor service levels)
Requested Resources	Requested processors, memory, swap, local disk, nodes, and processor-equivalents	Allows favoring of jobs which meet various requested resource constraints (i.e., favoring large processor jobs counters backfills proclivity for smaller jobs and improves overall system utilization)
Fairshare	User, group, account, QoS, and Class fairshare utilization	Allows favoring jobs based on historical usage associated with their credentials
Direct Priority Specification	User, group, account, QoS, and Class administrator specified priorities	Allows political priorities to be assigned to various groups
Target	Current delta between measured and target queue time and expansion factor values	Allows ability to specify service targets and enable non-linear priority growth to enable a job to reach this service target
Bypass	Job bypass count	Allows favoring of jobs bypassed by backfill to prevent backfill based job starvation

```
Priority = SERVICEWEIGHT * SERVICEFACTOR +
           RESOURCEWEIGHT * RESOURCEFACTOR +
           FAIRSHAREWEIGHT * FAIRSHAREFACTOR +
           DIRECTSPECWEIGHT * DIRECTSPECFACTOR +
           TARGETWEIGHT * TARGETFACTOR +
           BYPASSWEIGHT * BYPASSFACTOR
```

where each *WEIGHT value is a configurable parameter and each *FACTOR component is calculated from subcomponents as described in table 1. Note that the *CAP parameters below are also configurable parameters which allow a site to cap the contribution of a particular priority factor.

6   Fairshare

There are a number of interpretations of the term fairshare as applied to batch systems. In general, however, they each involve a mechanism which controls the distribution of delivered resources across various job attribute-based dimensions. They do this by tracking a utilization metric over time and using this historical data to adjust scheduling behavior so as to maintain resource usage within configured fairshare constraints. The above vague description of fairshare leaves great room for interpretation and leaves many algorithmic questions unanswered.

Table 2. Job Priority Component Equations. **NOTE:** XFactor/XF represents expansion factor information calculated as (QueueTime - ExecutionTime / (ExecutionTime)

Factor	Formula
Service	QueueTimeWeight * min(QueueTimeCap,QueueTime$_J$) + XFactorWeight * min(XFCap,XFactor$_J$)
Resource	MIN(RESOURCECAP, NODEWEIGHT * Nodes$_J$ + PROCWEIGHT * Processors$_J$ + MEMWEIGHT * Memory$_J$ + SWAPWEIGHT * Swap$_J$ + DISKWEIGHT * Disk$_J$ + PEWEIGHT * PE$_J$)
Fairshare	MIN(FSCAP, FSUSERWEIGHT * FSDeltaUserUsage[User$_J$] + FSGROUPWEIGHT * FSDeltaGroupUsage[Group$_J$] + FSACCOUNTWEIGHT * FSDeltaAccountUsage[Account$_J$] + FSQOSWEIGHT * FSDeltaQOSUsage[QOS$_J$] + FSCLASSWEIGHT * FSDeltaClassUsage[Class$_J$])
Directspec	USERWEIGHT * Priority[User$_J$] + GROUPWEIGHT * Priority[Group$_J$] + ACCOUNTWEIGHT * Priority[Account$_J$] + QOSWEIGHT * Priority[QOS$_J$] + CLASSWEIGHT * Priority[Class$_J$]
Target	$(\text{MAX}(.0001, \text{XFTarget} - \text{XFCurrent}_J)^{-2}$ + $(\text{MAX}(.0001, \text{QTTarget} - \text{QTCurrent}_J)^{-2}$ NOTE: XF is a unitless ratio while QT is reported in minutes.
Bypass	BypassCount$_J$

For example, it is not clear what the metric of utilization should be nor to which job attributes this correlation data should be correlated. Also, the method of compiling historical data in order to compare it to a particular target value is unclear. Finally, the significant issue of how fairshare targets are enforced is left completely open.

Maui offers flexibility in configuring fairshare in areas including the tracked utilization metric, the utilization to job correlation attributes, the historical period, and the method of fairshare enforcement. Figure 5 shows a typical Maui fairshare configuration.

```
FSPOLICY    PSDEDICATED # track fairshare usage by dedicated proc-seconds
FSINTERVAL    12:00:00 # maintain 12 hour fairshare utilization records
FSDEPTH             14 # track effective usage using last 14 records
FSDECAY           0.80 # decay historical records
FSWEIGHT           100 # specify relative fairshare priority weight
USERFSWEIGHT         2 # relative user fairshare impact
GROUPFSWEIGHT        1 # relative group fairshare impact
QOSFSWEIGHT         10 # relative QOS fairshare impact
CLASSFSWEIGHT        4 # relative class fairshare impact

UserCfg[BigKahuna]    FSTARGET=50    # target usage of 50% (target)
GroupCfg[staff]       FSTARGET=10.0- # target usage below 10% (ceiling)
QOSCfg[HighPriority]  FSTARGET=40.0+ # target usage above 40% (floor)
ClassCfg[interactive] FSTARGET=15.0^ # ignore interactive jobs
                                     # if usage exceeds 15% (cap)
```

Fig. 5. Sample Fairshare Configuration.

Fairshare target usage can be specified on a per user, group, account, QOS, or class basis by way of a fairshare target. Each target is specified as a percentage value where each value is interpreted as a percent of delivered utilization. The use of delivered utilization as the target basis as opposed to using percent of configured or available resources allows the fairshare system to transparently take into account factors such scheduling inefficiencies, system maintenance, job failures, etc.

Fairshare targets can be specified as floors, ceilings, targets, and caps. In the above example, Maui will adjust job priority in an attempt to deliver 50% of delivered processor-hours to user **BigKahuna**, no more than 10% to group staff, and at least 40% to QOS **HighPriority**. The config file also specifies a cap on the class **interactive** instructing Maui to block interactive class jobs from running if the weighted one week usage of the class ever exceeds 15%.

6.1   Fairshare Algorithm

The fairshare algorithm is composed of several parts. These parts handle tasks including the updating of historical fairshare usage information, managing fairshare windows, determining effective fairshare usage, and determining the impact of a job's various effective fairshare usage components.

Updating Historical Fairshare Usage Information. The first issue in a fairshare system is determining the metric of utilization measurement. Likely candidates include utilized cpu and dedicated cpu. The first metric, utilized cpu *charges* a job only for the cpu actually consumed by job processes. The latter, charges a job for all the processing cycles dedicated to the job, regardless of whether or not the job made effective use of them. In a multi-resource, time-sharing, or shared node system, these metrics may not be adequate as they ignore the consumption of non-processor resources. In addition to these CPU metrics, Maui includes an option to track resource consumption by *processor equivalent* metric (PE), where a job's requested PE value is equivalent to

```
PE = MAX(ProcsRequestedByJob / TotalConfiguredProcs,
MemoryRequestedByJob / TotalConfiguredMemory,
DiskRequestedByJob / TotalConfiguredDisk,
SwapRequestedByJob / TotalConfiguredSwap) *
TotalConfiguredProcs
```

This metric determines a job's most constraining resource consumption and translates it into an equivalent processor count. For example, a 1 processor 4 GB job running on a system with a total of 8 processors and 16 GB of RAM would have a PE of 2 (i.e. MAX(1/8,4/16)*8= 2). To update fairshare usage information, the algorithm steps through the list of active jobs and the list of credentials associated with each job. Typically, each job is associated with a user, group, class (or queue), quality of service (QOS) level, and an optional account. The fairshare usage for each recorded job credential is incremented by the job's fairshare metric amount multiplied by the time interval since the last fairshare measurement was taken as shown below:

```
for (J in JobList)
   for (C in J->CredentialList)
      FSUsage[C->Type][C->Name][0] += <FSMETRIC> * Interval
```

Determining Effective Fairshare Usage. If fairshare targets are to be used, a mechanism for compiling fairshare information collected over time into a single effective usage value is required. This mechanism must determine the timeframe covered and how this information is to be aged. Maui's fairshare algorithm utilizes the concept of fairshare windows each covering a particular period of time. The algorithm allows a site to specify how long each window should last, how fairshare usage in each window should be weighted, and how many windows should be evaluated in obtaining the final effective fairshare usage. For example. a site may wish to make fairshare adjustments based on usage of the previous 8 days. To do this, they may choose to evaluate 8 fairshare windows each consisting of 24 hour periods, with a decay, or aging factor of 0.75 as seen in Figure 6.

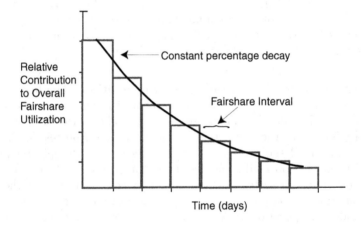

Fig. 6. Effective Fairshare Usage.

To maintain fairshare windows, Maui rolls its fairshare window information each time a fairshare window boundary is reached as shown in the algorithm below:

```
for (N=1->FSDepth)
{
    FSUsage[ObjectType][ObjectName][N] =
        FSUsage[ObjectType][ObjectName][N-1]
}
FSUsage[ObjectType][ObjectName][0] = 0.0;
```

The effective fairshare usage is then calculated at each scheduling algorithm using the following:

```
FSEffectiveUsage[ObjectType][ObjectIndex] = 0.0
for (N=0->FSDEPTH)
  FSEffectiveUsage[ObjectType][ObjectIndex] +=
FSUsage[ObjectType][ObjectIndex][N] * (FSDECAY ^ N)
```

Determining the Impact of Fairshare Information. Maui utilizes fairshare information in one of two ways. If a fairshare target, floor, or ceiling is specified, fairshare information is used to adjust job priority. If a fairshare cap is specified, fairshare utilization information is used to determine a job's acceptability to be scheduled. (See table 3)

Table 3. Fairshare Target Types

Target Type	Scheduler Action
Target	Always adjust job priority to favor target usage
Floor	Increase job priority if usage drops below target
Ceiling	Decrease job priority if usage exceeds target
Cap	Do not consider job for scheduling if usage exceeds target

As mentioned previously, Maui determines percentage fairshare utilization with respect to actual delivered utilization, not configured or available utilization. This is calculated using the following equation:

```
FSPercentUsage[ObjectType][ObjectIndex] =
FSEffectiveUsage[ObjectType][ObjectIndex] /
FSTotalEffectiveUsage
```

The impact of all relevant fairshare targets are considered and incorporated into the final priority adjustment of a job as described in section 3.

There is a common misperception about fairshare. Some sites initially believe that they can specify fairshare targets and that the scheduler can force these targets to be met. This is not the case. Since a fairshare system cannot control the mix of jobs submitted, it cannot guarantee successful fulfillment of targets. If a high target user does not submit jobs, then his target cannot be met regardless of how hard the scheduler tries and preventing other jobs from running will not help. The purpose of a fairshare system should be to *steer* existing workload, favoring jobs below the target so as to improve the turnaround time of these jobs and perhaps allow the associated users the opportunity to submit subsequent dependent jobs sooner. A fairshare system can only *push* submitted jobs so as to approach targets, hence the extensive use of priority adjustments.

The Maui fairshare system fits neatly in a time-based spectrum of resource distribution capabilities. At the short term end, a number of throttling policies are available allowing a specification of how many jobs, processors, nodes, etc. can be used by a given entity at a single time (i.e., the sum of processors simultaneously utilized by user John's jobs may not exceed 32). Fairshare allows resource usage targets to be specified over a given time frame, generally a few days to a few weeks. For longer time frames, Maui interfaces to powerful allocation management systems, such as PNNL's QBank, which allow per user allocations to be managed over an arbitrary time frame. Such systems allow Maui to check the *available balance* of a job, blocking those jobs with inadequate balances, and debiting allocations for successfully completed jobs.

6.2   Summary

The purpose of this paper was to present the backfill, job prioritization, and fairshare algorithms used within the Maui scheduler. While wide-spread use and numerous informal evaluations of the scheduler have demonstrated value in these algorithms, no formal or exhaustive analysis of the effectiveness of each algorithm has been published. These algorithms will be evaluated individually in forthcoming papers.

While the described backfill, priority, and fairshare systems appear to have met the needs of a wide spectrum of HPC architectures and site policies, research and development in these areas continue. Significant enhancements to Maui also continue in the realm of quality of service delivery and new preemption based backfill optimizations. Additional work is also ongoing in extending Maui's existing interface for grid applications and general metascheduling, with a near term focus on improving job start time estimations. Research regarding the effect of the quality of this start time information on the performance of multi-system load balancing systems is currently underway.

References

1. D. Jackson. The Maui Scheduler. Technical report.
   http://supercluster.org/projects/maui.
2. J.S. Skovira, W. Chen, and H. Zhou. The EASY - LoadLeveler API Project. *Job Scheduling Strategies for Parallel Processing, Lecture Notes in Computer Science 1162*, pages 41–47, 1996.
3. R.L. Henderson. Job scheduling under the Portable Batch System. *Job Scheduling Strategies for Parallel Processing, Lecture Notes in Computer Science*, 949, 1995.
4. J.M. Barton and N. Bitar. A scalable multi-discipline multiple processor scheduling framework for IRIX. *Job Scheduling Strategies for Parallel Processing, Lecture Notes in Computer Science*, 949, 1995.
5. D. Jackson. HPC workload repository. Technical report.
   http://www.supercluster.org/research/traces.
6. D. Feitelson and A. Mu'alem Weil. Utilization and predicability in scheduling the IBM SP2 with backfilling. In *Proceedings of IPPS/SPDP*, April 1998.
7. Q. Snell, M. Clement, D. Jackson, and C. Gregory. The performance impact of advance reservation metascheduling. *Lecture Notes in Computer Science: Job Scheduling Strategiew for Parallel Processing*, 1911, 2000.
8. John Jardine. Avoiding livelock using the Y Metascheduler and exponential backoff. Master's thesis, Brigham Young University, 2000.
9. D. Jackson, Q. Snell, and M. Clement. Simulation based HPC workload analysis. In *International Parallel and Distributed Processing Symposium*, 2001.

On the Development
of an Efficient Coscheduling System

B.B. Zhou[1] and R.P. Brent[2]

[1] School of Computing and Mathematics, Deakin University,
Geelong, VIC 3217, Australia
[2] Oxford University Computing laboratory, Wolfson Building, Parks Road,
Oxford OX1 3QD, UK

Abstract. Applying gang scheduling can alleviate the blockade problem caused by exclusively space-sharing scheduling. To simply allow jobs to run simultaneously on the same processors as in the conventional gang scheduling, however, may introduce a large number of time slots in the system. In consequence the cost of context switches will be greatly increased, and each running job can only obtain a small portion of resources including memory space and processor utilisation and so no jobs can finish their computations quickly. In this paper we present some experimental results to show that to properly divide jobs into different classes and to apply different scheduling strategies to jobs of different classes can greatly reduce the average number of time slots in the system and significantly improve the performance in terms of average slowdown.

1 Introduction

Scheduling strategies for parallel processing can be classified into either space sharing, or time sharing. Currently most clusters for parallel processing only adopt space-sharing strategies, in which each partitioned processor subset is dedicated to a single job and the job will exclusively occupy the subset until completion. However, one major drawback of space sharing is the blockade situation, that is, short jobs can easily be blocked for a long time by long jobs. Though the backfilling technique can be applied to alleviate this problem to certain extent [5,7], under heavy workload the blockade can still be a serious problem. As more parallel software packages have been developed for various kinds of applications and more and more ordinary users are getting familiar with multiple processor systems, it is expected that the workload on machines with multiple processors will become heavy in the near future. To alleviate this blockade problem, time-sharing strategies have to be considered.

Because processes of the same parallel job need to coordinate with each other during the computation, coordinated scheduling of parallel jobs across the processors is a critical factor to achieve efficient parallel execution in a time-shared environment. Currently the most popular scheme for coordinated scheduling is explicit coscheduling [6], or gang scheduling [4]. With gang scheduling time is

D.G. Feitelson and L. Rudolph (Eds.): JSSPP 2001, LNCS 2221, pp. 103–115, 2001.

divided into time slots and all parallel jobs, controlled by a global scheduler, take turns to receive the service in a coordinated manner.

One major fundamental problem associated with conventional gang scheduling is resource contention. Currently nearly all time-sharing strategies assume that the resources in a system are unlimited. This assumption is not true and makes the proposed strategies impractical. In a real system the processing speed of processors is limited. If there is a large number of jobs running simultaneously on the same set of processors, no job is able to complete quickly. Because the memory space in a real system is also limited, it is quite possible that the system can run out of memory space if a number of jobs are allowed to run simultaneously and then some jobs have to be paged or swapped out to the secondary memory. However, the experimental results show that simply applying the methods of paging and swapping may seriously harm the process coordination of parallel jobs and thus degrade the system and job performance [1]. Therefore, there is an urgent need to design new time-sharing strategies that take both processor and memory constraints into consideration.

Recently several methods have been proposed to alleviate this kind of contention problem. For example, the reported experimental results in [1] show that using a queue to delay job execution is more efficient than running jobs all together with paging applied. In [9], for another example, the authors first set a multiprogramming level, or a limit for the maximum number of jobs which are allowed to run simultaneously on the same processors. If the maximum level is reached, the new arrivals have to be queued. The authors then combine the gang scheduling and the backfilling technique to achieve a reasonably good performance.

Using a waiting queue to delay the execution of certain jobs is a good way to alleviate the problem of resource contention. The question is, however, which jobs should be queued. Conventionally, jobs are not distinguished according to their execution times when gang scheduling is considered. It should be pointed out that the simple round robin scheme used in gang scheduling works well only if the sizes of jobs are distributed in a wide range. Gang scheduling using the simple round robin may not perform as well as even a simple FCFS scheme in terms of average response time, or average slowdown, when all the incoming jobs are long. The results of our recent study show that limiting the number of long jobs to time-share the same processors can improve both the average job performance and processor utilisation [12]. To ensure an efficient utilisation of the limited computing power and at the same time to satisfy the performance requirements of various kinds of applications in a give parallel system, therefore, priorities need to be considered and assigned for different jobs.

Our project to develop an effective and practical coscheduling system is divided into three key stages. In the context of gang scheduling computing resources are two dimensional, that is, we have to consider resource allocation in both time and space dimensions. At the first stage we investigated effective resource allocation (packing) and re-allocation (re-packing) schemes for gang scheduling. We designed a job re-packing strategy for resource re-allocation and time slot reduction. Combining certain existing efficient allocation and re-allocation strategies, we can greatly enhance both resource utilisation and job performance [10,11].

At the second stage we try to introduce priority scheduling into gang schedul-ing by dividing jobs into classes, such as, long, medium and short according to their required execution times. Different allocation strategies are then used for jobs of different classes to satisfy performance requirements of different appli-cations. For example, we may queue long jobs to limit the number of long ones time-sharing the same processors and to allow short ones to be executed im-mediately without any delay. The method to classify jobs into classes and treat them differently is not new at all. However, it has not been studied systemati-cally in the context of gang scheduling. We believe that the performance of gang scheduling can significantly be improved by taking the priority scheduling into consideration. Since the computing power is limited, to give one class of jobs a special treatment will no doubt affect the performance of jobs in other classes. A hard question is how to design scheduling strategies such that the performance of jobs in one class can be improved without severely punishing the others.

To solve the problem of memory pressure we need to consider scheduling and memory management simultaneously. Another advantage of dividing jobs into classes is that we are able to choose a particular type of jobs for paging and swapping to alleviate the memory pressure without significantly degrade the overall job performance. Therefore, in our future work, that is, the third stage of our project we will consider to combine memory management with gang scheduling to directly solve the problem of memory pressure.

In this paper we shall present some simulation results from our second stage research, to show that, by properly classifying jobs (which are generated from a particular workload model) and choosing different scheduling strategies to different classes of jobs, we are able to improve the overall performance without severely degrading the performance of long jobs.

The paper is organised as follows: In Section 2 we briefly describe the gang scheduling system implemented for our experiments. A workload model used in our experiments is discussed in Section 3. Experimental results and discussions are presented in Sections 4. Finally the conclusions are given in Section 5.

2   Our Experimental System

The gang scheduling system implemented for our experiments is mainly based on a *job re-packing* allocation strategy which is introduced for enhancing both resource utilisation and job performance [10,11].

Conventional resource allocation strategies for gang scheduling only consider processor allocation within the same time slot and the allocation in one time slot is independent of the allocation in other time slots. One major disadvantage of this kind of allocation is the problem of fragmentation. Because processor allocation is considered independently in different time slots, freed processors due to job termination in one time slot may remain idle for a long time even though they are able to be re-allocated to existing jobs running in other time slots.

One way to alleviate the problem is to allow jobs to run in multiple time slots [3,8]. When jobs are allowed to run in multiple time slots, the buddy based allocation strategy will perform much better than many other existing allocation schemes in terms of average slowdown [3].

Another method to alleviate the problem of fragmentation is job re-packing. In this scheme we try to rearrange the order of job execution on the originally allocated processors so that small fragments of idle processors from different time slots can be combined together to form a larger and more useful one in a single time slot. Therefore, processors in the system can be utilised more efficiently. When this scheme is incorporated into the buddy based system, we can set up a *workload tree* to record the workload conditions of each subset of processors. With this workload tree we are able to simplify the search procedure for available processors, to balance the workload across the processors and to quickly determine when a job can run in multiple time slots and when the number of time slots in the system can be reduced.

With a combination of job re-packing, running jobs in multiple time slots, minimising time slots in the system, and applying buddy based scheme to allocate processors in each time slot we are able to achieve high efficiency in processor utilisation and a great improvement in job performance [11].

Our experimental system is based on the gang scheduling system described above. In this experimental system, however, jobs are classified and limits are set to impose restrictions on how many jobs are allowed to run simultaneously on the same processors.

To classify jobs we introduce two parameters. Assume the execution time of the longest job is t^e. A job will be considered "long" in each test if its execution time is longer than $\alpha_l t^e$ for $0.0 \leq \alpha_l \leq 1.0$. A job is considered "medium" if its execution time is longer than $\alpha_m t^e$, but shorter than or equal to $\alpha_l t^e$ for $0.0 \leq \alpha_m \leq \alpha_l$. Otherwise, the job will be considered "short". By varying these two parameters we are able to make different job classifications and to see how different classifications affect the system performance.

We introduce a waiting queue for medium and long jobs in our coscheduling system. To alleviate the blockade problem the backfilling technique is adopted. Because the backfilling technique is applied, a long job in front of the queue will not block the subsequent medium sized jobs from entering the system. Therefore, one queue is enough for both classes of jobs. A major advantage of using a single queue for two classes of jobs is that the jobs will be easily kept in a proper order based on their arriving times. Note that in our experimental system short jobs can be executed immediately on their arrivals without any delay.

To conduct our experiments we further set two other parameters. One parameter k_m is the limit for the number of both medium and long jobs to be allowed to time-share the same processors. If the limit is reached, the incoming medium and long jobs have to be queued. The other parameter k_l is the limit for the number of long jobs to be allowed to run simultaneously on the same processors. If that limit is reached, the incoming long jobs have to be queued. By varying these two parameters we are able to see how the added queue affects the system performance.

3   The Workload Model

In our experiment we adopted one workload model proposed in [2]. Both job run-times and sizes (the number of processors required) in this model are distributed uniformly in log space (or uniform-log distributed), while the interarrival times are exponentially distributed. This model was constructed based on observations from the Intel Paragon at the San Diego Supercomputer Center and the IBM SP2 at the Cornell Theory Center and has been used by many researchers to evaluate their parallel job scheduling algorithms. Since the model was originally built to evaluate batch scheduling policies, we made a few minor modifications in our simulation for gang scheduling.

In following sections we present some experimental results. We assume that there are 128 processors in the system. In each experiment we measure the average slowdown and the average number of time slots which are defined below.

Assume the execution time and the turnaround time for job i are t_i^e and t_i^r, respectively. The slowdown for job i is $s_i = t_i^r/t_i^e$. The average slowdown s is then $s = \sum_{i=0}^{m} s_i/m$ for m being the total number of jobs.

If t_i is the total time when there are i time slots in the system, the average number of time slots in the system during the operation can be defined as $n = \sum_{i=0}^{l} it_i / \sum_{i=0}^{l} t_i$ where l is the largest number of time slots encountered in the system during the computation.

For each estimated system workload, 10 different sets of 10000 jobs were generated using the workload model described above and the final result is the average of these 10 runs.

4   Experimental Results

We conducted four different experiments. Some of our experimental results are presented in the following subsections.

4.1   Experiment One

In our first experiment α_m and α_l are fixed, that is, $\alpha_m = 0.0$ and $\alpha_l = 1.0$. With this setting all jobs are treated as equal and they may have to enter the queue before being executed if k_m is not set to infinity. The number of jobs to be allowed to time-share the same processor is determined by k_m. Thus the system performance will be affected by varying this parameter. Some experimental results for average slowdown are given in Fig. 1.

When $k_m = 1$, it is just a simple FCFS scheduling system with backfilling. It can be seen from this figure that the slowdown is very dramatically increased

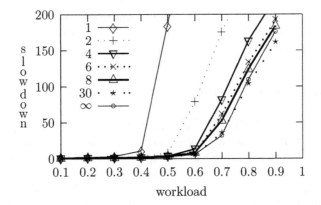

Fig. 1. Average slowdown when $\alpha_m = 0.0$ and $\alpha_l = 1.0$.

after workload becomes greater than 0.4. Therefore, exclusively space-sharing scheduling can only perform well under light workload. When the system workload becomes heavy, time sharing should be considered.

When k_m is increased, the performance is improved as indicated in the figure. After k_m reaches certain value, however, further increase in k_m will not lead to a great increase in performance. An interesting point is that the simple gang scheduling system (by setting $k_m = \infty$) will not perform as well as one with $k_m = 30$ when the system workload becomes heavy. This is because the computing power of a given system is limited. If too many jobs time-share the same set of processors, each job can only obtain a very small portion of processor utilisation and no job can complete quickly. Thus the system performance will be degraded.

4.2   Experiment Two

In our first experiment jobs are not distinguished based on their execution times. Though the performance is improved by increasing k_m, the improvement is not that significant.

As mentioned in Section 1, the simple round robin scheduling strategy will not perform well when a number of long jobs are running simultaneously on the same processors. To demonstrate this in our second experiment we set $\alpha_m = 0.8$ and $\alpha_l = 1$, which means jobs are divided into two classes, that is, "long" jobs whose execution time is longer than $0.8t^e$ for t^e the execution time of the longest job, and "short" jobs whose execution time is shorter than or equal to $0.8t^e$. By varying k_m we can determine how many long jobs can run simultaneously on the same processors.

Some experimental results are depicted in Fig. 2. We can see from the figure that the average slowdown, the average number of slots and the maximum slot number (i.e. the maximum number of jobs which are running simultaneously on the same processors during the computation) are all reduced when k_m decreases.

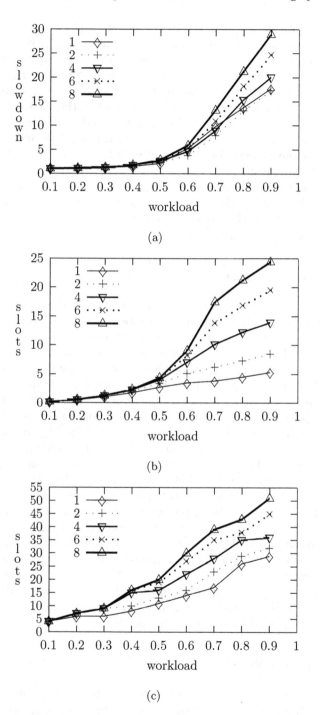

Fig. 2. (a) Average slowdown, (b) average number of time slots and (c) maximum number of time slots, when $\alpha_m = 0.8$ and $\alpha_l = 1.0$.

It is a clear indication that limiting the number of long jobs to run simultaneously on the same processors can indeed improve overall system performance.

Comparing Fig. 2(a) with Fig. 1, we see that a much smaller average slowdown can be obtained by only queueing long jobs, but allowing other jobs to run immediately on their arrivals. As depicted in Fig. 1, for example, the average slowdown will become greater than 150 when the workload is 0.9. This can be considered a very good result when the method of combining the gang scheduling with backfilling is applied. By queueing long jobs, however, the average slowdown can be even lower than 20 with $k_m = 1$ (or $k_m = 2$), which is a significant improvement.

It can also been seen from Fig. 2(b) that for $k_m = 1$ the average number of slots is only about 5 when the system workload is 0.9. thus queueing long jobs can also decrease the average number of time slots in contrast with the conventional gang scheduling.

4.3   Experiment Three

Although the average slowdown is significantly decreased by queueing long jobs in gang scheduling, the maximum slot number encountered during the computation is relatively high in contrast to the strategy which queues every incoming job once a hard limit for the number of time slots is reached. The question is if we can produce similar performance with reduced maximum slot number.

In our third experiment we first set $\alpha_m = 0.0$, $k_m = 6$ and $k_l = 1$, that is, we set a limit for maximum number of time slots to 6 and another limit for long jobs to be allowed to time-share the same processors to 1. Thus the maximum slot number will never exceed 6 during the computation. By varying α_l we can determine what jobs should be considered as long such that a good performance can be obtained by blocking them from running simultaneously on the same processors. Some experimental results are depicted in Fig. 3(a).

When $\alpha_l = 1.0$, no jobs are treated as long. This is the same as that in our first experiment by combining the gang scheduling with backfilling and then setting $k_m = 6$. The performance is first improved with α_l decreasing. However, further decreasing α_l will cause an increase in average slowdown. We can see from the figure that the best performance is obtained when $\alpha_l = 0.8$.

Next we set $\alpha_m = 0.0$, $k_m = 6$ and $\alpha_l = 0.8$. We want to see how the system performs by varying k_l. Some experimental results are depicted in Fig. 3(b) and (c). It is clearly shown in the figures that to allow more long jobs to time-share the same processors can only degrade the performance.

4.4   Experiment Four

The results obtained from the third experiment is not desirable, that is, these results are not as good as those obtained by only queueing long jobs in the second experiment. In contrast with the results obtained by using the combination of the gang scheduling and backfilling in our first experiment, however, both the

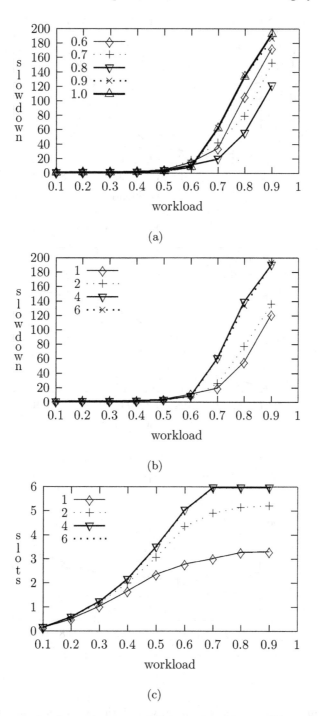

Fig. 3. (a) Average slowdown when $\alpha_m = 0.0$, $k_m = 6$ and $k_l = 1$, (b) average slowdown and (c) average number of slots when $\alpha_m = 0.0$ and $\alpha_l = 0.8$ and $k_m = 6$.

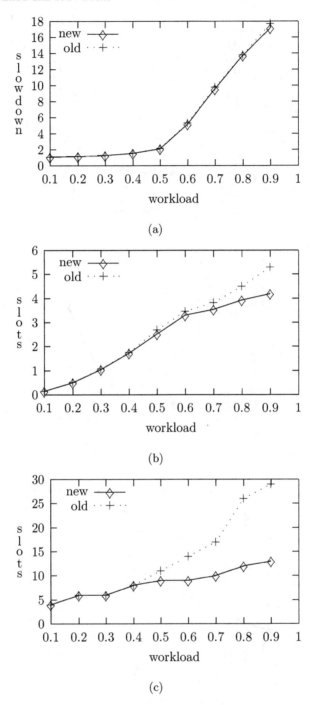

Fig. 4. Comparison of the new results (new) with the best results (old) obtained from experiment two. (a) average slowdown, (b) average number of slots and (c) maximum number of slots.

average slowdown and the average number of slots are reduced if we set limits both for all jobs and for long jobs to run simultaneously on the same processors.

In our fourth experiment we still set $\alpha_l = 0.8$, $k_m = 6$ and $k_l = 1$, that is, the same set of long jobs will be limited to time-share the same processors as that in the third experiment. However, we allow a (small) number of real short jobs to run immediately on their arrivals by setting $\alpha_m = 0.15$. In this way we hope that the number of time slots will not be increased greatly during the computation and at the same time the average slowdown will significantly be reduced. Some experimental results (new) are depicted in Fig. 4. In order to provide a clearer view about the performance, the best results (old) obtained by setting $\alpha_m = 0.8$ and $k_m = 1$ in our second experiment, are also presented in the figure. We can see that the two strategies (old and new) are comparable in terms of average slowdown. Under heavy system workload, however, a smaller average number of time slots and a much smaller maximum number of time slots is obtained in our fourth (or new) experiment.

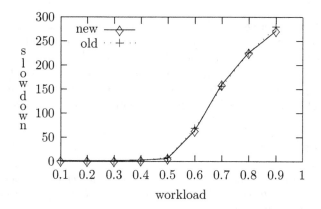

Fig. 5. Comparison of the two strategies (old and new) in average slowdown for long jobs

Since a number of short jobs are allowed to run immediately without delay, the performance of long jobs might be severely degraded. As depicted in Fig. 5, however, we find that no serious performance degradation for long jobs in terms of slowdown occurs in our experiment. To allow short jobs to run immediately may enhance the system utilisation. This may be the main reason why the overall system performance is enhanced in our fourth experiment.

5   Conclusions

It is known that exclusively space-sharing scheduling can cause blockade problem under heavy workload and that this problem can be alleviated by applying the gang scheduling strategy. Using gang scheduling to simply allow jobs to run simultaneously on the same processors, however, may introduce a large number of time slots in the system. In consequence the cost of context switches will be greatly increased, and each running job can only obtain a small portion of resources including memory space and processor utilisation and so no jobs can complete quickly. Therefore, the number of jobs allowed to run in the system should be limited. The question is what kind of jobs should be queued so that the overall performance can be improved, or at least will not be significantly degraded in comparison with the conventional gang scheduling. In this paper we presented some results obtained from our experiments to show that to properly divide jobs into different classes and to apply different scheduling strategies to jobs of different classes can greatly reduce the average number of time slots in the system and significantly improve the performance in terms of average slowdown.

In our experiments we showed that a good overall system performance can be obtained by first classifying jobs into short, medium and long and then using conventional gang scheduling for short, the combination of the gang and back-filling for medium and the combination of the FCFS and backfilling for long jobs.

Although the average number of time slots is significantly reduced, which may alleviate memory pressure, our method can only be considered as an indirect method for solving that problem because it does not directly take memory requirements into consideration. In our future research in the development of an efficient and practical coscheduling system we shall combine memory management with scheduling to directly solve the problem of memory pressure.

References

1. A. Batat and D. G. Feitelson, Gang scheduling with memory considerations, *Proceedings of 14th International Parallel and Distributed Processing Symposium*, Cancun, May 2000, pp.109-114.
2. A. B. Downey, A parallel workload model and its implications for processor allocation, *Proceedings of 6th International Symposium on High Performance Distributed Computing*, Aug 1997.
3. D. G. Feitelson, Packing schemes for gang scheduling, In *Job Scheduling Strategies for Parallel Processing*, D. G. Feitelson and L. Rudolph (eds.), Lecture Notes Computer Science, Vol. 1162, Springer-Verlag, 1996, pp.89-110.
4. D. G. Feitelson and L. Rudolph, Gang scheduling performance benefits for fine-grained synchronisation, *Journal of Parallel and Distributed Computing*, 16(4), Dec. 1992, pp.306-318.
5. D. Lifka, The ANL/IBM SP scheduling system, In *Job Scheduling Strategies for Parallel Processing*, D. G. Feitelson and L. Rudolph (Eds.), Lecture Notes Computer Science, Vol. 949, Springer-Verlag, 1995, pp.295-303.
6. J. K. Ousterhout, Scheduling techniques for concurrent systems, *Proceedings of Third International Conference on Distributed Computing Systems*, May 1982, pp.20-30.
7. J. Skovira, W. Chan, H. Zhou and D. Lifka, The EASY - LoadLeveler API project, In *Job Scheduling Strategies for Parallel Processing*, D. G. Feitelson and L. Rudolph (Eds.), Lecture Notes Computer Science, Vol. 1162, Springer-Verlag, 1996.

8. K. Suzaki, H. Tanuma, S. Hirano, Y. Ichisugi and M. Tukamoto, Time sharing systems that use a partitioning algorithm on mesh-connected parallel computers, *Proceedings of the Ninth International Conference on Distributed Computing Systems*, 1996, pp.268-275.

9. Y. Zhang, H. Franke, J. E. Moreira and A. Sivasubramaniam, Improving parallel job scheduling by combining gang scheduling and backfilling techniques, *Proceedings of 14th International Parallel and Distributed Processing Symposium*, Cancun, May 2000, pp.133-142.

10. B. B. Zhou, R. P. Brent, C. W. Johnson and D. Walsh, Job re-packing for enhancing the performance of gang scheduling, *Proceedings of 5th Workshop on Job Scheduling Strategies for Parallel Processing*, San Juan, April 1999, pp.129-143.

11. B. B. Zhou, D. Walsh and R. P. Brent, Resource allocation schemes for gang scheduling, *Proceedings of 6th Workshop on Job Scheduling Strategies for Parallel Processing*, Cancun, May 2000, pp.45-53.

12. B. B. Zhou and R. P. Brent, Gang scheduling with a queue for large jobs, accepted by *15th International Parallel and Distributed Processing Symposium*, San Francisco, April 2001.

Effects of Memory Performance
on Parallel Job Scheduling

G. Edward Suh, Larry Rudolph, and Srinivas Devadas

MIT Laboratory for Computer Science
Cambridge, MA 02139
{suh,rudolph,devadas}@mit.edu

Abstract. We develop a new metric for job scheduling that includes the
effects of memory contention amongst simultaneously-executing jobs that
share a given level of memory. Rather than assuming each job or process
has a fixed, static memory requirement, we consider a general scenario
wherein a process' performance monotonically increases as a function of
allocated memory, as defined by a miss-rate versus memory size curve.
Given a schedule of jobs in a shared-memory multiprocessor (SMP), and
an isolated miss-rate versus memory size curve for each job, we use an
analytical memory model to estimate the overall memory miss-rate for
the schedule. This, in turn, can be used to estimate overall performance.
We develop a heuristic algorithm to find a good schedule of jobs on a
SMP that minimizes memory contention, thereby improving memory and
overall performance.

1   Introduction

High performance computing is more than just raw FLOPS; it is also about
managing the memory among parallel threads so as to keep the operands flow-
ing into the arithmetic units. Hence, some high performance job schedulers are
beginning to consider the memory requirements of a job in addition to the traditional CPU requirements. But memory is spread across a hierarchy, it is difficult
to know the real requirements of each job, and underallocation of space to one
job can adversely affect the performance of other jobs. Allocating a fixed amount
of space to a job regardless of the needs of the other concurrently executing jobs
can result in suboptimal performance. We argue that a scheduler must compare
the marginal utility or marginal gain accrued by a job to the gains accrued by
other jobs, when giving more memory to a job.

Shared-memory multiprocessors (SMPs) [2,8,9], have become a basic building
block for modern high performance computer systems, and in the near future,
other layers of the memory hierarchy will be shared as well, with multiple processors (MPC) on a chip [3] and simultaneous multithreading (SMT) systems
[13,10,4]. So, in nearly all high performance systems, there will be either threads,
processes, or jobs that execute simultaneously and share parts of the memory
system. But how many jobs should execute simultaneously? There is no magic
number, rather it depends on the individual memory requirements of the jobs.

D.G. Feitelson and L. Rudolph (Eds.): JSSPP 2001, LNCS 2221, pp. 116–132, 2001.

Sometimes, it is even beneficial to let some processors remain idle so as to improve the overall performance.

Although most research on job scheduling for high performance parallel processing is concerned only with the allocation of processors in order to maximize processor utilization [6,5], scheduling with memory considerations is not new. Parsons [11] studied bounds on the achievable system throughput considering memory demand of parallel jobs. Batat [1] improved gang scheduling by imposing admission control based on the memory requirement of a new job and the available memory of a system. The modified gang scheduler estimates the memory requirement for each job, and assigns a job into a time slice only if the memory is large enough for all jobs in the time slice. Although these works have pointed out the importance of considering memory in job scheduling problems, they did not provide a way of scheduling jobs to optimize the memory performance.

Rather than assuming each job or process has a fixed, static memory requirement, this paper considers a general scenario wherein a process' performance monotonically increases as a function of allocated memory. The characteristics of each process' memory usage are given by the miss-rate as a function of memory size when the process is executed in isolation (which can be easily obtained either in an on-line or off-line manner). With this information, an analytical memory model for time-shared systems [12] can be used to estimate the memory miss-rate for each job and the processor idle time for a given schedule. Therefore, our approach provides a good memory performance metric for job scheduling problems.

The new approach based on the miss-rate curves and the analytical model can be used to evaluate a schedule including the effects of memory performance. If multiple processors share the same memory, our method can effectively schedule a given set of processes to minimize memory contention. Finally, the length of time slices can be determined for time-shared systems so as to minimize pollution effects.

The paper is organized as follows. In Section 2, we present a case study of scheduling SPEC CPU2000 benchmarks, which demonstrates the importance and challenges of job scheduling with memory considerations. Section 3 motivates isolated miss-rate curves, and describes how an analytical memory model evaluates the effect of a given schedule on the memory performance. Section 4 discusses new challenges that memory considerations impose on parallel job scheduling, and suggests possible solutions using the miss-rate curves and the model. Finally, Section 5 concludes the paper.

2   Case Study: SPEC CPU2000

This section discusses the results of trace-driven simulations that estimate the miss-rate of main memory when six jobs execute on a shared-memory multiprocessor system with three processors. The results demonstrate the importance of memory-aware scheduling and the problem of naive approaches based on footprint sizes.

Table 1. The descriptions and Footprints of benchmarks used for the simulations. All benchmarks are from SPEC CPU2000 [7] benchmark suite.

Name	Description	Footprint (MB)
bzip2	Compression	6.2
gcc	C Programming Language Compiler	22.3
gzip	Compression	76.2
mcf	Image Combinatorial Optimization	9.9
vortex	Object-oriented Database	83.0
vpr	FPGA Circuit Placement and Routing	1.6

Six jobs, which have various footprint sizes, are selected from SPEC CPU2000 benchmark suite [7] (See Table 1). Here, footprint size represents the memory size that a benchmark needs to achieve the minimum possible miss-rate. Benchmarks in the SPEC CPU2000 suite are not parallel jobs, however, the insights obtained from the experiments are also valid for parallel processing of multi-threaded jobs since all threads (or processes) from a job can be considered as one large process from the main memory standpoint.

Concurrent execution of six jobs by three processors requires time-sharing. We assume that there are two time slices long enough to render context switching overhead negligible. In the first time slice, three out of the six jobs execute sharing the main memory and in the second time slice the three remaining jobs execute. Processors are assumed to have 4-way 16-KB L1 instruction and data caches and a 8-way 256-KB L2 cache, and 4-KB pages are assumed for the main memory.

All possible schedules are simulated for various memory sizes. We compare the average miss-rate of all possible schedules with the miss-rates of the worst and the best schedule. The miss-rate only considers accesses to main memory, not accesses that hit on either L1 or L2 caches. The simulation results are summarized in Table 2 and Figure 1. In the table, a corresponding schedule for each case is also shown. In the 128-MB and 256-MB cases, many schedules result in the same miss-rate. A schedule is represented by two sets of letters. Each set represents a time slice, and each letter represents a job: A-bzip2, B-gcc, C-gzip, D-mcf, E-vortex, F-vpr. In the figure, the miss-rates are normalized to the average miss-rate.

The results demonstrate that job scheduling can have significant effects on the memory performance, and thus the overall system performance. For 16-MB memory, the best case miss-rate is about 30% better than the average case, and about 53% better than the worst case. Given a very long page fault penalty, performance can be significantly improved due to this large reduction in miss-rate. As the memory size increases, scheduling becomes less important since the entire workload fits into the memory. However, the smart schedule can still improve the memory performance significantly even for the 128-MB case (over 20% better than the average case, and 40% better than the worst case).

Memory traces used in this experiment have footprints smaller than 100 MB. As a result, scheduling of simultaneously executing processes is relevant to the

Table 2. The miss-rates for various job schedules. A schedule is represented by two sets of letters. Each set represents a time slice, and each letter represents a job: A-**bzip2**, B-**gcc**, C-**gzip**, D-**mcf**, E-**vortex**, F-**vpr**.

Memory Size (MB)		Average of All Cases	Worst Case	Best Case
8	Miss-Rate(%)	1.379	2.506	1.019
	Schedule		(ADE,BCF)	(ACD,BEF)
16	Miss-Rate(%)	0.471	0.701	0.333
	Schedule		(ADE,BCF)	(ADF,BCE)
32	Miss-Rate(%)	0.187	0.245	0.148
	Schedule		(ADE,BCF)	(ACD,BEF)
64	Miss-Rate(%)	0.072	0.085	0.063
	Schedule		(ABF,CDE)	(ACD,BEF)
128	Miss-Rate(%)	0.037	0.052	0.029
	Schedule		(ABF,CDE)	(ACD,BEF)
256	Miss-Rate(%)	0.030	0.032	0.029
	Schedule		(ABF,CDE)	(ACD,BEF)

main memory performance only for the memory up to 256 MB. However, many parallel applications have very large footprints often larger than main memory. For these applications, the memory size where scheduling matters should scale up.

An intuitive way of scheduling with memory considerations is to use footprint sizes. Since the footprint size of each job indicates its memory space needs, one can try to balance the total footprint size for each time slice. It also seems to be reasonable to be conservative and keep the total footprint size smaller than available physical memory. The experimental results show that these naive approaches do not work.

Balancing the total footprint size for each time slice may not work for memory smaller than the entire footprint. The footprint size of each benchmark only provides the memory size that the benchmark needs to achieve the best performance, however, it does not say anything about having less memory space. For example, in our experiments, executing **gcc**, **gzip** and **vpr** together and the others in the next time slice seems to be reasonable since it balances the total footprint size for each time slice. However, this schedule is actually the worst schedule for memory smaller than 128-MB, and results in a miss-rate that is over 50% worse than the optimal schedule.

If the replacement policy is not ideal, even being conservative and having larger physical memory than the total footprint may not be enough to guarantee the best memory performance. Smart scheduling can still improve the miss-rate by about 10% over the worst case even for 256-MB memory that is larger than the total footprint size of any three jobs from Table 1. This happens because the LRU replacement policy does not allocate the memory properly. (For a certain job, the LRU policy may allocate memory larger than the footprint of the job).

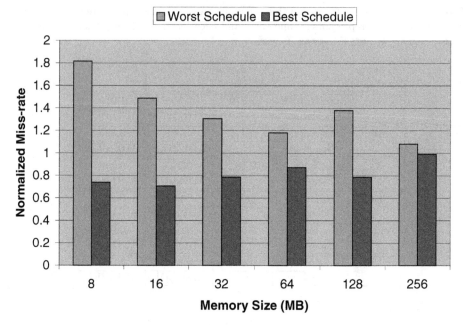

Fig. 1. The comparison of miss-rates for various schedules: the worst case, the best case, and the average of all possible schedules. The miss-rates are normalized to the average miss-rate of all possible schedules for each memory size. Notice that even when the memory is large enough to hold all the footprints of the executing jobs, the set of jobs that execute together has an effect on the miss-rate.

3   New Approach Based on Miss-Rate Curves

The previous section pointed out that the conventional scheduling approaches based on static footprints are very limited. This section proposes a new approach based on the *isolated miss-rate curve*, $m_i(x)$. After defining the isolated miss-rate curve, an analytical model is developed that incorporates the effect of time-sharing and memory contention based on the miss-rate curves. Using these curves and the model, we show how to evaluate a given schedule.

3.1   Miss-Rate Curves

The *isolated miss-rate curve* for process i, namely $m_i(x)$, is defined as the miss-rate when process i is isolated without other competing processes using the memory of size x. Effectively, this miss-rate curve represents the miss-rate when a process occupies only a part of the entire memory.

The advantage of having a miss-rate curve rather than static footprints is clear for the problem of scheduling processes for shared-memory systems. Consider the case of scheduling three processes, whose miss-rate curves are shown in Figure 2, on a shared-memory system with two processors. *Which two processes*

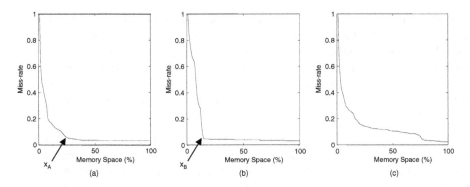

Fig. 2. (a) Miss-rate curve for process P_A (**gcc**). (b) Miss-rate curve for process P_B (**swim**). (c) Miss-rate curve for process P_C (**bzip2**). Clearly, process P_A's miss-rate does not reduce very much after the point marked x_A. Similarly, for process P_B after the point marked x_B. If $x_A + x_B$ is less than the total memory size available, then it is likely that processes P_A and P_B can both be run together, achieving good performance, especially if they are restricted to occupy an appropriate portion of the cache. On the other hand, process P_C has a different type of miss-rate curve, and will likely not run well with either P_A or P_B.

should run together? This question cannot be answered based on the static foot-prints since the memory is smaller than the individual footprints. However, from the miss-rate curves, it is clear that running both P_A and P_B simultaneously and P_C separately will result in a lower miss-rate than running P_A or P_B with P_C.

3.2   Estimating the Miss-Rate Curves

The miss-rate curves can be obtained either on-line or off-line. Here, an on-line method to estimate a miss-rate curve $m_i(x)$ is described. We use the LRU information of each page and count the number of hits in the kth most recently used page for each process ($counter_i[k]$). For example, $counter_i[1]$ is the number of hits in the most recently used page of process i, and $counter_i[2]$ is the number of hits in the second most recently used page. If we count hits for one time slice, $m_j(x)$ and $counter_j[k]$ have the following relation.

$$counter_i[k] = (m_i(k-1) - m_i(k)) \cdot r_i. \tag{1}$$

where r_i is the number of memory accesses for process i over one time slice. Since $m_j(0) = 1$, we can calculate the miss-rate curve recursively.

3.3   Modeling Memory Contention

Although isolated miss-rate curves provide much more information than static footprints, the miss-rate curves alone are still not enough to predict the effects of memory contention under a non-ideal replacement policy or under the effects of time-sharing. This subsection explains how a previously developed analytical model can be extended to accurately estimate the overall miss-rate incorporating both space-sharing effects and time-sharing effects. First, the original uniprocessor model of [12] is briefly summarized. Then, we discuss how this original model can be applied to parallel jobs on shared-memory multiprocessor systems.

Uniprocessor Model. The cache model from [12] estimates the overall miss-rate for a fully-associative cache when multiple processes time-share the same cache (memory) on a uniprocessor system. There are three inputs to the model: (1) the memory size (C) in terms of the number of memory blocks (pages), (2) job sequences with the length of each process' time slice (T_i) in terms of the number of memory references, and (3) the miss-rate curve for each process ($m_i(x)$). The model assumes that the least recently used (LRU) replacement policy is used, and that there are no shared data structures among processes.

Let us consider a case when N processes execute with a given schedule (sequences of processes) and fixed time quanta for each process (T_i). First, the number of misses for each process' time quantum is estimated. Then, the overall miss-rate is obtained by combining the number of misses for each process.

Define the footprint of process i, $x_i(t)$, as the amount of process i's data in the memory at time t where time t is 0 at the beginning of the process' time quantum. Then, $x_i(t)$ is approximated by the following recursive equation, once $x_i(0)$ is known [1];

$$x_i(t+1) = MIN[x_i(t) + m_i(x_i(t)), C], \qquad (2)$$

where C is the size of memory in terms of the number of blocks.

The miss-rate curve, $m_i(x)$, can be considered as the probability to miss when x valid blocks are in the memory. Therefore, the number of misses that process i experiences over one time quantum is estimated from the footprint of the process $x_i(t)$ as follows;

$$\text{miss}_i = \int_0^{T_i} m_i(x_i(t))dt. \qquad (3)$$

Once the number of misses for each process is estimated, the overall miss-rate is straightforwardly calculated from those numbers.

$$\text{miss-rate}_{\text{overall}} = \frac{\sum_{i=1}^{N} \text{miss}_i}{\sum_{i=1}^{N} T_i} \qquad (4)$$

Extension to Multiprocessor Cases. The original model assumes only one process executes at a time. Here, we describe how the original model can be

---

[1] The estimation of $x_i(0)$ and more accurate $x_i(t)$ can be found in our previous work [12].

applied to multiprocessor systems where multiple processes can execute simultaneously sharing the memory. Although the model can be applied to more general cases, we consider the situation where all processors context switch at the same time; more complicated cases can be modeled in a similar manner.

No matter how many processes are executing simultaneously sharing the memory, all processes in a time slice can be seen as one big process from the standpoint of memory. Therefore, we take a two-step approach to model shared-memory multiprocessor cases. First, define a conceptual process for each time slice that includes memory accesses from all processes in the time slice, which we call a *combined process*. Then, the miss-rate for the combined process of each time slice is estimated using the original model. Finally, the uniprocessor model is used again to incorporate the effects of time-sharing assuming only the combined process executes for each time slice.

What should be the miss-rate curve for the combined process of a time slice? Since the original model for time-sharing needs *isolated* miss-rate curves, the miss-rate curve of each time-slice s is defined as the overall miss-rate of all processes in time slice s when they execute together without context switching on the memory of size x. We call this miss-rate curve for a time slice as a combined miss-rate curve $m_{combined,s}(x)$. Next we explain how to obtain the combined miss-rate curves.

The simultaneously executing processes within a time slice can be modeled as time-shared processes with very short time quanta. Therefore, the original model is used to obtain the combined miss-rate curves by assuming the time quantum is $ref_{s,p}/\sum_{i=1}^{P} ref_{s,i}$ for processor p in time-slice s. $ref_{s,p}$ is the number of memory accesses that processor p makes over time slice s. The following paragraphs summarize this derivation of the combined miss-rate curves. Here, we use $m_{s,p}$ to represent the isolated miss-rate curve for the process that executes on processor p in time slice s.

Let $x_{s,p}(k_{s,p})$ be the number of memory blocks that processor p brings into memory after $k_{s,p}$ memory references in time slice s. The following equation estimates the value of $x_{s,p}(k_{s,p})$:

$$k_{s,p} = \int_{0}^{x_{s,p}(k_{s,p})} \frac{1}{m_{s,p}(x')} dx'. \tag{5}$$

Considering all P processors, the system reaches the steady-state after K_s memory references where K_s satisfies the following equation.

$$\sum_{p=1}^{P} x_{s,p}(\alpha(s,p) \cdot K_s) = x. \tag{6}$$

In the above equation, x is the number of memory blocks, and $\alpha(s,p)$ is the length of a time slice for processor p, which is equal to $ref_{s,p}/\sum_{i=1}^{P} ref_{s,i}$. In steady-state, the combined miss-rate curve is given by

$$m_{combined,s}(x) = \sum_{p=1}^{P} \alpha(s,p) \cdot m_{s,p}(x_p(\alpha(s,p) \cdot K_s)). \tag{7}$$

Now we have the combined miss-rate curve for each time-slice. The overall miss-rate is estimated by using the original model assuming that only one process executes for a time slice whose miss-rate curve is $m_{combined,s}(x)$.

Dealing with Shared Memory Space. The model described so far assumes that there is no shared memory space among processes. However, processes from the same parallel job often communicate through shared memory space. The analytical model can be modified to be used in the case of parallel jobs synchronizing through shared memory space, as described below.

The accesses to shared memory space can be excluded from the miss-rate curve of each process, and considered as a separate process from the viewpoint of memory. For example, if P processes are simultaneously executing and share some memory space, the multiprocessor model in the previous subsection can be used considering $P + 1$ conceptual processes. The first P miss-rate curves are from the accesses of the original P processes excluding the accesses to the shared memory space, and the $(P + 1)^{th}$ miss-rate curve is from the accesses to the shared memory space. Since the $P + 1$ conceptual processes do not have shared memory space, the original model can be applied.

3.4   Evaluating a Schedule

A poor schedule has lots of idle processors, and a schedule can be better evaluated in terms of a processor idle time rather than a miss-rate. A processor is idle for a time slice if no job is assigned to it for that time slice or it is idle if it is waiting for the data to be brought into the memory due to a "miss" or page fault. Although modern superscalar processors can tolerate some cache misses, it is reasonable to assume that a processor stalls and therefore idles on every page fault.

Let the total processor idle time for a schedule be as follows:

$$
\begin{aligned}
\mathrm{Idle}(\%) = \{ &\sum_{s=1}^{S} \sum_{p=1}^{N(s)} miss(p, s) \cdot l \\
&+ \sum_{s=1}^{S} (P - N(s) \cdot T(s)\} / \{\sum_{s=1}^{S} T(s)\} \\
= \{&(\text{total misses}) \cdot l \\
&+ \sum_{s=1}^{S} (P - N(s)) \cdot T(s)\} / \{\sum_{s=1}^{S} T(s)\}
\end{aligned}
\tag{8}
$$

where $miss(p, s)$ is the number of misses on processor p for time slice s, l is the memory latency, $T(s)$ is the length of time slice s, and $N(s)$ is the number of processes scheduled in time slice s.

In Equation 8, the first term represents the processor idle time due to page faults and the second term represents the idle time due to processors with no job scheduled on. Since the number of idle processors is given with a schedule, we can evaluate a given schedule once we know the total number of misses, which can be estimated from the model in the previous subsection.

4   The Effects of Memory Performance on Scheduling

This section discusses new considerations that memory performance imposes on parallel job scheduling and their solutions based on the miss-rate curves and the analytical model. First, we discuss scheduling problems to optimize memory performance for the space-shared systems. Then, scheduling considerations for time-sharing the memory are studied.

4.1   Processes to Space-Share Memory

In shared-memory multiprocessor systems, processes in the same time slice space-share the memory since they access the memory simultaneously. In this case, the amount of memory space allocated to each process is determined by the other processes that are scheduled in the same time slice. Therefore, the performance (execution time) of each process can be significantly affected by which processes are scheduled to space-share the memory (see Section 2). The main consideration of memory-aware schedulers in space-shared systems is to group jobs in a time slice properly so as to minimize the performance degradation caused by the memory contention.

A schedule can be evaluated using the isolated miss-rate curves and the analytical model. Effectively, the model provides a new cost function of memory performance, and any scheduler can be modified to incorporate memory considerations by adding this new cost function from the model. As an example, here we show how a simple gang scheduler can be modified to consider the memory performance. The modification of more complicated schedulers is left for future studies.

Consider the problem of scheduling J jobs on a P_{tot} processor system, which consists of SMPs with P_{node} processors. Gang scheduling is assumed, i.e., all processes from one job are scheduled in the same time slice, and context switch at the end of the time slice. All P_{tot} processors are assumed to context switch at the same time. A processor does not context switch even on a page fault, but only when the time slice expires. The problem is to determine the number of time slices S to schedule all jobs, and assign each job to a time slice so that the processor idle time is minimized. Also, each process should be mapped to a SMP node considering memory contention.

The most obvious way of scheduling with memory consideration is to use the analytical model detailed in Section 3. If the isolated miss-rate curves are obtained either on-line or off-line, the model can easily compare different schedules. The problem is to search for the optimal schedule with the given evaluation method. For a small number of jobs, an exhaustive search can be performed to find the best schedule. As the number of jobs increases, however, the number of possible schedules increases exponentially, which makes exhaustive search impractical. Unfortunately, there appears to be no polynomial-time algorithm that guarantees an optimal solution.

A number of search algorithms can be developed to find a sub-optimal schedule in polynomial time using the analytical model directly. Alternately, we can just utilize the miss-rate curves and incorporate better memory considerations into existing schedulers. Although the analytical model is essential to accurately compare different schedules and to find the best schedule, we found that a heuristic algorithm based only on the miss-rate curves is often good enough for optimizing memory performance for space-sharing cases. The following subsection presents the heuristic search algorithm.

A Heuristic Algorithm. For most applications, the miss rate curve as a function of memory size has one prominent knee (See Figure 2). That is, the miss rate quickly drops and then levels off. As a rough approximation, this knee is considered as a *relative footprint* of the process. Then, processes are scheduled to balance the total size of relative footprints for each node. Although this algorithm cannot consider the complicated effects of memory contention, it is much cheaper than computing the model and often results in a reasonable schedule.

The algorithm works in three steps; First, the *relative footprints* are determined considering the number of processes and the size of memory. At the same time, we decide the number of time slices S. Then, jobs are assigned to a time slice to balance the total relative footprints for each time slice. Finally, processes are assigned to a node to balance the relative footprints for each node.

In the explanation of the algorithm, we make use of the following notations:

- P_{tot}: the total number of processors in the entire system.
- P_{node}: the number of processors in a node.
- J: the total number of jobs to be scheduled.
- $Q(j)$: the number of processors that job j requires.
- m_j: the miss-rate curve for job j.
- r_j: the number of memory references of job j for one time slice.
- S: the number of time slices to schedule all jobs.

The relative footprint for job j, $fp(j)$ is defined as the number of memory blocks allocated to the job when the memory with $C \cdot S \cdot P/P_{node}$ blocks is partitioned among all jobs so that the marginal gain for all jobs is the same. Effectively, the relative footprint of a job represents the optimal amount of memory space for that job when all jobs execute simultaneously sharing the entire memory resource over S time slices.

To compute the relative footprints, the number of time slices S should also be decided. First, make an initial, optimistic guess; $S = \lceil \sum_{j=1}^{J} Q(j)/P \rceil$. Then, compute the relative footprints for that S and approximate the processor idle time using Equation 8 assuming that each job experiences $m_j(fp(j)) \cdot r_j$ misses over a time slice. Finally, increase the number of time slices and try again until the resultant idle time increases. For a given S, the following greedy algorithm determines the relative footprints.

1. Compute the marginal gain $g_j(x) = (m_j(x-1) - m_j(x)) \cdot r_j$. This function represents the number of additional hits for the job j, when the allocated memory blocks increases from $x-1$ to x.
2. Initialize $fp(1) = fp(2) = ... = fp(J) = 0$.
3. Assign a memory block to the job that has the maximum marginal gain. For each job, compare the marginal gain $g_j(fp(j)+1)$ and find the job that has the maximum marginal gain j_{max}. Increase the allocation for the job $fp_{j_{max}}$ by one.
4. Repeat step 3 until all memory blocks are assigned.

Once the relative footprints are computed, assigning jobs to time slices is straightforward. In a greedy manner, the unscheduled job with the largest relative footprint is assigned to a time slice with the smallest total footprint at the time. After assigning jobs to time slices, we assume that each process from job j has the relative footprint of $fp(j)/Q(j)$. Then, assign processes to nodes in the same manner.

Notice that the analytic model is not used by this algorithm. However, the model is needed to validate the heuristic. For jobs that have significantly different miss-rate curves, new heuristics are needed and the model will be required to validate those as well.

Experimental Validation. The model-based algorithm and the heuristic algorithm are applied to solve a scheduling problem in Section 2. The problem is to schedule six SPEC CPU2000 benchmarks using three processors and two time slices. Figure 3 compares the miss-rates of the model-based algorithm and the heuristic algorithm with miss-rates of the best schedule and the worst schedule, which are already shown in Section 2. The best schedule and the worst schedule are found by simulating all possible schedules and comparing their miss-rates. For the model-based algorithm, the average isolated miss-rate curves over the entire execution are obtained by trace-driven simulations. Then, the schedule is found by an exhaustive search based on the analytical model. The heuristic algorithm uses the same average isolated miss-rate curves, but decides the schedule using the algorithm in the previous subsection. Once the schedules are decided by either the model-based algorithm or the heuristic algorithm, the actual miss-rates for those schedules are obtained by trace-driven simulations.

The results demonstrate that our scheduling algorithms can effectively find a good schedule. In fact, the model-based algorithm found the best schedule except for the 16-MB and 64-MB cases. Even for these cases, the model-based schedule found by the algorithm shows a miss-rate very close to the best case.

The heuristic algorithm also results in good schedules in most cases with significantly less computation than the model-based algorithm. However, the heuristic algorithm shows worse performance than the model-based algorithm because it cannot accurately estimate the effects of the LRU replacement policy.

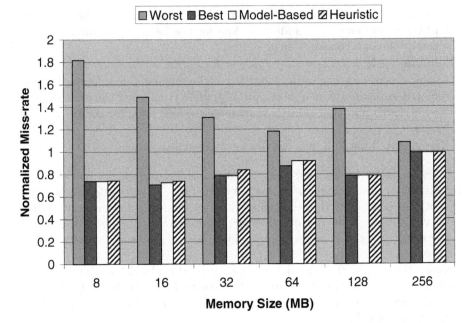

Fig. 3. The performance of the model-based scheduling algorithm and the heuristic scheduling algorithm. The miss-rates are normalized to the average miss-rate of all possible schedules for each memory size.

4.2   The Length of Time Slices

When available processors are not enough to execute all jobs in parallel, processors should be time-shared amongst jobs. In conventional batch processing, each job runs to completion before giving up the processor(s). However, this approach may block short jobs from executing and significantly degrade the response time. Batch processing may also cause significant processor fragmentation. Therefore, many modern job scheduling methods such as gang scheduling use time slices shorter than the entire execution time to share processors.

Unfortunately, shorter time slices often degrade the memory performance since each job should reload the evicted data every time it restarts the execution. To amortize this context switching cost and achieve reasonable performance in time-shared systems, schedulers should ensure that time slices are long enough to reload data and reuse them. Time slices should be long to reduce the context switch overhead, but short to improve response time and processor fragmentation.

The proper length of time slices still remains as a question. Conventionally, the length of time slices are determined empirically. However, the proper length of time slices depends on the characteristics of concurrent jobs and changes as jobs and/or memory configuration vary. For example, a certain length of time slice may be long enough for jobs with a small working set, but not long enough for larger jobs. Since the proposed analytical model can predict the miss-rate for a given length of time slices, it can be used to determine the proper length once another cost function such as response time or fragmentation is given.

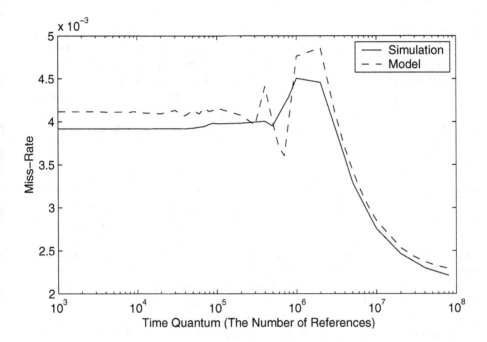

Fig. 4. The overall miss-rate when three processes (`gzip`, `vortex`, `vpr`) are sharing the memory (64 MB). The solid line represents the simulation results, and the dashed line represents the miss-rates estimated by the analytical model. The length of a time quantum is assumed to be the same for all three processes.

Figure 4 shows the overall miss-rate as a function of the length of time slices when three SPEC CPU2000 benchmarks, `gzip`, `vortex`, and `vpr`, are concurrently executing with a round-robin schedule. The solid line represents the simulation results, and the dashed line represents the miss-rates estimated by the model. The figure shows a very interesting fact that a certain range of time slices can be very problematic for memory performance. Conventional wisdom assumes that the miss-rate will monotonically decrease as the length of time slices increase. However, the miss-rate may increase for some cases since more data of processes that will run next are evicted as the length of time slices increase. The problem occurs when a time slice is long enough to pollute the memory but not long enough to compensate for the misses caused by context switches.

It is clear that time slices should always be long enough to avoid the problematic bump. Fortunately, the analytical model can estimate the miss-rate very close to the simulation results. Therefore, we can easily evaluate time slices and choose ones that are long enough.

5   Conclusion

Modern multiprocessor systems commonly share the same physical memory at some levels of memory hierarchy. Sharing memory provides fast synchronization and communication amongst processors. Sharing memory also enables flexible management of the memory. However, it is clear that sharing memory can exacerbate the memory latency problem due to conflicts amongst processors. Currently, users of high performance computing systems prefer to "throw out the baby with the bathwater" and fore-go virtual memory and sharing of memory resources. We believe such extreme measures are not needed. Memory-aware scheduling can solve the problem.

This paper has studied the effects of the memory contention amongst processors that share the same memory on job scheduling. The case study of SPEC CPU2000 benchmarks has shown that sharing the memory can significantly degrade the performance unless the memory is large enough to hold the entire working set of all processes. Further, memory performance is heavily dependent on job scheduling. We have shown that the best schedule that minimizes memory contention cannot be found based on conventional footprints.

Miss-rate curves and an analytical model has been proposed as a new method to incorporate the effects of memory contention in job scheduling. The analytical model accurately estimates the overall miss-rate including both space-sharing effects and time-sharing effects from the miss-rate curves. Therefore, they provide a new cost function of memory performance, and any scheduler can be modified to incorporate memory considerations by adding this new cost function.

As an example, a simple gang scheduler is modified to optimize the memory performance. Applying theory to practice is not straightforward: First, some mechanism is needed to estimate the miss-rate characteristics at run-time since it is unreasonable to expect the user to provide an accurate function. Second, a heuristic algorithm is required to find a solution in polynomial time. Simulation results have validated our approach that can effectively find a good schedule that results in low miss-rates. Both a model-based algorithm and a heuristic algorithm were simulated and evaluated. Although the exhaustive search algorithm based on the model showed slightly better performance than the heuristic algorithm, the difference is minimal. Therefore, we believe that anything more than an inexpensive heuristic is overkill.

The paper is mainly focused on optimizing the performance for simultaneously executing processes. However, the approach based on the miss-rate curves and the analytical model is also applicable to scheduling problems related to time-sharing. In time-shared systems, there is a tradeoff in the length of time slices. Our model provides the metric of memory performance for this tradeoff. Especially, it is shown that a certain range of time slices can be very harmful for memory performance and this range can be avoided using the model.

The development of more realistic memory-aware schedulers is left for future studies. Practical schedulers have many considerations other than memory performance, thus it is more complicated to incorporate memory considerations into these schedulers as compared to a simple gang scheduler. However, we believe that the miss-rate curves and the analytical model provide a good metric for memory performance and existing schedulers can be modified to optimize the memory performance utilizing the given degrees of freedom.

Acknowledgements

Funding for this work is provided in part by the Defense Advanced Research Projects Agency under the Air Force Research Lab contract F30602-99-2-0511, titled "Malleable Caches for Data-Intensive Computing". Funding was also provided in part by a grant from the NTT Corporation. Thanks also to David Chen, Derek Chiou, Prahbat Jain, Josh Jacobs, Vinson Lee, Peter Portante, and Enoch Peserico.

References

1. A. Batat and D. G. Feitelson. Gang scheduling with memory considerations. In *14th International Parallel and Distributed Processing Symposium*, 2000.
2. Compaq. Compaq AlphaServer series.
   http://www.compaq.com/alphaserver/platforms.html.
3. W. J. Dally, S. Keckler, N. Carter, A. Chang, M. Filo, and W. S. Lee. M-Machine architecture v1.0. Technical Report Concurrent VLSI Architecture Memo 58, Massachusetts Institute of Technology, 1994.
4. S. J. Eggers, J. S. Emer, H. M. Levy, J. L. Lo, R. L. Stamm, and D. M. Tullsen. Simultaneous multithreading: A platform for next-generation processors. *IEEE Micro*, 17(5), 1997.
5. D. G. Feitelson and L. Rudolph. Evaluation of design choices for gang scheduling using distributed hierarchical control. *Journal of Parallel and Distributed Computing*, 1996.
6. D. G. Feitelson and A. M. Weil. Utilization and predictability in scheduling the ibm sp2 with backfilling. In *12th International Parallel Processing Symposium*, 1998.
7. J. L. Henning. SPEC CPU2000: Measuring CPU performance in the new millennium. *IEEE Computer*, July 2000.
8. HP. HP 9000 superdome specifications. http://www.hp.com/products1/unixservers/highend/superdome/specifications.html.
9. IBM. RS/6000 enterprise server model S80.
   http://www-1.ibm.com/servers/eserver/pseries/hardware/enterprise/s80.html.
10. J. L. Lo, J. S. Emer, H. M. Levy, R. L. Stamm, D. M. Tullsen, and S. J. Eggers. Converting thread-level parallelism to instruction-level parallelism via simultaneous multithreading. *ACM Transactions on Computer Systems*, 15, 1997.
11. E. W. Parsons and K. C. Sevcik. Coordinated allocation of memory and processors in multiprocessors. In *the ACM SIGMETRICS conference on Measurement & modeling of computer systems*, 1996.

12. G. E. Suh, S. Devadas, and L. Rudolph. Analytical cache models with applications to cache partitioning. In *15th ACM International Conference on Supercomputing*, 2001.
13. D. M. Tullsen, S. J. Eggers, and H. M. Levy. Simultaneous multithreading: Maximizing on-chip parallelism. In *22nd Annual International Symposium on Computer Architecture*, 1995.

An Integrated Approach to Parallel Scheduling Using Gang-Scheduling, Backfilling, and Migration

Y. Zhang[1], H. Franke[2], J. E. Moreira[2], and A. Sivasubramaniam[1]

[1] Department of Computer Science & Engineering
The Pennsylvania State University
University Park PA 16802
{yyzhang, anand}@cse.psu.edu
[2] IBM Thomas J. Watson Research Center
Yorktown Heights NY 10598-0218
{frankeh, jmoreira}@us.ibm.com

Abstract. Effective scheduling strategies to improve response times, throughput, and utilization are an important consideration in large supercomputing environments. Such machines have traditionally used space-sharing strategies to accommodate multiple jobs at the same time. This approach, however, can result in low system utilization and large job wait times. This paper discusses three techniques that can be used beyond simple space-sharing to greatly improve the performance figures of large parallel systems. The first technique we analyze is backfilling, the second is gang-scheduling, and the third is migration. The main contribution of this paper is an evaluation of the benefits from combining the above techniques. We demonstrate that, under certain conditions, a strategy that combines backfilling, gang-scheduling, and migration is always better than the individual strategies for all quality of service parameters that we consider.

1 Introduction

Large scale parallel machines are essential to meet the needs of demanding applications at supercomputing environments. In that context, it is imperative to provide effective scheduling strategies to meet the desired quality of service parameters from both user and system perspectives. Specifically, we would like to reduce response and wait times for a job, minimize the slowdown that a job experiences in a multiprogrammed setting compared to when it is run in isolation, maximize the throughput and utilization of the system, and be fair to all jobs regardless of their size or execution times.

Scheduling strategies can have a significant impact on the performance characteristics of a large parallel system [2,3,4,7,10,13,14,17,18,21,22]. Early strategies used a space-sharing approach, wherein jobs can run concurrently on different nodes of the machine at the same time, but each node is exclusively assigned to a job. Submitted jobs are kept in a priority queue which is always traversed according to a priority policy in search of the next job to execute. Space sharing in isolation can result in poor utilization since there could be nodes that are unutilized despite a waiting queue of jobs. Furthermore, the wait and response times for jobs with an exclusively space-sharing strategy can be relatively high.

D.G. Feitelson and L. Rudolph (Eds.): JSSPP 2001, LNCS 2221, pp. 133–158, 2001.
© Springer-Verlag Berlin Heidelberg 2001

We analyze three approaches to alleviate the problems with space sharing scheduling. The first is a technique called backfilling [6,14], which attempts to assign unutilized nodes to jobs that are behind in the priority queue (of waiting jobs), rather than keep them idle. To prevent starvation for larger jobs, (conservative) backfilling requires that a job selected out of order completes before the jobs that are ahead of it in the priority queue are scheduled to start. This approach requires the users to provide an estimate of job execution times, in addition to the number of nodes required by each job. Jobs that exceed their execution time are killed. This encourages users to overestimate the execution time of their jobs.

The second approach is to add a time-sharing dimension to space sharing using a technique called gang-scheduling or coscheduling [16,22]. This technique virtualizes the physical machine by slicing the time axis into multiple virtual machines. Tasks of a parallel job are coscheduled to run in the same time-slices (same virtual machines). In some cases it may be advantageous to schedule the same job to run on multiple virtual machines (multiple time-slices). The number of virtual machines created (equal to the number of time slices), is called the multiprogramming level (MPL) of the system. This multiprogramming level in general depends on how many jobs can be executed concurrently, but is typically limited by system resources. This approach opens more opportunities for the execution of parallel jobs, and is thus quite effective in reducing the wait time, at the expense of increasing the apparent job execution time. Gang-scheduling does not depend on estimates for job execution time.

The third approach is to dynamically migrate tasks of a parallel job. Migration delivers flexibility of adjusting your schedule to avoid fragmentation [3,4]. Migration is particularly important when collocation in space and/or time of tasks is necessary. Collocation in space is important in some architectures to guarantee proper communication among tasks (e.g., Cray T3D, CM-5, and Blue Gene). Collocation in time is important when tasks have to be running concurrently to make progress in communication (e.g., gang-scheduling).

It is a logical next step to attempt to combine these approaches – gang-scheduling, backfilling, and migration – to deliver even better performance for large parallel systems. Progressing to combined approaches requires a careful examination of several issues related to backfilling, gang-scheduling, and migration. Using detailed simulations based on stochastic models derived from real workloads, this paper analyzes (i) the impact of overestimating job execution times on the effectiveness of backfilling, (ii) a strategy for combining gang-scheduling and backfilling, (iii) the impact of migration in a gang-scheduled system, and (iv) the impact of combining gang-scheduling, migration, and backfilling in one scheduling system.

We find that overestimating job execution times does not really impact the quality of service parameters, regardless of the degree of overestimation. As a result, we can conservatively estimate the execution time of a job in a coscheduled system to be the multiprogramming level (MPL) times the estimated job execution time in a dedicated setting after considering the associated overheads, such as context-switch overhead. These results help us construct a backfilling gang-scheduling system, called BGS, which fills in holes in the Ousterhout scheduling matrix [16] with jobs that are not necessarily in first-come first-serve (FCFS) order. It is clearly demonstrated that, under certain conditions, this combined strategy is always better than the individual gang-scheduling or backfilling strategies for all the quality of service parameters that we consider. By combining gang-scheduling and migration we can further improve the system performance parameters. The improvement is larger when applied to plain gang-scheduling (without backfilling), although the absolute best performance was achieved by combining all three techniques: gang-scheduling, backfilling, and migration.

The rest of this paper is organized as follows. Section 2 describes our approach to modeling parallel job workloads and obtaining performance characteristics of scheduling systems. It also characterizes our base workload quantitatively. Section 3 analyzes the impact of job execution time estimation on the overall performance from system and user perspectives. We show that relevant performance parameters are almost invariant to the accuracy of average job execution time estimation. Section 4 describes gang-scheduling, and the various phases involved in computing a time-sharing schedule. Section 5 demonstrates the significant improvements in performance that can be achieved with time-sharing techniques, particularly when enhanced with backfilling and migration. Finally, Section 6 presents our conclusions and possible directions for future work.

2   Evaluation Methodology

When selecting and developing job schedulers for use in large parallel system installations, it is important to understand their expected performance. The first stage is to have a characterization of the workload and a procedure to synthetically generate the expected workloads. Our methodology for generating these workloads, and from there obtaining performance parameters, involves the following steps:

1. Fit a typical workload with mathematical models.
2. Generate synthetic workloads based on the derived mathematical models.
3. Simulate the behavior of the different scheduling policies for those workloads.
4. Determine the parameters of interest for the different scheduling policies.

We now describe these steps in more detail.

2.1   Workload Modeling

Parallel workloads often are over-dispersive. That is, both job interarrival time distribution and job service time (execution time on a dedicated system) distribution have coefficients of variation that are greater than one. Distributions with coefficient of variation greater than one are also referred to as long-tailed distributions, and can be fitted adequately with Hyper Erlang Distributions of Common Order. In [12] such a model was developed, and its efficacy demonstrated by using it to fit a typical workload from the Cornell University Theory Center. Here we use this model to fit a typical workload from the ASCI Blue-Pacific System at Lawrence Livermore National Laboratory (LLNL), an IBM RS/6000 SP.

Our modeling procedure involves the following steps:

1. First we group the jobs into classes, based on the number of nodes they require for execution. Each class is a bin in which the upper boundary is a power of 2.
2. Then we model the interarrival time distribution for each class, and the service time distribution for each class as follows:
   (a) From the job traces, we compute the first three moments of the observed inter-arrival time and the first three moments of the observed service time.
   (b) Then we select the Hyper Erlang Distribution of Common Order that fits these 3 observed moments. We choose to fit the moments of the model against those of the actual data because the first 3 moments usually capture the generic features of the workload. These three moments carry the information on the mean, variance, and skewness of the random variable, respectively.

Next, we generate various synthetic workloads from the observed workload by vary-ing the interarrival rate and service time used. The Hyper Erlang parameters for these synthetic workloads are obtained by multiplying the interarrival rate and the service time each by a separate multiplicative factor, and by specifying the number of jobs to generate. From these model parameters synthetic job traces are obtained using the pro-cedure described in [12]. Finally, we simulate the effects of these synthetic workloads and observe the results.

Within a workload trace, each job is described by its arrival time, the number of nodes it uses, its execution time on a dedicated system, and an overestimation factor. Backfilling strategies require an estimate of the job execution time. In a typical system, it is up to each user to provide these estimates. This estimated execution time is always greater than or equal to the actual execution time, since jobs are terminated after reaching this limit. We capture this discrepancy between estimated and actual execution times for parallel jobs through an *overestimation factor*. The overestimation factor for each job is the ratio between its estimated and actual execution times. During simulation, the estimated execution time is used exclusively for performing job scheduling, while the actual execution time is used to define the job finish event.

In this paper, we adopt what we call the Φ model of overestimation. In the Φ model, Φ is the fraction of jobs that terminate at exactly the estimated time. This typically corresponds to jobs that are killed by the system because they reach the limit of their allocated time. The rest of the jobs $(1 - \Phi)$ are distributed such that the distribution of jobs that end at a certain fraction of their estimated time is uniform. This distribution is shown in Figure 1. It has been shown to represent well actual job behavior in large systems [6]. To obtain the desired distribution for execution times in the Φ model, in our simulations we compute the overestimation factor as follows: Let y be a uniformly distributed random number in the range $0 \le y < 1$. If $y < \Phi$, then the overestimation factor is 1 (*i.e.*, estimated time = execution time). If $y \ge \Phi$, then the overestimation factor is $(1 - \Phi)/(1 - y)$.

2.2   Workload Characteristics

The baseline workload is the synthetic workload generated from the parameters directly extracted from the actual ASCI Blue-Pacific workload. It consists of 10,000 jobs, varying

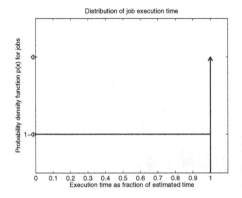

Fig. 1. The Φ models for overestimation.

in size from 1 to 256 nodes, in a system with a total of 320 nodes. Some characteristics of this workload are shown in Figures 2 and 3. Figure 2 reports the distribution of job sizes (number of nodes). For each job size, between 1 and 256, Figure 2(a) shows the number of jobs of that size, while Figure 2(b) plots the number of jobs with *at most* that size. (In other words, Figure 2(b) is the integral of Figure 2(a).) Figure 3 reports the distribution of total CPU time, defined as job execution time on a dedicated setting times its number of nodes. For each job size, Figure 3(a) shows the sum of the CPU times for all jobs of that size, while Figure 3(b) is a plot of the sum of the CPU times for all jobs of *at most* that size. (In other words, Figure 3(b) is the integral of Figure 3(a).) From Figures 2 and 3 we observe that, although large jobs (defined as those with more than 32 nodes), represent only 30% of the number of jobs, they constitute more than 80% of the total work performed in the system. This baseline workload corresponds to a system utilization of $\rho = 0.55$. (System utilization is defined in Section 2.3.)

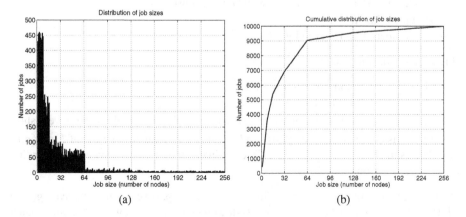

(a)   (b)

Fig. 2. Workload characteristics: distribution of job sizes.

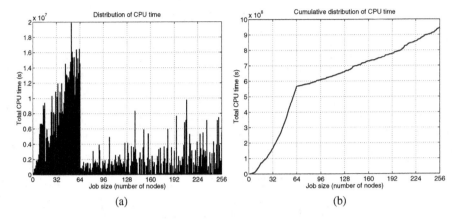

Fig. 3. Workload characteristics: distribution of cpu time.

In addition to the baseline workload of Figures 2 and 3 we generate 8 additional workloads, of 10,000 jobs each, by varying the model parameters so as to increase average job execution time. More specifically, we generate the 9 different workloads by multiplying the average job execution time by a factor from 1.0 to 1.8 in steps of 0.1. For a fixed interarrival time, increasing job execution time typically increases utilization, until the system saturates.

2.3   Performance Metrics

The synthetic workloads generated as described in Section 2.1 are used as input to our event-driven simulator of various scheduling strategies. We simulate a system with 320 nodes, and we monitor the following parameters:

- t_i^a: arrival time for job i.
- t_i^s: start time for job i.
- t_i^e: execution time for job i (in a dedicated setting).
- t_i^f: finish time for job i.
- n_i: number of nodes used by job i.

From these we compute:

- $t_i^r = t_i^f - t_i^a$: response time for job i.
- $t_i^w = t_i^s - t_i^a$: wait time for job i.
- $s_i = \frac{\max(t_i^r, \Gamma)}{\max(t_i^e, \Gamma)}$: the slowdown for job i. To reduce the statistical impact of very short jobs, it is common practice [5,6] to adopt a minimum execution time of Γ seconds. This is the reason for the $\max(\cdot, \Gamma)$ terms in the definition of slowdown. According to [6], we adopt $\Gamma = 10$ seconds.

To report quality of service figures from a user's perspective we use the average job slowdown and average job wait time. Job slowdown measures how much slower than a dedicated machine the system appears to the users, which is relevant to both interactive and batch jobs. Job wait time measures how long a job takes to start execution and therefore it is an important measure for interactive jobs. In addition to objective measures of quality of service, we also use these averages to characterize the fairness of a scheduling strategy. We evaluate fairness by comparing average and standard deviation of slowdown and wait time for small jobs, large jobs, and all jobs combined. As discussed in Section 2.2, large jobs are those that use more than 32 nodes, while small jobs use 32 or fewer nodes.

We measure quality of service from the system's perspective with two parameters: utilization and capacity loss. Utilization is the fraction of total system resources that are actually used during the execution of a workload. Let the system have N nodes and execute m jobs, where job m is the last job to finish execution. Also, let the first job arrive at time $t = 0$. Utilization is then defined as

$$\rho = \frac{\sum_{i=1}^{m} n_i t_i^e}{t_m^f \times N} \tag{1}$$

A system incurs loss of capacity when (i) it has jobs waiting in the queue to execute, and (ii) it has empty nodes (either physical or virtual) but, because of fragmentation, it still cannot execute those waiting jobs. Before we can define loss of capacity, we need to introduce some more concepts. A *scheduling event* takes place whenever a new job arrives or an executing job terminates. By definition, there are $2m$ scheduling events, occurring at times ψ_i, for $i = 1, \ldots, 2m$. Let e_i be the number of nodes left empty between scheduling events i and $i + 1$. Finally, let δ_i be 1 if there are any jobs waiting in the queue after scheduling event i, and 0 otherwise. Loss of capacity in a purely space-shared system is then defined as

$$\kappa = \frac{\sum_{i=1}^{2m-1} e_i(\psi_{i+1} - \psi_i)\delta_i}{t_m^f \times N} \tag{2}$$

To compute the loss of capacity in a gang-scheduling system, we have to keep track of what happens in each time-slice. Please note that here one time-slice is not exactly equal to one row in the matrix since the last time-slice could be shorter than a row in time due to the fact that a scheduling event could happen in the middle of a row. Let s_i be the number of time slices between scheduling event i and scheduling event $i + 1$. We can then define

$$\kappa = \frac{\sum_{i=1}^{2m-1} [e_i(\psi_{i+1} - \psi_i) + T \times CS \times s_i \times n_i]\delta_i}{t_m^f \times N} \tag{3}$$

where

- T is the duration of one row in the matrix;
- CS is the context-switch overhead (as a fraction of T);
- n_i is the number of occupied nodes between scheduling events i and $i + 1$, more specifically, $n_i + e_i = N$.

A system is in a saturated state when increasing the load does not result in an increase in utilization. At this point, the loss of capacity is equal to one minus the maximum achievable utilization. More specifically, $\kappa = 1 - \rho_{max}$.

3 The Impact of Overestimation on Backfilling

Backfilling is a space-sharing optimization technique. With backfilling, we can bypass the priority order imposed by the job queuing policy. This allows a lower priority job j to be scheduled before a higher priority job i as long as this reschedule does not incur a delay on the start time of job i for that particular schedule. This requirement of not delaying higher priority jobs is exactly what imposes the need for an estimate of job execution times. The effect of backfilling on a particular schedule can be visualized in Figure 4. Suppose we have to schedule five jobs, numbered from 1 to 5 in order of arrival. Figure 4(a) shows the schedule that would be produced by a FCFS policy without backfilling. Note the empty space between times T_1 and T_2, while job 3 waits for job 2 to finish. Figure 4(b) shows the schedule that would be produced by a FCFS policy with backfilling. The empty space was filled with job 5, which can be executed before job 3 without delaying it.

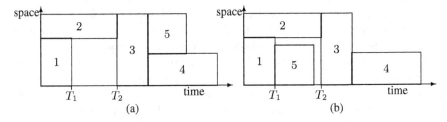

Fig. 4. FCFS policy without (a) and with (b) backfilling. Job numbers correspond to their position in the priority queue.

A common perception with backfilling is that one needs a fairly accurate estimation of job execution time to perform good backfilling scheduling. Users typically provide an estimate of job execution time when jobs are submitted. However, it has been shown in [6] that there is not necessarily correlation between estimated and actual execution times. Since jobs are killed when the estimated time is reached, users have an incentive to overestimate the execution time. This is indeed a major impediment to applying backfilling to gang-scheduling. The effective rate at which a job executes under gang-scheduling depends on many factors, including: (i) what is the effective multiprogramming level of the system, (ii) what other jobs are present, and (iii) how many time slices are occupied by the particular job. This makes it even more difficult to estimate the correct execution time for a job under gang-scheduling.

We conducted a study of the effect of overestimation on the performance of backfilling schedulers using a FCFS prioritization policy. The results are summarized in Figure 5 for the $\varPhi$ model. Figures 5(a) and 5(b) plot average job slow down and average job wait time, respectively, as a function of system utilization for different values of $\varPhi$. We observe very little impact of overestimation. For utilization up to $\rho = 0.90$, overestimation actually helps in reducing job slowdown. However, we can see a little benefit in wait time from more accurate estimates.

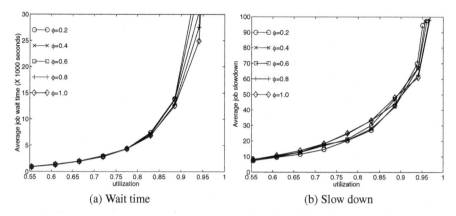

Fig. 5. Average job slowdown and wait time for backfilling under Φ model of overestimation.

We can explain why backfilling is not that sensitive to the estimated execution time by the following reasoning: On average, overestimation impacts both the jobs that are running and the jobs that are waiting. The scheduler computes a later finish time for the running jobs, creating larger holes in the schedule. The larger holes can then be used to accommodate waiting jobs that have overestimated execution times. The probability of finding a backfilling candidate effectively does not change with the overestimation.

Even though the average job behavior is insensitive to the average degree of overestimation, individual jobs can be affected. To verify that, we group the jobs into 10 classes based on how close is their estimated time to their actual execution time. For the Φ model, class i, $i = 0, \ldots, 9$ includes all those jobs for which their ratio of execution time to estimated time falls in the range $(i \times 10\%, (i + 1) \times 10\%]$. Figure 6 shows the average job wait time for (i) all jobs, (ii) jobs in class 0 (worst estimators) and (iii) jobs in class 9 (best estimators) when $\Phi = 0.2$. We observe that those users that provide good estimates are rewarded with a lower average wait time. The conclusion is that the "quality" of an estimation is not really defined by how close it is to the actual execution time, but by how much better it is compared to the average estimation. Users do get a benefit, and therefore an encouragement, from providing good estimates.

Our findings are in agreement with the work described in [19]. In that paper, the authors describe mechanisms to more accurately predict job execution times, based on historical data. They find that more accurate estimates of job execution time lead to more accurate estimates of wait time. The authors do observe an improvement in average job wait time, for a particular Argonne National Laboratory workload, when using their predictors instead of previously published work [1,9].

4   Gang-Scheduling

In the previous sections we only considered space-sharing scheduling strategies. An extra degree of flexibility in scheduling parallel jobs is to share the machine resources not only spatially but also temporally by partitioning the time axis into multiple time

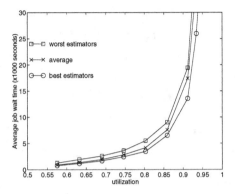

Fig. 6. The impact of good estimation from a user perspective for the Φ model of overestimation.

slices [2,4,8,11,20]. As an example, time-sharing an 8-processor system with a multi-programming level of four is shown in Figure 7. The figure shows the scheduling matrix (also called the *Ousterhout matrix*) that defines the processors and each time-slice. J_i^j represents the j-th task of job J_i. The matrix is cyclic in that time-slice 3 is followed by time-slice 0. One cycle through all the rows of the matrix defines a *scheduling cycle*. Each row of the matrix defines an 8-processor virtual machine, which runs at 1/4th of the speed of the physical machine. We use these four virtual machines to run two 8-way parallel jobs (J_1 and J_2) and several smaller jobs (J_3, J_4, J_5, J_6). All tasks of a parallel job are always coscheduled to run concurrently, which means that all tasks of a job should be assigned to the same row in the matrix. This approach gives each job the impression that it is still running on a dedicated, albeit slower, machine. This type of scheduling is commonly called *gang-scheduling* [2]. Note that some jobs can appear in multiple rows (such as jobs J_4 and J_5).

	P_0	P_1	P_2	P_3	P_4	P_5	P_6	P_7
time-slice 0	J_1	J_1	J_1	J_1	J_1	J_1	J_1	J_1
time-slice 1	J_2	J_2	J_2	J_2	J_2	J_2	J_2	J_2
time-slice 2	J_3	J_3	J_3	J_3	J_4	J_4	J_5	J_5
time-slice 3	J_6	J_6	J_6	J_6	J_4	J_4	J_5	J_5

Fig. 7. The scheduling matrix defines spatial and time allocation.

4.1 Considerations in Building a Scheduling Matrix

Creating one more virtual machine for the execution of a new 8-way job in the case of Figure 7 requires, in principle, only adding one more row to the Ousterhout matrix. However, there is a cost associated with time-sharing, due mostly to: (i) the cost of the context-switches themselves, (ii) additional memory pressure created by multiple jobs sharing nodes, and (iii) additional swap space pressure caused by more jobs executing concurrently. For that reason, the degree of time-sharing is usually limited by a parameter that we call, in analogy to uniprocessor systems, the multiprogramming level (MPL). A gang-scheduling system with multiprogramming level of 1 reverts back to a space-sharing system.

In our particular simulation of gang-scheduling, we make the following assumptions and scheduling strategies:

1. Multiprogramming levels are kept at modest levels, in order to guarantee that the images of all tasks in a node remain in core. This eliminates paging and significantly reduces the cost of context switching. Furthermore, the time slices are sized so that the cost of the resulting context switches are small. More specifically, in our simulations, we use MPL ≤ 5, and CS (context switch overhead fraction) $\leq 5\%$.
2. Assignments of tasks to processors are static. That is, once spatial scheduling is performed for the tasks of a parallel job, they cannot migrate to other nodes.
3. When building the scheduling matrix, we first attempt to schedule as many jobs for execution as possible, constrained by the physical number of processors and the multiprogramming level. Only after that we attempt to *expand* a job, by making it occupy multiple rows of the matrix. (See jobs J_4 and J_5 in Figure 7.)
4. For a particular instance of the Ousterhout matrix, each job has an assigned *home row*. Even if a job appears in multiple rows, one and only one of them is the home row. The home row of a job can change during its life time, when the matrix is recomputed. The purpose of the home row is described in Section 4.2.

Gang-scheduling is a time-sharing technique that can be applied together with any prioritization policy. In particular, we have shown in previous work [7,15] that gang-scheduling is very effective in improving the performance of FCFS policies. This is in agreement with the results in [4,17]. We have also shown that gang-scheduling is particularly effective in improving system responsiveness, as measured by average job wait time. However, gang scheduling alone is not as effective as backfilling in improving average job response time, unless very high multiprogramming levels are allowed. These may not be achievable in practice by the reasons mentioned in the previous paragraphs.

4.2   The Phases of Scheduling

Every job arrival or departure constitutes a *scheduling event* in the system. For each scheduling event, a new scheduling matrix is computed for the system. Even though we analyze various scheduling strategies in this paper, they all follow an overall organization for computing that matrix, which can be divided into the following steps:

1. **CleanMatrix:** The first phase of a scheduler removes every instance of a job in the Ousterhout matrix that is not at its assigned home row. Removing duplicates across rows effectively opens the opportunity of selecting other waiting jobs for execution.
2. **CompactMatrix:** This phase moves jobs from less populated rows to more populated rows. It further increases the availability of free slots within a single row to maximize the chances of scheduling a large job.
3. **Schedule:** This phase attempts to schedule new jobs. We traverse the queue of waiting jobs as dictated by the given priority policy until no further jobs can be fitted into the scheduling matrix.

4. **FillMatrix:** This phase tries to fill existing holes in the matrix by replicating jobs from their home rows into a set of replicated rows. This operation is essentially the opposite of **CleanMatrix**.

The exact procedure for each step is dependent on the particular scheduling strategy and the details will be presented as we discuss each strategy.

5   Scheduling Strategies

When analyzing the performance of the time-shared strategies we have to take into account the context-switch overhead. Context switch overhead is the time used by the system in suspending a currently running job and resuming the next job. During this time, the system is not doing useful work from a user perspective, and that is why we characterize it as overhead. In the IBM RS/6000 SP, context switch overhead includes the protocol for detaching and attaching to the communication device. It also includes the operations to stop and continue user processes. When the working set of time-sharing jobs is larger than the physical memory of the machine, context switch overhead should also include the time to page in the working set of the resuming job. For our analysis, we characterize context switch overhead as a percentage of time slice. Typically, context switch overhead values should be between 0 to 5% of time slice.

5.1   Gang-Scheduling (GS)

The first scheduling strategy we analyze is plain gang-scheduling (GS). This strategy is described in Section 4. For gang-scheduling, we implement the four scheduling steps of Section 4.2 as follows.

CleanMatrix: The implementation of CleanMatrix is best illustrated with the following algorithm:

```
for i = first row to last row
  for all jobs in row i
    if row i is not home of job, remove job
```

It eliminates all occurrences of a job in the scheduling matrix other than the one in its home row.

CompactMatrix: We implement the CompactMatrix step in gang-scheduling according to the following algorithm:

```
for i = least populated row to most populated row
  for j = most populated row to i+1
    for each job in row i
      if it can be moved to row j, then move job
```

We traverse the scheduling matrix from the least populated row to the most populated row. We attempt to find new homes for the jobs in each row. The goal is to pack the most jobs in the least number of rows.

Schedule: The Schedule phase for gang-scheduling traverses the waiting queue in FCFS order. For each job, it looks for the row with the least number of free columns in the scheduling matrix that has enough free columns to hold the job. This corresponds to a best fit algorithm. The row to which the job is assigned becomes its home row. We stop when the next job in the queue cannot be scheduled right away.

FillMatrix: After the schedule phase completes, we proceed to fill the holes in the matrix with the existing jobs. We use the following algorithm in executing the FillMatrix phase.

```
do{
  for each job in starting time order
    for each row in matrix,
      if job can be replicated in same columns
        do it and break
} while matrix changes
```

The algorithm attempts to replicate each job at least once (In the algorithm, once a chance of replicating a job is found, we stop looking for more chances of replicating the same job, but instead, we start other jobs) , although some jobs can be replicated multiple times. We go through the jobs in starting time order, but other ordering policies can be applied.

5.2   Backfilling Gang-Scheduling (BGS)

Gang-scheduling and backfilling are two optimization techniques that operate on orthogonal axes, space for backfilling and time for gang scheduling. It is tempting to combine both techniques in one scheduling system that we call *backfilling gang-scheduling* (BGS). In principle this can be done by treating each of the virtual machines created by gang-scheduling as a target for backfilling. The difficulty arises in estimating the execution time for parallel jobs. In the example of Figure 7, jobs J_4 and J_5 execute at a rate twice as fast as the other jobs, since they appear in two rows of the matrix. This, however, can change during the execution of the jobs, as new jobs arrive and executing jobs terminate.

Fortunately, as we have shown in Section 3, even significant average overestimation of job execution time has little impact on average performance. Therefore, it is reasonable to attempt to use a worst case scenario when estimating the execution time of parallel jobs under gang-scheduling. We take the simple approach of computing the estimated time under gang-scheduling as the product of the estimated time on a dedicated machine and the multiprogramming level.

In backfilling, each waiting job is assigned a maximum starting time based on the predicted execution times of the current jobs. That start time is a reservation of resources for waiting jobs. The reservation corresponds to a particular time in a particular row of the matrix. It is possible that a job will be run before its reserved time and in a row different than reserved. However, using a reservation guarantees that the start time of a job will not exceed a certain limit, thus preventing starvation.

The issue of reservations impact both the CompactMatrix and Schedule phases. When moving jobs in CompactMatrix we must make sure that the moved job does not conflict with any reservations in the destination row. In the Schedule phase, we first attempt to schedule each job in the waiting queue, making sure that its execution does not violate any reservations. If we cannot start a job, we compute the future start time for that job in each row of the matrix. We select the row with the lowest starting time, and make a reservation for that job in that row. This new reservation could be different from the previous reservation of the job. The reservations do not impact the FillMatrix phase, since the assignments in this phase are temporary and the matrix gets cleaned in the next scheduling event.

To verify that the assumption that overestimation of job execution times indeed do not impact overall system performance, we experimented with various values of Φ. Results are shown in Figure 8. For those plots, BGS with all four phases and MPL=5 was used. We observe that differences in wait time are insignificant across the entire range of utilization. For moderate utilizations of up to 75%, job slowdown differences are also insignificant. For utilizations of 85% and higher, job slowdown exhibits larger variation with respect to overestimation, but the variation is nonmonotonic and perfect estimation is not necessarily better.

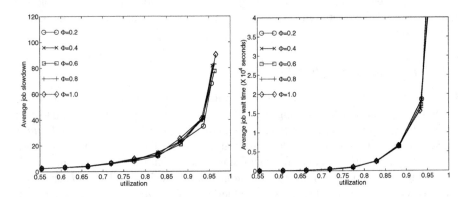

Fig. 8. Average job wait time and slow down for BGS (best) with Φ model of overestimation.

5.3   Comparing GS, BGS, and BF

We compare three different scheduling strategies, with a total of seven configurations. They all use FCFS as the prioritization policy. The first strategy is a space-sharing policy that uses backfilling to enhance the performance parameters. We identify this strategy as BF. We also use three variations of the gang-scheduling strategy, with multiprogramming levels 2, 3, and 5. These configurations are identified by GS-2, GS-3, GS-5, respectively. Finally, we consider three configurations of the backfilling gang-scheduling strategy. That is, backfilling is applied to each virtual machine created by gang-scheduling. These are referred to as BGS-2, BGS-3. and BGS-5, for multiprogramming level 2, 3, and 5. The results presented here are based on the Φ-model, with $\Phi = 0.2$. We use the performance parameters described in Section 2.3, namely (i) average slow down, (ii) average wait time, and (iii) average loss of capacity, to compare the strategies.

Figure 9 shows the average job slow down for all our seven configurations. Each plot ((a), (b), (c), and (d)) is for a different value of context switch overhead as a fraction of time slice. The time slice is 200 seconds. If we look only at the case of zero context switch overhead, we observe that regular gang scheduling (GS strategies) results in very high slow downs, even at low or moderate (less than $\rho = 0.75$) utilizations. BF always performs better than GS-2 and GS-3. It also performs better than GS-5 when utilization is greater than 0.65. The combined approach (BGS) is always better than its individual components (BF and GS with corresponding multiprogramming level). The improvement in average slow down is monotonic with the multiprogramming level. This observation also applies most of the time for the standard deviation. Given a highest tolerable slow down, BGS allows the system to be driven to much higher utilizations. We want to emphasize that significant improvements can be achieved even with the low multiprogramming level of 2. For instance, if we choose a maximum acceptable slow down of 20, the resulting maximum utilization is $\rho = 0.67$ for GS-5, $\rho = 0.76$ for BF and $\rho = 0.82$ for BGS-2. That last result represents an improvement of 20% over GS-5 with a much smaller multiprogramming level. With BGS-5, we can drive utilization as high as $\rho = 0.87$.

At all combinations of context switch overhead and utilization, BGS outperforms GS with the same multiprogramming level. BGS also outperforms BF at low context switch overheads 0% or 1%. Even at context switch overhead of 2% or 5%, BGS has significantly better slowdown than BF in an important operating range. For 2%, BGS-5 saturates at $\rho = 0.93$ whereas BF saturates at $\rho = 0.95$. Still, BGS-5 is significantly better than BF for utilization up to $\rho = 0.92$. For context switch overhead of 5%, BGS-5 is superior to BF only up to $\rho = 0.83$. Therefore, we have two options in designing the scheduler system: we either keep the context switch overhead low enough that BGS is always better than BF or we use an adaptive scheduler that switches between BF and BGS depending on the utilization of the system. Let $\rho_{critical}$ be the utilization at which BF starts performing better than BGS. For utilization smaller than $\rho_{critical}$, we use BGS. When utilization goes beyond $\rho_{critical}$, we use BF. Further investigation of adaptive scheduling is beyond the scope of this paper.

Figure 10 shows the average job wait time for all our seven configurations. Again, each plot is for a different value of context-switch overhead. We observe that regular gang-scheduling (GS strategies) results in very high wait times, even at low or moderate (less than $\rho = 0.75$) utilizations. Even with 0% context switching overhead, saturation takes place at $\rho = 0.84$ for GS-5 and at $\rho = 0.79$ for GS-3. At 5% overhead, the saturations occur at $\rho = 0.73$ and $\rho = 0.75$ for GS-3 and GS-5 respectively. Backfilling performs better than gang-scheduling with respect to wait time for utilizations above $\rho = 0.72$. It saturates at $\rho = 0.95$. The combined approach (BGS) is always better than its individual components (BF and GS with corresponding multiprogramming level) for a zero context switch overhead. The improvement in average job wait time is monotonic with the multiprogramming level. This observation also applies most of the time for the standard deviation. With BGS and zero context switch overhead, the machine appears faster, more responsive and more fair.

We further analyze the scheduling strategies by comparing the behavior of the system for large and small jobs. (As defined in Section 2.2, a small job uses 32 or fewer nodes,

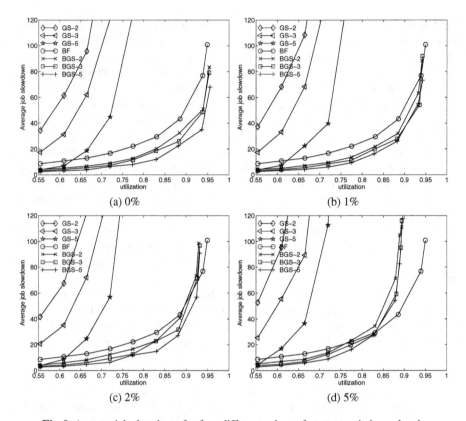

Fig. 9. Average job slowdown for four different values of context switch overhead.

while a large job uses more than 32 nodes.) The results for slowdown and wait times are shown in Figure 11, when a 0% context switch overhead is used. With respect to slowdown, we observe that, BGS-5 always performs better than BF for either large or small jobs. With respect to wait time, we observe that the improvement generated by BGS is actually larger for large jobs. In other words, for any given utilization, the difference in wait time between large and small jobs is less in BGS-5 than in BF. Both for BF and BGS, the machine appears less responsive to large jobs than to small jobs as utilization increases. However, the difference is larger for BF.

At first, the BF results for slow down and wait time for large and small jobs may seem contradictory: small jobs have smaller wait times but larger slow down. Slow down is a relative measure of the response time normalized by the execution time. Since smaller jobs tend to have shorter execution time, the relative cost of waiting in the queue can be larger. We note that BGS is very effective in affecting the wait time for large and small jobs in a way that ends up making the system feel more equal to all kinds of jobs.

Whereas Figures 9 through 11 report performance from a user's perspective, we now turn our attention to the system's perspective. Figure 12 is a plot of the average capacity loss as a function of utilization for all our seven strategies. By definition, all strategies

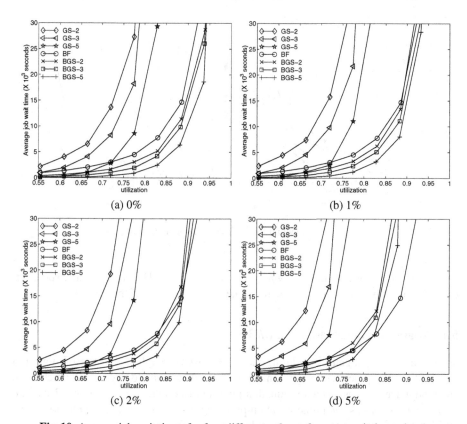

Fig. 10. Average job wait times for four different values of context switch overhead.

saturate at the line $\kappa = 1 - \rho_{max}$, which is indicated by the dashed line in Figure 12. Again, the combined policies deliver consistently better results than the pure backfilling and gang scheduling (of equal MPL) policies. The improvement is also monotonic with the multiprogramming level. However, all backfilling based policies (pure or combined) saturate at essentially the same point. Loss of capacity comes from holes in the scheduling matrix. The ability to fill those holes actually improves when the load is very high. We observe that the capacity loss for **BF** actually starts to decrease once utilization goes beyond $\rho = 0.83$. At very high loads ($\rho > 0.95$) there are almost always small jobs to backfill holes in the schedule. Looking purely from a system's perspective, we note that pure gang-scheduling can only be driven to utilization between $\rho = 0.82$ and $\rho = 0.87$, for multiprogramming levels 2 through 5. On the other hand, the backfilling strategies can be driven to up to $\rho = 0.95$ utilization.

To summarize our observations, we have shown that the combined strategy of backfilling with gang-scheduling (**BGS**) can consistently outperforms the other strategies (backfilling and gang-scheduling separately) from the perspectives of responsiveness, slow down, fairness, and utilization. For **BGS** to realize this advantage, context switch

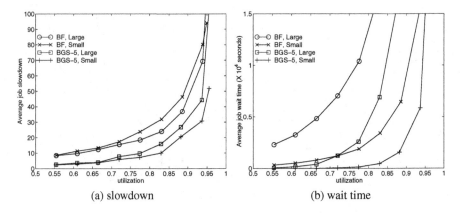

(a) slowdown   (b) wait time

Fig. 11. Slowdown and wait time for large and small jobs.

cost must be kept low. We have shown **BGS** to be superior to **BF** over the entire spectrum of workloads when the context switch overhead is 1% or less of the time slice.

5.4 Migration Gang-Scheduling (MGS)

We now analyze how gang-scheduling can be improved through the addition of migration capabilities. The process of migration embodies moving a job to any row in which there are enough free processors to execute that job (not just on the same columns). There are basically two options each time we attempt to migrate a job A from a source row r to a target row p (in either case, row p must have enough free nodes):

- *Option 1*: We migrate the jobs in row p that execute on the CPUs where the processes of A reside, to make space for A in row p. This is shown pictorially in figure 13 where 3 processes of job J in row 2 occupy the same columns as job A in row 1. Job J is migrated to 4 other processes in the same row and job A is replicated in this row. Consequently when we move from row 1 to row 2 in the scheduling cycle, job A does not need to be migrated (one-time effort).
- *Option 2*: Instead of migrating job J to make space for A, we can directly migrate job A to those slots in row p that are free. This approach lets other jobs in row p proceed without migration, but the down side is that each time we come to row p, job A incurs migration costs (recurring). This is again shown pictorially in figure 13.

We can quantify the cost of each of these two options based on the following model. For the distributed system we target, namely the IBM RS/6000 SP, migration can be accomplished with a checkpoint/restart operation. Let $S(A)$ be the set of jobs in target row p that overlap with the nodes of job A in source row r. Let C be the total cost of migrating one job, including the checkpoint and restart operations. We consider the case in which (i) checkpoint and restart each have the same cost $C/2$, (ii) the cost C is independent of the job size, and (iii) checkpoint and restart are dependent operations

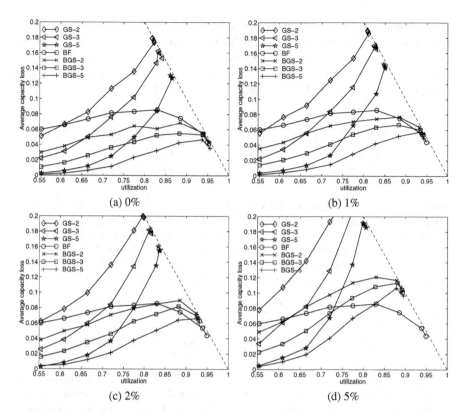

Fig. 12. Loss of capacity for BGS, GS, and BF, with different context-switch overheads.

(*i.e.*, you have to finish checkpoint before you can restart). During the migration process, nodes participating in the migration cannot make progress in executing a job. The total amount of resources (processor × time) wasted during this process is the overhead for the migration operation.

The overhead for option 1 is

$$\left(\frac{C}{2} \times |A| + C \times \sum_{J \in S(A)} |J|\right), \tag{4}$$

where $|A|$ and $|J|$ denote the number of tasks in jobs A and J, respectively. The operations for option 1 are illustrated in Figure 13(a), with a single job J in set $S(A)$. The first step is to checkpoint job J in its current set of nodes. This checkpointing operation takes time $C/2$. As soon as the checkpointing is complete we can resume execution of job A. Therefore, job A incurs an overhead $\frac{C}{2} \times |A|$. To resume job J in its new set of nodes requires a restart step of time $\frac{C}{2}$. Therefore, the total overhead for job J is $C \times |J|$.

The overhead for option 2 is estimated by

$$\left(C \times |A| + \frac{C}{2} \times \sum_{J \in S(A)} |J|\right). \tag{5}$$

The migration for option 2 is illustrated in Figure 13(b), with a single job J in set $S(A)$. The first step is to checkpoint job A. This checkpoint operation takes time $\frac{C}{2}$. After job A is checkpointed we can resume execution of job J. Therefore, the overhead for job J is $\frac{C}{2} \times |J|$. To resume job A we need to restart it in its new set of processors, which again takes time $\frac{C}{2}$. The overhead for job A is then $C \times |A|$.

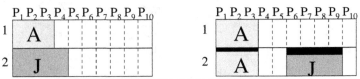

(a) Migration option 1: J is migrated to CPUs P6-P9 in row 2 so that A can executed in CPUs P1-P3 in row 2. This requires checkpointing J at the beginning of the time quantum (for row 2) incurring $C/2$ cost, and then the restart cost for those processes in the destination CPUs incurring another $C/2$ cost. Note that A can start executing in row 2 after $C/2$ time while J can start only after C time units. The migration cost is indicated by the black region. Whether A is removed from row 1 or not is optional (depends on the steps of the algorithm).

(b) Migration option 2: A is directly migrated to CPUs P7-P9. This requires checkpoint A at the beginning of the time quantum for row 2 (incurring $C/2$ cost), and restarting A in the destination CPUs subsequently (incurring another $C/2$ cost). Even though only A's processes are being migrated at P1-P3, J has to wait for $C/2$ time before it can execute (on all four of its CPUs). A can begin execution after C time units in CPUs P7-P9. The migration cost is indicated by the black region. Again, whether A is removed from row 1 or not is optional (depends on the steps of the algorithm). If it is not removed, a recurring migration cost is incurred each time we transition from row 1 to row 2 in the schedule.

Fig. 13. The two migration options.

As discussed, migration in the IBM RS/6000 SP requires a checkpoint/restart operation. Although all tasks can perform a checkpoint in parallel, resulting in a C that is independent of job size, there is a limit to the capacity and bandwidth that the file system can accept. Therefore we introduce a parameter Q that controls the maximum number of tasks that can be migrated in any time-slice.

When migration is used, the scheduling proceeds along the following steps:

step	reason
ClearMatrix	Maximize holes
CollapseMatrix-1	Compaction without migration
Schedule-1	Accommodate new jobs after compaction
CollapseMatrix-2	Compaction with migration
Schedule-2	Accommodate new jobs after migration
FillMatrix-1	Replicate jobs without migration
FillMatrix-2	Replicate jobs after migrating destination

The ordering results in applying optimizations without incurring unnecessary costs. We first attempt to optimize without migration (CollapseMatrix-1,Schedule-1). After Schedule-1, we then attempt to collapse with migration (CollapseMatrix-2) and repeat scheduling (Schedule-2) to accommodate new jobs. After we are done accommodating new jobs, we do FillMatrix-1 first because it does not incur a migration cost. Then we try FillMatrix-2 with migration.

The algorithm for CollapseMatrix-2 is the same as for CollapseMatrix-1 in GS. The only difference are the conditions for moving a job. With migration, a job can be moved to any row and any set of columns, provided that (i) enough empty columns are available in the destination row, (ii) number of migrated tasks does not violate the Q parameter, and (iii) a job must make progress, that is, it must execute in at least one row for every cycle of scheduling. The last requirement is identical as for gang-scheduling (GS). If migration is required to move a job to a new target row, we consider the two options described above (option 1 and option 2) and choose the one with the least estimated cost. FillMatrix-2 uses the same algorithm as FillMatrix-1, with the following constraints when deciding to replicate a job in a new row. First, the job must not already be replicated in that row. Second, the row must have sufficient empty columns to execute the job and the total number of migrated tasks must not exceed parameter Q. Only option 1 (move jobs in target row) is considered for FillMatrix-2, and therefore those jobs must not be present in any other row of the schedule. Given these algorithms, we ensure that migration never incurs recurring cost. That is, a job will not ping-pong between different columns within the same scheduling matrix.

5.5   Migration Backfilling Gang-Scheduling (MBGS)

Just as we augmented plain gang-scheduling (GS) with migration, the same can be done with backfilling gang-scheduling (BGS). This creates the migration backfilling gang-scheduling (MBGS). The differences between MGS and MBGS are in the Collapse-Matrix and Schedule steps. MBGS use the same scheduling as BGS, that is, backfilling is performed in each row of the matrix, and reservations are created for jobs that cannot be immediately scheduled. When compacting the matrix, MBGS must make sure that reservations are not violated.

5.6   Comparing GS, BGS, MGS, and MBGS

Table 1 summarizes some of the results from migration applied to gang-scheduling and backfilling gang-scheduling. For each of the nine workloads (numbered from 0 to 8) we present achieved utilization (ρ) and average job slowdown (s) for four different scheduling policies: (i) backfilling gang-scheduling without migration (BGS), (ii) backfilling gang-scheduling with migration (MBGS), (iii) gang-scheduling without migration (GS), and (iv) gang-scheduling with migration (MGS). We also show the percentage improvement in job slowdown from applying migration to gang-scheduling and backfilling gang-scheduling. Those results are from the best case for each policy: zero cost and unrestricted number of migrated tasks, with an MPL of 5.

We can see an improvement from the use of migration throughout the range of workloads, for both gang-scheduling and backfilling gang-scheduling. We also note that the improvement is larger for mid-to-high utilizations between 70 and 90%. Improvements for low utilization are less because the system is not fully stressed, and the matrix is relatively empty. Therefore, there are not enough jobs to fill all the time-slices, and expanding without migration is easy. At very high loads, the matrix is already very full and migration accomplishes less than at mid-range utilizations. Improvements for backfilling gang-scheduling are not as impressive as for gang-scheduling. Backfilling gang-scheduling already does a better job of filling holes in the matrix, and therefore the potential benefit from migration is less. With backfilling gang-scheduling the best improvement is 50% at a utilization of 89%, whereas with gang-scheduling we observe benefits as high as 92%, at utilization of 88%.

We note that the maximum utilization with gang-scheduling increases from 86% without migration to 94% with migration. Maximum utilization for backfilling gang-scheduling increases from 96% to 98% with migration. Migration is a mechanism that significantly improves the performance of gang-scheduling without the need for job execution time estimates. However, it is not as effective as backfilling in improving plain gang-scheduling. The combination of backfilling and migration results in the best overall gang-scheduling system.

Table 1. Percentage improvements from migration.

work load	backfilling gang-scheduling BGS		MBGS		% s better	gang-scheduling GS		MGS		% s better
	ρ	s	ρ	s		ρ	s	ρ	s	
0	0.55	2.5	0.55	2.1	19.2%	0.55	3.9	0.55	2.6	33.7%
1	0.61	3.2	0.61	2.5	23.9%	0.61	7.0	0.61	4.0	42.5%
2	0.66	3.8	0.66	2.9	24.8%	0.66	18.8	0.66	6.9	63.4%
3	0.72	6.5	0.72	3.7	43.1%	0.72	44.8	0.72	13.5	69.9%
4	0.77	8.0	0.77	5.1	36.6%	0.78	125.6	0.77	29.4	76.6%
5	0.83	11.9	0.83	7.6	36.2%	0.83	405.6	0.83	54.4	86.6%
6	0.89	22.4	0.88	11.0	50.8%	0.86	1738.0	0.88	134.2	92.3%
7	0.94	34.9	0.94	20.9	40.2%	0.86	4147.7	0.94	399.3	90.4%
8	0.96	67.9	0.98	56.8	16.4%	0.86	5941.5	0.97	1609.9	72.9%

Figure 14 shows average job slowdown and average job wait time as a function of the parameter Q, the maximum number of task that can be migrated in any time slice. Each line is for a different combination of scheduling mechanism and migration cost (*e.g.*, BGS/10 represents backfilling gang-scheduling with migration cost of 10 seconds. The time slice is 200 seconds). We consider two representative workloads, 2 and 5, since they define the bounds of the operating range of interest. Beyond workload 5, the system reaches unacceptable slowdowns for gang-scheduling, and below workload 2 there is little benefit from migration. We note that migration can significantly improve the performance of gang-scheduling even with as little as 64 tasks migrated. (Note that the case without migration is represented by the parameter $Q = 0$ for number of migrated tasks.) We also observe a monotonic improvement in slowdown and wait time with the number of migrated tasks, for both gang-scheduling and backfilling gang-scheduling.

Even with migration costs as high as 30 seconds, or 15% of the time slice, we still observe a benefit from migration. Most of the benefit of migration is accomplished at $Q = 64$ migrated tasks, and we choose that value for further comparisons. Finally, we note that the behaviors of wait time and slowdown follow approximately the same trends. Thus, for the next analysis we focus on slowdown.

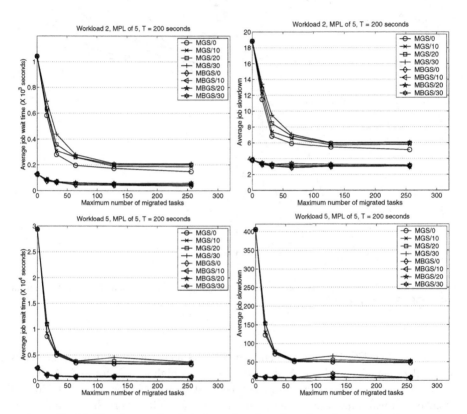

Fig. 14. Slowdown and wait time as a function of number of migrated tasks.

Figure 15 compares loss of capacity, slowdown, and wait time for all four time-sharing strategies: **GS**, **BGS**, **MGS** and **MBGS**. Results shown are for MPL of 5, $\Phi = 0.2$, and (for **MGS** and **MBGS**) a migration cost of 10 seconds (5% of the time-slice). We observe that **MBGS** is always better than the other strategies, for all three performance parameters and across the spectrum of utilization. Correspondingly, GS is always worse than the other strategies. The relative behavior of **BGS** and **MGS** deserves a more detailed discussion.

With respect to loss of capacity, **MGS** is consistently better than **BGS**. **MGS** can drive utilization up to 98% while **BGS** saturates at 96%. With respect to wait time, **BGS** is consistently better than **MGS**. Quantitatively, the wait time with **MGS** is 50-100% larger than with **BGS** throughout the range of utilizations. With respect to slowdown,

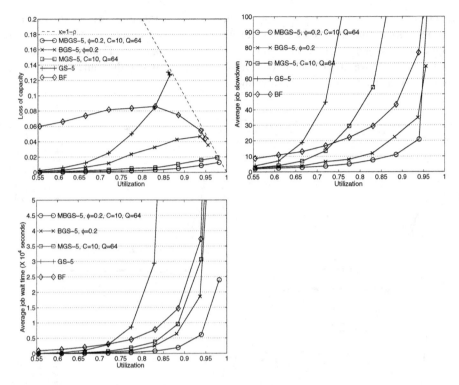

Fig. 15. Average loss of capacity, job slowdown, and job wait time as a function of utilization for GS, MGS, BGS, and MBGS.

we observe that BGS is always better than MGS and that the difference increases with utilization. For workload 5, the difference is as high as a factor of 5. At first, it is not intuitive that BGS can be so much better than MGS in the light of the loss of capacity and wait time results. The explanation is that BGS favors short-running jobs when backfilling, thus reducing the average job slowdown. To verify that, we further investigated the behavior of MGS and BGS in two different classes of jobs: one class is comprised of the jobs with running time shorter than the median (680 seconds) and the other class of jobs with running time longer than or equal to the median. For the shorter jobs, slowdown with BGS and MGS are 18.9 and 104.8, respectively. On the other hand, for the longer jobs, slowdown with BGS and MGS are 4.8 and 4.1, respectively. These results confirm that BGS favors short running jobs. We note that the penalty for longer jobs in BGS (as compared to MGS) is very small, whereas the benefit for shorter jobs is quite significant.

We emphasize that MBGS, which combines all techniques (gang-scheduling, back-filling, and migration), provides the best results. In particular, it can drive utilization higher than MGS, and achieves better slow down and wait times than BGS. Quantitatively, wait times with MBGS are 2 to 3 times shorter than with BGS, and slowdown is 1.5 to 2 times smaller.

6   Conclusions

This paper has reviewed several techniques to enhance job scheduling for large parallel systems. We started with an analysis of two commonly used strategies: backfilling and gang-scheduling. We showed how the two could be combined into a backfilling gang-scheduling (BGS) strategy that is always superior to its two components when the context switch overhead is kept low. With BGS, we observe a monotonic improvement in job slowdown, job wait time, and maximum system utilization with the multiprogramming level.

Further improvement in scheduling efficacy can be accomplished with the introduction of migration. We have demonstrated that both plain gang-scheduling and backfilling gang-scheduling benefit from migration. The scheduling strategy that incorporates all our techniques: gang-scheduling, backfilling, and migration consistently outperforms the others for average job slow down, job wait time, and loss of capacity. It also achieves the highest system utilization, allowing the system to reach up to 98% utilization. When a maximum acceptable slowdown of 20 is adopted, the system can achieve 94% utilization.

References

1. A. B. Downey. **Using Queue Time Predictions for Processor Allocation**. In *IPPS'97 Workshop on Job Scheduling Strategies for Parallel Processing*, volume 1291 of *Lecture Notes in Computer Science*, pages 35–57. Springer-Verlag, April 1997.
2. D. G. Feitelson. **A Survey of Scheduling in Multiprogrammed Parallel Systems**. Technical Report RC 19790 (87657), IBM T. J. Watson Research Center, October 1994.
3. D. G. Feitelson. Packing schemes for gang scheduling. In *Job Scheduling Strategies for Parallel Processing, IPPS'96 Workshop*, volume 1162 of *Lecture Notes in Computer Science*, pages 89–110, Berlin, March 1996. Springer-Verlag.
4. D. G. Feitelson and M. A. Jette. **Improved Utilization and Responsiveness with Gang Scheduling**. In *IPPS'97 Workshop on Job Scheduling Strategies for Parallel Processing*, volume 1291 of *Lecture Notes in Computer Science*, pages 238–261. Springer-Verlag, April 1997.
5. D. G. Feitelson, L. Rudolph, U. Schwiegelshohn, K. C. Sevcik, and P. Wong. **Theory and Practice in Parallel Job Scheduling**. In *IPPS'97 Workshop on Job Scheduling Strategies for Parallel Processing*, volume 1291 of *Lecture Notes in Computer Science*, pages 1–34. Springer-Verlag, April 1997.
6. D. G. Feitelson and A. Mu'alem Weil. **Utilization and predictability in scheduling the IBM SP2 with backfilling**. In *12th International Parallel Processing Symposium*, pages 542–546, April 1998.
7. H. Franke, J. Jann, J. E. Moreira, and P. Pattnaik. **An Evaluation of Parallel Job Scheduling for ASCI Blue-Pacific**. In *Proceedings of SC99, Portland, OR*, November 1999. IBM Research Report RC21559.
8. H. Franke, P. Pattnaik, and L. Rudolph. **Gang Scheduling for Highly Efficient Multiprocessors**. In *Sixth Symposium on the Frontiers of Massively Parallel Computation, Annapolis, Maryland*, 1996.
9. R. Gibbons. **A Historical Application Profiler for Use by Parallel Schedulers**. In *IPPS'97 Workshop on Job Scheduling Strategies for Parallel Processing*, volume 1291 of *Lecture Notes in Computer Science*, pages 58–77. Springer-Verlag, April 1997.

10. B. Gorda and R. Wolski. **Time Sharing Massively Parallel Machines**. In *International Conference on Parallel Processing*, volume II, pages 214–217, August 1995.
11. N. Islam, A. L. Prodromidis, M. S. Squillante, L. L. Fong, and A. S. Gopal. **Extensible Resource Management for Cluster Computing**. In *Proceedings of the 17th International Conference on Distributed Computing Systems*, pages 561–568, 1997.
12. J. Jann, P. Pattnaik, H. Franke, F. Wang, J. Skovira, and J. Riordan. **Modeling of Workload in MPPs**. In *Proceedings of the 3rd Annual Workshop on Job Scheduling Strategies for Parallel Processing*, pages 95–116, April 1997. In Conjuction with IPPS'97, Geneva, Switzerland.
13. H. D. Karatza. **A Simulation-Based Performance Analysis of Gang Scheduling in a Distributed System**. In *Proceedings 32nd Annual Simulation Symposium*, pages 26–33, San Diego, CA, April 11-15 1999.
14. D. Lifka. **The ANL/IBM SP scheduling system**. In *IPPS'95 Workshop on Job Scheduling Strategies for Parallel Processing*, volume 949 of *Lecture Notes in Computer Science*, pages 295–303. Springer-Verlag, April 1995.
15. J. E. Moreira, W. Chan, L. L. Fong, H. Franke, and M. A. Jette. **An Infrastructure for Efficient Parallel Job Execution in Terascale Computing Environments**. In *Proceedings of SC98, Orlando, FL*, November 1998.
16. J. K. Ousterhout. **Scheduling Techniques for Concurrent Systems**. In *Third International Conference on Distributed Computing Systems*, pages 22–30, 1982.
17. U. Schwiegelshohn and R. Yahyapour. **Improving First-Come-First-Serve Job Scheduling by Gang Scheduling**. In *IPPS'98 Workshop on Job Scheduling Strategies for Parallel Processing*, March 1998.
18. J. Skovira, W. Chan, H. Zhou, and D. Lifka. **The EASY-LoadLeveler API project**. In *IPPS'96 Workshop on Job Scheduling Strategies for Parallel Processing*, volume 1162 of *Lecture Notes in Computer Science*, pages 41–47. Springer-Verlag, April 1996.
19. W. Smith, V. Taylor, and I. Foster. **Using Run-Time Predictions to Estimate Queue Wait Times and Improve Scheduler Performance**. In *Proceedings of the 5th Annual Workshop on Job Scheduling Strategies for Parallel Processing*, April 1999. In conjunction with IPPS/SPDP'99, Condado Plaza Hotel & Casino, San Juan, Puerto Rico.
20. K. Suzaki and D. Walsh. **Implementation of the Combination of Time Sharing and Space Sharing on AP/Linux**. In *IPPS'98 Workshop on Job Scheduling Strategies for Parallel Processing*, March 1998.
21. K. K. Yue and D. J. Lilja. **Comparing Processor Allocation Strategies in Multiprogrammed Shared-Memory Multiprocessors**. *Journal of Parallel and Distributed Computing*, 49(2):245–258, March 1998.
22. B. B. Zhou, R. P. Brent, C. W. Jonhson, and D. Walsh. **Job Re-packing for Enhancing the Performance of Gang Scheduling**. In *Job Scheduling Strategies for Parallel Processing, IPPS'99 Workshop*, pages 129–143, April 1999. LNCS 1659.

Characteristics of a Large Shared Memory Production Workload

Su-Hui Chiang and Mary K. Vernon

Computer Sciences Department
University of Wisconsin
1210 W. Dayton Street, Madison, Wisconsin
{suhui, vernon}@cs.wisc.edu

Abstract. This paper characterizes the production workload that highly utilizes the NCSA Origin 2000. The characterization includes the distributions of job interarrival time, requested number of processors, requested memory, requested runtime, actual runtime as a fraction of requested runtime, and the ratio of memory usage to memory request. Conditional distributions are defined as needed for generating a synthetic workload with the same characteristics, including the key correlations observed among the job parameters. Characteristics of the O2K workload that differ from previously reported production workload characteristics are also noted.

1 Introduction

To better understand the performance of job scheduling policies, and to create realistic synthetic workloads for evaluating the performance of alternative policies, it is useful to understand the characteristics of workloads that occur in actual production systems.

Several production parallel workloads have been analyzed previously [1,2,3,4], [5,6,7,8,9,10,11]. Some characteristics are similar across most of these previous workloads. For example, most jobs request power-of-two processors and a large fraction of the jobs are serial. Other characteristics have varied. For example, some workloads have a positive correlation between job runtime and the number of processors [1,8], while the correlation is more complex in other workloads [2].

In this paper, we analyze six one-month production workloads on the Origin 2000 (O2K) at the National Computational Science Alliance (NCSA). This system is interesting for several reasons. First, the system (i.e., 1520 processors, 616 GB of memory) is larger than systems previously studied. Second, the jobs have longer running times (i.e., up to 400 hours or 16 days 16 hours) compared to a maximum runtime of only a few tens of hours in the systems previously studied. Third, the jobs collectively require a higher fraction (i.e., 90-100%) of the available processing time than in previous workloads. Finally, the O2K is a shared memory system; thus individual jobs may request a different fraction of the memory than the processors on the system. Most systems previously studied

D.G. Feitelson and L. Rudolph (Eds.): JSSPP 2001, LNCS 2221, pp. 159–187, 2001.

schedule processors only, with a default memory allocation equal to the memory associated with the processors allocated to the job.

The contributions of this paper are threefold. First, characteristics of the NCSA O2K workload that differ from previous workloads are identified. Second, we provide significant new measures and analysis. Third, we provide conditional distributions and a "roadmap" for creating a synthetic workload that has the observed distributions as well as the key correlations among the distributions of requested processors, requested runtime, requested memory, actual runtime, and peak memory usage. To our knowledge, the roadmap and requisite conditional distributions have not been provided in previous workload studies.

Characteristics of the O2K workload that differ from previously reported workloads include the following.

- The coefficient of variation (CV) of the job interarrival time is in the range of 1-2 during each period of approximately stationary hourly arrival rate.
- Jobs require an *average* of 50-100 processor hours, depending on the month.
- 10-15% of the jobs run for over 20 hours.
- 15-20% of the jobs each month request a higher fraction of memory than processors.
- Jobs that request more processors tend to request and use less memory per processor.
- Greater than 50% of the jobs have actual runtime less than 20% of their requested runtime.
- There is not an appreciable correlation between the number of processors requested and the job runtime.

The new measures and analyses provided include:

- Memory demand, equal to the product of the amount of memory requested and the actual job runtime, is provided as a measure of system load.
- A comparison of the workload mix from month to month.
- We identify peak, intermediate, and low periods of approximately stable job arrival rate per hour, rather than using the (12-hour) "day" and "night" periods in [1,8,6].
- We examine whether the jobs submitted on different days or during different periods of the day are statistically similar or not.
- Distributions of requested total memory, requested runtime, and processor utilization, are provided.
- We provide a more extensive analysis of the correlations among the job characteristics. For example, the correlations between requested number of processors and requested memory, or between the ratio of actual to requested runtime and the requested runtime have, to our knowledge, not been studied in previous workload analyses.
- Characteristics of the fifteen largest jobs submitted each month are provided.

The remainder of the paper is organized as follows. Section 2 provides an overview of the NCSA O2K job classes and resources as well as a brief review of

Table 1. NCSA O2K Space Shared Hosts

Host Name	Number of Processors	Memory	
		Total (GB)	Per Processor (MB)
eir	128	64	512
nerthus	128	64	512
hod1	128	64	512
jord1	128	32	256
saga1	128	32	256
huldra	128	32	256
mimir	128	32	256
modi2	64	16	256

related work. Section 3 provides an overview of the system load. Sections 4 and 5 characterize the O2K workload in terms of requested resources and resource usage, respectively, pointing out the differences compared to previous workloads, and providing a roadmap for creating a synthetic workload. Section 6 provides the characteristics of the fifteen jobs that used the largest processing time each month. Section 7 concludes the paper and identifies topics for future research.

2   Background

2.1   NCSA O2K System and Job Traces

The NCSA O2K processors are partitioned into twelve hosts. Eight hosts, with a total of 960 processors, are used for space-shared scheduling of batch jobs that do not request exclusive use of a (dedicated) host. Table 1 shows the processor and memory resources of each of these eight space-shared hosts. Three other hosts, with a total of 512 processors, have a higher priority for running batch jobs that request a dedicated host, one at a time. Each of the three hosts will run other batch jobs with short requested run-time (i.e., less than five hours) in space-shared mode if there are no jobs waiting to run that have requested a dedicated host. The remaining one host runs interactive jobs only.

The paper provides the characteristics of all of the batch jobs that do not request a dedicated host. These jobs have more widely varying processor and memory requests than the jobs that request a dedicated host.

The jobs analyzed were submitted in the six one-month periods (i.e., January - March and October - December 2000). The LSF job scheduler [12], locally tuned for the NCSA workload, was used during the first three months. A priority-backfill scheduler similar to the Maui Scheduler [13] replaced the LSF scheduling algorithm at the end of June 2000 [14], although LSF continues to log information about each job.

Each job requests a number of processors, an amount of memory, and a maximum running time. Based on these requests, the job is classified in one of four time classes (i.e., vst, st, mt, or lt) and one of three size classes (i.e., sj, mj,

Table 2. NCSA O2K Job Class Definitions

Class Name		Resource Request	
Time Component		Job Run Time	
vst	(very short)	$\leq$ 5 hrs	
st	(short)	$\leq$ 50 hrs	
mt	(medium)	$\leq$ 200 hrs	
lt	(long)	$\leq$ 400 hrs	
Size Component		# Processors	Memory
sj	(small)	$\leq$ 8	$\leq$ 2 GB
mj	(medium)	$\leq$ 16	$\leq$ 4 GB
lj	(large)	$\leq$ 64	$\leq$ 16 GB*

(* $\leq$ 25 GB in October-December 2000)

or lj), as defined in Table 2. For example, a job that requests 16 processors and 2 gigabytes of memory is an mj job. Jobs that require more than 64 processors can request a dedicated host. Table 4 shows that each month on the eight space shared hosts, the submitted mj and lj jobs typically require 65-70% of the total processing time available while upwards of 5500 sj jobs also need to be scheduled.

A job is killed if it exceeds its requested run time by one hour or has a number of processes greater than the number requested plus one.[1] Only a small fraction (under 2%) of the jobs each month exceed their requested processors. The jobs that are killed are included in the workload characterization.

The LSF log contains the arrival time, actual and requested job runtime, and requested processors and memory of each job. Jobs that have zero runtime (i.e., they failed or were aborted immediately) are excluded in our analysis. A software daemon (JMD) developed at NCSA records the actual resource usage of each job every 30 seconds during its execution. The memory and cpu usage of each job is obtained from the JMD log.

2.2   Related Work

Several workload studies [1,3,2,5,4,8,15,16] report the measured distributions of the number of requested processors and actual job runtime, on various production systems (e.g., NASA Ames Intel iPSC/860, Argonne SP/1, Cornell Theory Center (CTC) SP/2, SDSC Intel Paragon, PSC T3D). Several of these studies also report the distribution of job interarrival time [1,5,8], and the relationship between the average or distribution of runtime and requested number of processors [1,2,5,16]. The studies in [7,11] focus on the memory usage of jobs on the

---

[1] A process is counted if it has used a cpu for at least 6 seconds (i.e., 20%) during a 30-second window. Under LSF scheduling, for the purpose of determining whether a job has exceeded its requested maximum runtime, the job's runtime was computed as its total cpu time, divided by the number of requested processors. For all other purposes, and for the Maui scheduler, job runtime is defined simply as the amount of (wall clock) time the job occupies the processors.

Table 3. Notation

Symbol	Definition
M	Requested Memory
P	Requested Processors
T	Actual Runtime
M×T	Memory Demand
P×T	Processor Demand

LANL CM-5 and SDSC CRAY T3E. [7] also reports the distribution of the fraction of requested memory used by a job. [5] reports the distribution of requested memory per node on the CTC SP/2.

Based on job traces from production systems, several previous papers propose mathematical distribution functions that closely approximate the observed distributions. In particular, [3] proposes distributions of the job interarrival time, the requested number of processors, and the actual runtime conditioned on the requested number of processors, derived from an analysis of six workloads. Four papers analyze the CTC SP/2 workload and propose distributions of job interarrival time [9], the requested number of processors [6], runtime [16], the product of requested number of processors and runtime [9,6,16], and the runtime conditioned on number of requested processors [16]. [10] characterizes the arrival patterns observed on the CTC SP/2. The study in [17] proposes a distribution for the requested runtime as a multiple of actual runtime for a different SP/2 system.

The differences between these previous workloads and the workload analyzed in this paper are noted as results are presented in Section 3- 5.

3   Overview of the O2K Workload

This section provides an overview of the total load on the O2K as well as the load due to the large jobs submitted during each month studied. The fifteen largest jobs each month are further characterized in Section 6. Table 3 defines some notation that will be used in the remainder of the paper. Note that the processor demand for a job is the product of the number of requested processors and the actual runtime of the job. Similarly, the memory demand is the product of the amount of requested memory and the job runtime.

3.1   Monthly System Load

Table 4 summarizes the overall load on the NCSA O2K during each of the six one-month periods. The processor demand (proc demand) is summed over all jobs or all jobs in one of the twelve job classes, and expressed as a fraction of the total processing time available on the eight space-shared hosts during the month (i.e., the product of the total number of processors and the total time during the month). Note that processor demand can be greater than 100%

Table 4. Total Monthly Processor and Memory Demand By Job Class

Month	Overall	Job Class											
		vst_sj	st_sj	mt_sj	lt_sj	vst_mj	st_mj	mt_mj	lt_mj	vst_lj	st_lj	mt_lj	lt_lj
Jan 2000													
#jobs	9652	3622	2606	553	71	950	589	163	61	671	252	91	23
proc demand	88%	2%	9%	11%	3%	2%	9%	13%	6%	4%	8%	12%	10%
mem demand	76%	1%	6%	7%	3%	1%	5%	10%	6%	1%	11%	10%	17%
Feb 2000													
#jobs	11290	5296	2269	466	71	1128	698	219	33	686	314	90	20
proc demand	96%	2%	9%	11%	3%	3%	10%	13%	3%	6%	18%	12%	5%
mem demand	78%	1%	7%	7%	3%	2%	5%	11%	5%	1%	10%	12%	15%
Mar 2000													
#jobs	12101	4671	2678	472	57	1808	631	216	70	850	500	123	25
proc demand	94%	2%	11%	9%	3%	4%	11%	15%	4%	4%	14%	14%	3%
mem demand	83%	1%	7%	6%	3%	2%	7%	9%	8%	2%	16%	18%	4%
Oct 2000													
#jobs	9768	3012	2488	580	278	881	627	241	50	957	367	209	78
proc demand	90%	1%	11%	9%	7%	2%	10%	11%	2%	5%	14%	13%	4%
mem demand	84%	1%	6%	7%	9%	1%	6%	6%	2%	2%	6%	18%	20%
Nov 2000													
#jobs	8708	2982	2279	416	60	711	497	187	16	912	513	110	25
proc demand	91%	2%	10%	8%	3%	2%	9%	12%	3%	6%	20%	13%	3%
mem demand	63%	1%	5%	5%	2%	1%	5%	6%	1%	2%	10%	11%	14%
Dec 2000													
#jobs	7798	2581	2190	565	164	801	252	215	59	667	176	113	15
proc demand	102%	2%	11%	10%	9%	2%	5%	18%	4%	6%	11%	13%	12%
mem demand	68%	1%	6%	8%	5%	1%	2%	10%	6%	2%	4%	13%	9%

Table 5. Summary of the Load of Various Large Job Classes

Month	Job Class	#Jobs	(%)	Demand/Demand All		Job Size			Avg P×T
				Processor Demand	Memory Demand	Avg Processors Requested	Avg Memory Requested (GB)	Avg Actual Runtime (hours)	
Oct 2000	P×T > avg P×T = 66h	1793	(18%)	89.3%	79.0%	15.2	2.3	42.5	319
	T > 20hr	1312	(13%)	71.3%	80.9%	6.7	1.9	59.6	348
	P > 16, T>10m	695	(7%)	35.7%	9.7%	42.2	4.7	8.5	329
	M > 4GB, T>10m	653	(7%)	15.8%	51.5%	22.0	10.1	15.0	154
	P > 16, M >4, T>10m	265	(3%)	10.7%	7.0%	47.0	9.8	6.1	258
Nov 2000	P×T > avg P×T = 72h	1495	(17%)	89.4%	83.3%	19.4	2.6	35.5	376
	T > 20hr	1065	(12%)	70.7%	79.6%	8.0	1.6	53.1	418
	P > 16, T>10m	767	(9%)	40.7%	21.7%	42.1	4.9	9.2	333
	M > 4GB, T>10m	502	(6%)	20.9%	53.7%	27.5	9.4	16.8	261
	P > 16, M > 4, T>10m	246	(3%)	14.4%	17.1%	46.8	12.0	8.6	367
Dec 2000	P×T > avg P×T = 93h	1188	(15%)	87.8%	76.0%	14.6	1.9	63.7	537
	T > 20hr	1293	(17%)	82.2%	87.7%	6.5	1.5	69.5	462
	P > 16, T>10m	455	(6%)	36.1%	21.2%	39.2	4.2	16.8	577
	M > 4GB, T>10m	310	(4%)	15.9%	36.1%	23.2	9.5	19.4	372
	P>16, M > 4, T>10m	97	(1%)	11.8%	15.9%	53.0	14.4	16.6	882

because in a typical month 50% of the vst jobs (collectively having a total of 4-9% processor demand) run on the three hosts that give priority to dedicated jobs. The memory demand is similarly reported as a fraction of total available memory on the eight space-shared hosts. We use the resources on eight space shared hosts for measuring processor and memory demand because these are the only hosts that are guaranteed to be available for running the batch jobs that are characterized.

The key observations from Table 4 are:

- The total processor demand each month is extremely high, i.e., typically 90-100% of the total available processing time on the eight hosts.
- The overall memory demand is somewhat lower than the processor demand each month, but is still in the range of 70-80% during most months.
- The job mix is similar from month to month. That is, with a few exceptions, the number of jobs in each class and the processor and memory demands of each job class are fairly similar from month to month. One exception is the December 2000 workload, which has fewer jobs but higher processor demand (overall and in several job classes) than in the other months.
- The vast majority (i.e., 95%) of the total processor demand is due to (st,mt,or lt) jobs that request runtimes greater than five hours. On the other hand, a large number of vst jobs must also be scheduled.
- The large (lj) jobs have a relatively high processor and memory demand (typically equal to 35% or more). This is a challenging workload for the job scheduling policy, as it is difficult to find free resources for these large jobs when total system load is above 90%.

3.2   Monthly Load Due to Large Jobs

Previous work has shown that a large fraction of the processor demand is due to a small fraction of the jobs. For example, on an iPSC/860 90% of the jobs had runtime under 15 minutes, but the remaining 10% of the jobs account for 90% of the total processor demand by all jobs [1]. Hotovy [2] reported that, fewer than 50% of the jobs on the CTC SP/2 use more than 1 processor, but they account for over 90% of the total processor demand of all jobs.

The characteristics of the NCSA O2K workload are somewhat different. For example, 65-70% of the jobs request more than one processor (Figure 4) and 40% of the jobs have runtime greater than one hour (Figure 12). Table 4 shows that 50-55% of the O2K jobs are in the vst class, and the other 45-50% of the jobs account for approximately 90% of the processor demand each month.

To determine the extent to which various small sets of jobs dominate processing and/or memory demand on the O2K, five classes of large jobs are summarized in Table 5. The class "P×T > avg P×T", is the set of jobs that each have processor demand (P×T) greater than the average processor demand over all jobs in the given month. The average processor demand for the month is given in parentheses (e.g., 93 processor hours in December 2000). In addition, T > 20 hours, P>16, M>4 GB, and T>10 minutes are used to define four classes, three of which are subsets of the 'lj' class. For each job class, the table shows the total number of jobs (and the fraction of all submitted jobs), the processor and memory demand expressed as a fraction of the respective demand of all submitted jobs, and the average of each of four size measures for jobs in the class.

Key observations from Table 5 include the following.

- Average processor demand per job is in the range of 50-100 processor hours, depending on the month.
- The load of each large job class is very similar across different months.
- Processor and memory usage are dominated by the 10-15% of jobs with running time greater than 20 hours or by the 15-18% of jobs with higher than average processor demand.
- No more than 3% of the jobs in the months we analyzed have P > 16, M > 4 GB, and T > 10 minutes.

4   Resource Request Characteristics

This section analyzes job arrival characteristics, and the observed distributions of requested number of processors, memory, and runtime. The analysis includes identifying periods per day of approximately stationary arrival rate, and determining whether resource request distributions vary among different months, days of the week, or periods of the day. Conditional distributions that capture the key correlations among the workload parameters are also provided. Section 5 will provide actual job runtime and memory usage distributions, as well as correlations between the usage distributions and the requested resources.

This section and Section 5 provide a "roadmap" for creating a synthetic workload with characteristics similar to the observed O2K workload. In other words, the workload characteristics are presented in the order in which synthetic job characteristics could be assigned so as to capture the key correlations among the distributions. Sections 4.6 and 5.4 summarize the roadmap.

4.1   Job Arrival Rate

Figure 1 shows the number of job arrivals each day during October 2000, with the number submitted on each particular day of the week (e.g., Monday) grouped

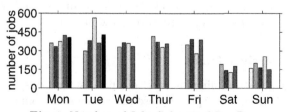

Fig. 1. Number of Jobs Submitted Per Day
(October 2000)

together. The figure shows that the number of arrivals is typically 350-400 per weekday and 150-200 per weekend day. Occasionally there are weekdays that have greater than 500 arrivals. Other months have similar arrivals per day, except that (1) in February 2000, the number of arrivals per weekend day was closer to 350, (2) during the last 2-3 weeks of December the number of arrivals per weekday is 150-200, and (3) on holidays (e.g., Thanksgiving, Christmas, New Years day), the number of arrivals is lower than a typical weekend day.

Several previous papers have provided the average number of jobs that arrive during each hour on weekdays and weekends on various parallel systems [1,8,5] including a network of workstations [18]. The pattern of job arrivals is very similar on each of these systems other than the Paragon in [8]. That is, during weekdays there is a peak arrival period between 8am-6pm, a very low arrival period before 8am, and an intermediate arrival period after 6pm, with less variation in the number of job arrivals per hour during weekends. The previous papers have noted the higher arrival rate from 8am-6pm, but not the intermediate arrival rate after 6pm. They also do not comment on whether the job arrival pattern is similar or different across different days of the week, and do not examine whether other job characteristics (such as runtime) differ depending on period of the day or day of the week (e.g., Monday vs Friday).

Plots of the number of jobs that arrive each hour for each day in the six months of O2K workload did not reveal any distinct characteristics for any particular day during the work week or during the weekend. Figure 2 shows that the arrival pattern varies somewhat from one weekday to another (Figure 2 (a-c)) or one weekend day to another (Figure 2(g),(h)), but the average number of arrivals each hour is approximately the same whether computed over all Fridays (or other day of the week) in a given month (e.g., Figure 2(d)), or over Monday through Friday in a given week (e.g., Figure 2(e)), or over all weekdays in any given month (e.g., Figure 2(f)).

The figure shows that when the average number of arrivals per hour is computed over a large sample, such as all weekdays in a month, three periods of approximately stationary average arrival rate are identified. The three periods are labeled peak, intermediate, and low in the figures. Allowing for statistical fluctuations due to finite sample sizes, as well as for fluctuations due to occasional system downtimes, these three periods appear to be present during each weekday in the six months studied. Analogously, two periods (intermediate and low) of approximately stationary arrival rate were identified on weekend days, as shown in the figure.

The arrive rate per hour on weekdays is typically around 30 during peak, 15-20 during intermediate, and 5-10 during low periods.

4.2 Job Interarrival Times

For the purpose of determining interarrival time distributions, we consider weekday peak periods from 9am-5pm because the 8-9am and 5-6pm periods have average arrival rate that is slightly lower than the other peak hours. For analyzing all other job characteristics, the weekday peak period is defined to be 8am-6pm.

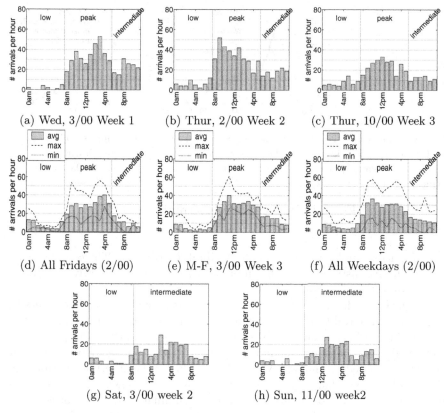

Fig. 2. Number of Job Arrivals Each Hour
(peak: 30-35/hr, intermediate: 15-20/hr, low: 5-10/hr)

Excluding periods when the O2K is down, during each period of approximately stationary hourly arrival rate, the coefficient of variation (CV) of the interarrival time is in the range of 1-2. Higher CVs (i.e., CV = 2.5-6) have been reported in other systems [1,8,9,10] for the distribution of interarrival times during 12-hour day and night periods (rather than during periods of stationary arrival rate).

We have investigated several models for the observed O2K interarrival time distribution in each period, including the exponential with the same mean interarrival time, a two-stage hyperexponential with the same mean and CV, the Weibull, and the gamma distribution.[2] The fit of these distributions is illustrated for two different periods in Figure 3(a) and (c). The fit of the gamma distribution

---

[2] In each period, the parameters of the two-stage hyperexponential distribution are computed using the standard algorithm such that the products of the probability and the mean service time for each stage are equal [19]. The maximum likelihood estimates of the Weibull and gamma distribution parameters, with 95% confidence intervals, are computed using Matlab [20,21].

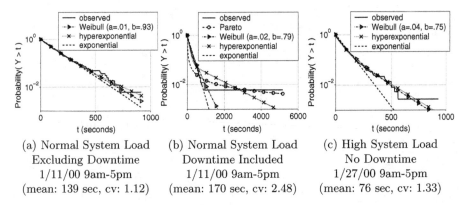

(a) Normal System Load
Excluding Downtime
1/11/00 9am-5pm
(mean: 139 sec, cv: 1.12)

(b) Normal System Load
Downtime Included
1/11/00 9am-5pm
(mean: 170 sec, cv: 2.48)

(c) High System Load
No Downtime
1/27/00 9am-5pm
(mean: 76 sec, cv: 1.33)

Fig. 3. Distributions of Job Interarrival Time (Y)

(not shown) is similar to the fit of the Weibull distribution. The complement of the cumulative distribution is shown on a log scale, to more clearly show the fit of the tail of the distribution.

As shown in the figure, the two-stage hyperexponential distribution fits the observed interarrival time distribution better than the exponential distribution, even during periods when the CV is quite close to 1. In fact, in all periods (including all peak, intermediate, and low periods), the two-stage hyperexponential with the measured mean and CV had the best fit for the observed distribution.[3] Figure 3(b) shows that if periods when the system is down[4] (e.g., the period during 10:12-11:38am on January 11), are not eliminated from the measured interarrival time distribution, one might erroneously conclude that the interarrival times are better approximated by a heavy-tailed distribution such as the Pareto distribution.

4.3   Number of Requested Processors

Figure 4(a) plots a typical distribution of the number of requested processors for jobs submitted during weekday peak periods in a given month. The distribution is similar for other months and for most intermediate and low periods on weekdays and weekends.[5] Occasionally during one of the intermediate or low ar-

---

[3] The two-stage hyperexponential with CV close to 3 was found to have a good fit for the distribution of all interarrival times, not separately measured over periods of approximately stationary arrival rate, for the CTC SP/2 in [9]

[4] Downtime is often not recorded in the job logs. We implemented a special daemon process that tracks system downtime on the O2K since the O2K job logs do not contain the down time information.

[5] On a system with restricted processor availability during 6am-8pm on weekdays, the fraction of submitted jobs that request the maximum number of processors was reported to be significantly higher during other hours [1]. The O2K does not restrict batch job sizes during weekday peak periods.

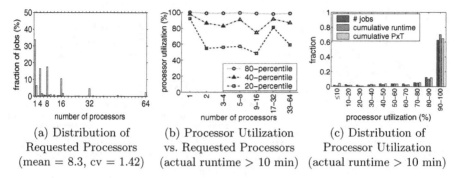

(a) Distribution of
Requested Processors
(mean = 8.3, cv = 1.42)

(b) Processor Utilization
vs. Requested Processors
(actual runtime > 10 min)

(c) Distribution of
Processor Utilization
(actual runtime > 10 min)

Fig. 4. Processor Requests and Utilization

rival rate periods, the number of jobs that request 32 or 64 processors is slightly higher than typical.

As in previous workloads [1,2,3,8,15,4,6], a large fraction (i.e., 30-40%) of the O2K jobs are serial, and most jobs request power-of-two processors. The distribution is similar to the log-uniform distribution proposed in [6], except that fewer jobs request 2 or 4 processors, and a small but not insignificant fraction of jobs request numbers of processors that are not a power of two. Thus, a harmonic distribution constructed to emphasize small numbers and powers of two, as proposed in [3], is a better characterization of the processor requests on the O2K.

Each O2K job is allocated its number of requested processors until it terminates. Figures 4(b) and (c) show that a high fraction of jobs utilize over 80% requested processors, including jobs that request 32-64 processors, jobs that have dominant actual runtimes, and jobs that have dominant processor demand (P×T). This leads to high total utilization of allocated processors on the O2K, as will be shown in Figure 18(c).

4.4   Requested Memory

The normalized requested memory for a job is defined as the amount of requested memory divided by the number of processors requested. Figures 5(a) - (c) show that the distribution of normalized or total requested memory is very similar during different months and during different periods of the weekday.[6] It is also very similar for different days of the week and during weekend periods (not shown). Note that only a very small fraction (i.e., <1%) of jobs each month request the maximum of 25 GB (or previously 16 GB) of memory.

Figure 6 shows that the requested memory (as measured by the mean, or the 20th, 50th or 80th percentile) has a significant correlation with the requested

---

[6] Jobs submitted during weekday intermediate periods request 256 MB to 1 GB of memory slightly more often, and 2-4 GB slightly less often, but the weekday peak distribution is still a fairly good approximation for the intermediate period.

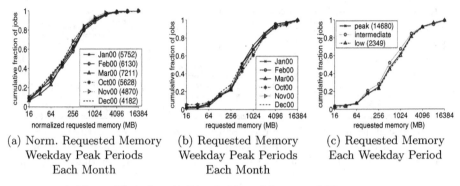

(a) Norm. Requested Memory
Weekday Peak Periods
Each Month

(b) Requested Memory
Weekday Peak Periods
Each Month

(c) Requested Memory
Each Weekday Period

Fig. 5. Variations in Distribution of Requested Memory
(Norm. Requested Memory = Requested Memory/Number of Requested Processors)

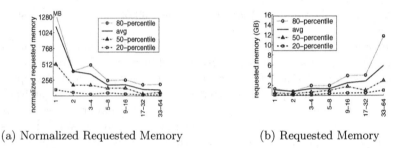

(a) Normalized Requested Memory

(b) Requested Memory

Fig. 6. Requested Memory vs. Requested Processors

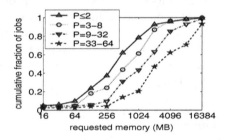

Fig. 7. Conditional Distributions of Requested Memory

number of processors. Specifically, total requested memory is positively correlated with the requested number of processors, while normalized requested memory is negatively correlated the requested number of processors. To our knowledge, the correlations between these parameters of previous workloads have not
been investigated. The curves shown in the figure were observed for both the
January - March 2000 and October - December 2000 workloads.

    Based on the curves in Figure 6(b), Figure 7 provides the measured condi-
tional distributions of requested memory for four different ranges of the requested
number of processors, which can be used to create memory requests that have
the observed correlation with job parallelism.

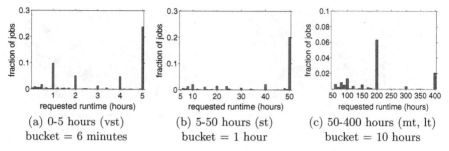

(a) 0-5 hours (vst)
bucket = 6 minutes

(b) 5-50 hours (st)
bucket = 1 hour

(c) 50-400 hours (mt, lt)
bucket = 10 hours

Fig. 8. Distribution of Requested Runtime During Weekday Peak Periods

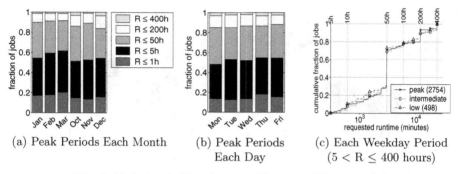

(a) Peak Periods Each Month

(b) Peak Periods
Each Day

(c) Each Weekday Period
(5 < R ≤ 400 hours)

Fig. 9. Variation in Distribution of Requested Runtime (R)

Recall from Table 1 that the average memory available per processor on the O2K is either 256 MB or 512 MB, depending on the host. As shown in Figures 5(a) and 6(a), 35-40% of all jobs have normalized requested memory greater than 256 MB; furthermore 15-20% of all jobs and 50% of the sequential jobs have normalized requested memory greater than 0.5 GB. In contrast, in an SP/2 system where more than 80% of the nodes had 128 MB of memory, 85% of the jobs requested this smallest possible normalized memory [2].

4.5 Requested Runtime

To our knowledge, previous papers have not reported the distribution of requested job runtime, although this parameter is used by many job scheduling policies.

Figure 8 shows the distribution of requested runtime for jobs submitted during weekday peak periods, and Figure 9 compares the distributions of requested runtime for jobs submitted during different periods of approximately stationary arrival rate. General observations about these distributions include the following.

– A large fraction of jobs request the default runtime for the job class (i.e., 5, 50, 200, or 400 hours). These requested runtimes have no special meaning for the current scheduler on the O2K, except that jobs that request up to

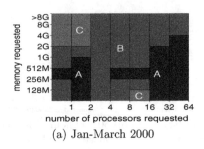
(a) Jan-March 2000

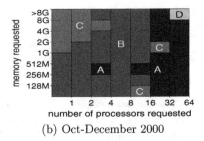
(b) Oct-December 2000

Fig. 10. Conditional Distributions (A-D) of Requested Runtime

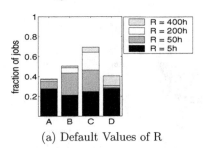
(a) Default Values of R

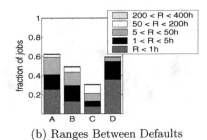
(b) Ranges Between Defaults

Fig. 11. The Distribution Functions

5 hours of runtime are eligible to run on the three hosts that have higher priority for jobs that request a dedicated host.

– Nearly all other jobs request some 'round' number such as 1, 2, 10, 20, or 300 hours, with approximately *uniform frequency* for each such requested runtime between a pair of default values.

– The distribution of requested runtime is similar for jobs submitted in different months, although a somewhat larger fraction of jobs request 50 - 400 hours during October through December 2000.

– The distribution of requested runtime is similar for different days of the week. Over each three month period, but not during each month within the period, there are slightly fewer vst jobs submitted on Mondays.

– Allowing for statistical variations in finite sample sizes, the distribution of requested runtime is very similar for jobs submitted during different days of the week, and different weekday arrival rate periods. The distributions during weekend intermediate and low periods, not shown in the figure, are also similar.

Analysis of the distribution of requested runtime for each range of requested processors paired with each range of requested memory, reveals four distributions (named A through D) that are conditioned on the requested processors and requested memory as shown in Figure 10. The distributions are provided in Figure 11. Although the ranges of processor and memory requests over which each conditional distribution applies are complex, the similarities between Figures 10(a) and (b) are also significant. That is, the recurrence of the distributions in the two different three-month periods suggests that the identified distributions are meaningful.

The conditional distributions can be used to generate a synthetic requested runtime after determining the processor and memory requests. Distribution A has a high fraction of jobs that request less than or equal to 5 hours of runtime, and smaller fractions that request 10, 20, or 50 hours. Distribution B has significant fractions of jobs that request 5 hours, 50 hours, and non-default values smaller than 50 hours; a smaller fraction request 200 hours. Distribution C has significant fractions of requests for 5, 50, and 200 hours, and a smaller but noticeable fraction that request 400 hours. Distribution D has the highest fractions of jobs that request 1-5 hours and 400 hours. Since most jobs request less than 2 GB of memory, and since distribution A has a significantly lower average requested runtime than distributions B and C, jobs that request greater than 16 processors have a significantly lower average requested runtime than jobs that request fewer processors. For example, the average requested runtime is approximately ten hours larger for serial jobs than that for the 64-processor jobs.

4.6   Summary of Requested Resources

The procedure for creating a synthetic workload that approximates the resource requests of the O2K weekday peak workloads can be summarized as follows:

- Job interarrival times have a two-stage hyperexponential distribution, with mean approximately equal to two minutes and CV in the range of 1-2.
- Requested number of processors has a specialized harmonic distribution that emphasizes powers of two and small numbers, as shown in Figure 4(a).
- The distributions of requested memory, conditioned on the requested number of processors, are given in Figure 7.
- The requested runtime distributions, conditioned on both the requested number of processors and requested memory, are given in Figures 10 - 11. These specialized distributions have significant probability mass at 5, 50, 200, and/or 400 hours, and relatively uniform probability for round numbers between these values, as illustrated in Figure 8.

To create a synthetic workload for intermediate and low arrival rate periods, only the mean interarrival time needs to be modified. Arrival rates for the non-peak arrival periods are provided in Figure 2.

5   Execution Characteristics

Sections 5.1 and 5.3 provide the distributions of actual job runtime and memory usage, respectively. Relationships among these quantities and the job resource requests for processors, memory, and runtime are also provided. Overall average utilization of allocated memory per month is compared against overall average utilization of allocated processors per month. Distribution of processor utilization was analyzed in Section 4.3. Section 5.4 summarizes the execution characteristics.

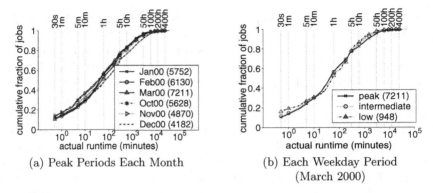

(a) Peak Periods Each Month

(b) Each Weekday Period
(March 2000)

Fig. 12. Distribution of Actual Runtime

5.1   Distribution of Actual Runtime

Many previous papers report distributions of actual runtime over a collection of
jobs that arrived over a period of several months, without establishing whether
the workload is (approximately) stationary over those months.

Figures 12(a) and (b) show that the distribution of actual runtime on the O2K
is similar for jobs submitted during weekday peak periods in different months and
for jobs submitted during non-peak arrival rate periods, although the coefficient
of variation (CV) is slightly lower for jobs submitted during low arrival rate
periods. The distribution is also similar for jobs submitted during different days
of the week (not shown).

The CV of the overall runtime distribution for the O2K workloads is approximately equal to 3; a runtime CV in the range of 2-5 has been reported for
several previous parallel workloads [1,8,22].

Plots of the complement of the runtime distribution on a log-log scale (not
shown) reveal that the observed distributions of runtime are not heavy tailed,
in contrast to the process runtimes observed on Unix systems [23] and a hypo-
thetical model of parallel job runtimes in [24]. The two-stage hyperexponential
distribution has been used to model the observed runtime distribution in a previous parallel workload [3]. As shown in Figure 13, the Weibull distribution
provides a significantly better fit for actual runtimes on the O2K.[7] The gamma
distribution (not shown) does not fit the tail of the observed distribution. Since
the observed distribution is approximately piecewise linear in the logarithm of

---

[7] The hyperexponential distribution shown in the figure matches only the first two moments of the observed distribution. Using the algorithm in [9] to fit a hyperErlang
distribution to the observed O2K runtime distribution, results in a two-stage hyperexponential distribution that matches the first three non-central moments of the
observed data, but this distribution has a slightly worse fit to the full distribution
than the fit of the hyperexponential distribution shown in the figure. Note that if a
linear scale is used for the x axis in the figure the hyperexponential distribution will
appear to be more accurate.

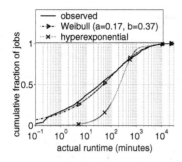

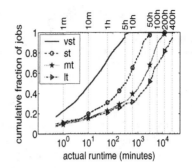

Fig. 13. Example Curve Fit
(Weekdays Peak, Oct 2000)
(mean = 566 minutes, cv = 3)

Fig. 14. Distribution of Actual Runtime
for Each Requested Runtime Class

the observed actual runtime, a piecewise log-uniform distribution as proposed
in [16] fits the observed distribution nearly as well as the Weibull distribution.

Similar results are obtained for modeling the distribution of total processing time (i.e., total number of cpu hours rather than total runtime) per job.
That is, the Weibull and piecewise log-uniform distributions closely approximate
the observed distribution, whereas the gamma, two-stage hyperexponential, and
heavy-tailed Pareto distributions do not.

Plots of the average and percentiles of the actual runtime for each range of
requested processors (omitted to conserve space) reveal that there is no appreciable correlation between the actual runtime and requested number of processors,
in contrast to previous workloads on an iPSC/860 [1], a Paragon [8], and an
SP/2 [2].

5.2   Actual vs. Requested Runtime

Previous workload studies report on the correlation between actual runtime and
number of requested processors [1,8,2] as well as the distribution of the ratio of
actual to requested runtime [17], but not (to our knowledge) on the correlation
between requested runtime and the ratio of actual runtime to requested runtime.

Figure 14 shows that there is a large discrepancy between actual and requested runtime for most jobs. For example, approximately 10% of the st, mt,
and lt jobs (which request over 5, 50, or 200 hours of runtime, respectively) actually complete in under one minute. These premature job completions may be
due to unanticipated errors in the application codes, but it's surprising that 10%
of all jobs that request over 5 hours would terminate due to an unanticipated
error in the code. Furthermore, more than 20actually run for 10-50 hours, and
30use 10-100 hours. Thus, a significant fraction of the of the inaccurate runtime
requests appear to be due to simple misestimation of the actual runtime, perhaps
encouraged by the existence of default runtime request values in the system.

Figures 15(a)-(c) show that more than 50% of all jobs have actual runtime
that is less than 20% of their requested runtime, and 50% of the jobs that re-

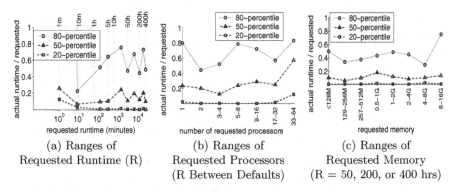

(a) Ranges of
Requested Runtime (R)

(b) Ranges of
Requested Processors
(R Between Defaults)

(c) Ranges of
Requested Memory
(R = 50, 200, or 400 hrs)

Fig. 15. Actual Runtime/Requested Runtime for Various Resource Request Classes
(October–December 2000)

quest default runtimes have actual runtime less than 10-12% of their requested
runtime. In contrast, Feitelson and Weil [17] reported that the ratio of the actual to requested runtime on an SP/2 ranges uniformly from 0-99%. They also
simulated the SP/2 job trace with accurate requested runtimes and showed that
the average of the job turnaround time divided by actual runtime (i.e., the mean
slowdown) improved for a non-preemptive scheduler similar to the current O2K
scheduler. This suggests that mean turnaround time and mean slowdown for jobs
on the O2K might be improved if requested runtimes could be specified more
accurately.

A key question is how to generate actual runtimes in a synthetic workload if
requested runtimes are generated as discussed in Section 4.5. The percentiles in
Figure 15(a) were computed for the default requested runtimes (i.e., 5,50,200,
and 400 hours), each range between the defaults, and the following ranges of
requested runtime (R): R=1 minute, 1 min. < R ≤ 10 min., 10 min < R < 5
hrs.[8]. This figure shows that the ratio of actual to requested runtime is statistically somewhat higher for jobs that request greater than 5 hours of runtime but
not one of the default values than for jobs that request one of the default values. Figure 15(b) shows that the distribution for the former category of runtime
requests is similar for each number of requested processors up to 32, but has a
much higher fiftieth percentile if the requested number of processors is greater
than 32. A similar graph (not shown) shows that the distribution for jobs that
request 5 hours of runtime is similar for each number of requested processors
greater than 16. For each category of requested runtime and requested number
of processors that has a similar distribution of the ratio of actual to requested
runtime, we plotted the distribution as a function of requested memory, as illustrated in Figure 15(c) for requested runtime equal to 5 hours and requested
processors greater than 16. In Figure 15(c) the distribution is different for re-

---

[8] The value of each percentile for each range of runtime is plotted against the average
requested runtime in the range.

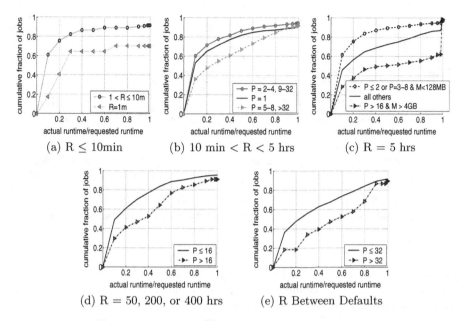

Fig. 16. Conditional Distributions of Actual Runtime/Requested Runtime
(R: Requested Runtime)

quested memory greater than 4 GB; in all other cases, the distribution is not significantly sensitive to the requested memory.

Based on these considerations, Figure 16 provides distributions of the ratio of actual to requested runtime conditioned on the requested runtime, requested processors, and requested memory. Recall that actual runtime can exceed requested runtime by one hour before the job is killed. The results in Figure 16(a) show that a significant fraction of the jobs that request one minute of runtime exceed their request. The results in Figure 16(c) show that a significant fraction of the jobs that request 5 hours of runtime are tuned to run for exactly 5 hours.

A synthetic workload generator can use the distributions provided in Figure 16 to generate the actual runtime as a fraction of requested runtime after requested runtime and number of processors have been generated.

5.3 Memory Usage

For each job the JMD logs record the job's peak memory usage during each 30 second interval of runtime. A small percentage (i.e., 0-4%) of the jobs that have at least one minute of actual runtime during each month do not have JMD log information about actual cpu and memory usage; these jobs are not included in the analysis of memory usage characteristics in this section.

The peak memory used by the job is the maximum of these 30-second peak values. The average memory used by the job is computed as the average of the 30-second peak values. The *normalized* peak memory used is defined to be the

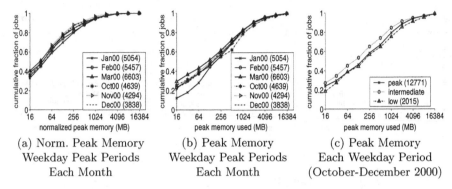

(a) Norm. Peak Memory
Weekday Peak Periods
Each Month

(b) Peak Memory
Weekday Peak Periods
Each Month

(c) Peak Memory
Each Weekday Period
(October-December 2000)

Fig. 17. Variations in Distribution of Peak Memory Used
(Norm. Peak Memory = Peak Memory Used/Number of Requested Processors)

ratio of the peak memory used divided by the number of processors requested. The peak (or average) *memory efficiency* is defined as the ratio of peak (or average) memory used to memory requested.

Figure 17 shows that there is some variability in the distributions of peak memory usage over different months and over different arrival rate periods. In particular, jobs submitted during intermediate arrival rate periods tend to have somewhat lower peak memory usage. In the remainder of this section we focus on further characterizing representative peak memory usage for jobs submitted during weekday peak arrival rate periods in October through December 2000. Parameters of the representative distributions for these periods could be adjusted to reflect the observed variations for different months or for the intermediate arrival rate period.

Similar to previous workloads [7,11], Figure 17(a) shows that a large fraction (i.e., approximately 50%) of the jobs on the O2K have a very small (i.e., under 32 MB) peak memory usage per processor. On the other hand, another significant fraction (about 5%) of the jobs on the O2K have normalized peak memory usage greater than 1 GB per processor.

Figure 18 shows that there is a large discrepancy between requested memory and memory utilized per job. In particular, Figures 18(a) and (b) show that the respective ratio of average or peak memory usage to the requested memory is distributed fairly uniformly over each 10% range from 10-100%, and 15-20% of the jobs have peak memory usage higher than their requested memory. A similar result was reported for a CM-5 workload in [7]. Figure 18(c) shows that the average memory efficiency varies between 40-55% from month to month, which is significantly lower than the time-average utilization of the requested processors. As with the large errors in requested runtime on the O2K, jobs might be scheduled more efficiently if memory requests were more accurate.

Peak memory usage is an important job characteristic in that it defines the amount of memory that must be allocated to the job (in a shared memory system such at the O2K) in order to guarantee that the job doesn't experience any

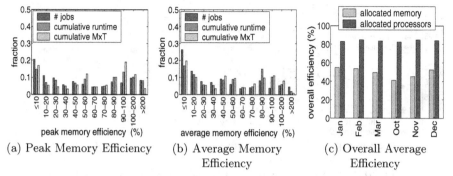

(a) Peak Memory Efficiency   (b) Average Memory Efficiency   (c) Overall Average Efficiency

Fig. 18. Memory Efficiency

memory interference during execution. To further characterize peak memory usage for the purpose of creating synthetic workloads, we analyze the correlations between peak memory efficiency and other job characteristics. To that end, Figures 19 - 20 plot the percentiles of the peak memory efficiency per job, for ranges of requested number of processors, requested memory, and actual runtime.

Figure 19(a) shows that the peak memory efficiency per job is fairly insensitive to the requested number of processors. An implication of this result is that peak memory usage is positively correlated with the number of requested processors, since requested memory and requested processors are positively correlated (see Figure 6(b)). Similarly, there is a negative correlation between the normalized peak memory usage and the number of requested processors ((see Figure 6(a)). In contrast, in the CM-5 [7] workload, the jobs with a larger number of processors not only use a larger amount of memory, but also a larger amount of per-processor memory.

Figure 19(b) shows that the distribution of peak memory efficiency is significantly different for jobs that request fewer than 128 MB of memory than for jobs that request more than 128 MB of memory. From this figure, noting that very few jobs request 33-64 MB of memory and that the 80-percentile value for

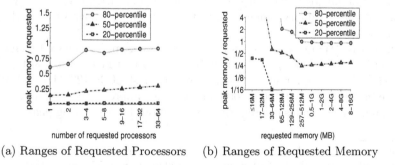

(a) Ranges of Requested Processors   (b) Ranges of Requested Memory

Fig. 19. Peak Memory/Requested Memory For Various Resource Request Classes

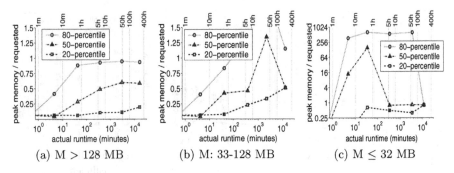

(a) M > 128 MB   (b) M: 33-128 MB   (c) M ≤ 32 MB

Fig. 20. Peak Memory/Requested Memory Versus Actual Runtime

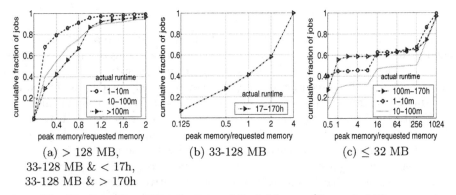

(a) > 128 MB,   (b) 33-128 MB   (c) ≤ 32 MB
33-128 MB & < 17h,
33-128 MB & > 170h

Fig. 21. Conditional Distributions of Peak Memory/Requested Memory
(Weekday Peak Periods, October-December 2000)

these memory requests is unreliable based on the small number of jobs, we partition the jobs into three classes according to their memory request (i.e., ≤ 32
MB, 33-128 MB, and > 128 MB) and provide the percentiles of peak memory
efficiency as a function of actual job runtime for each class in Figures 20(a) -
(c).[9]

Note that all jobs that have runtime under one minute use a very small
fraction of their memory request; in fact, nearly all such jobs use less than 64
MB of memory.

The distribution of peak memory used as a fraction of requested memory is
very similar for runtime greater than 10 minutes and memory request greater
than 32 MB, except for jobs with memory request of 33-128 MB and actual
runtime in the range of 1,000-10,000 minutes (i.e., approximately 17-170 hours).
Thus, Figure 21 provides the requisite distributions for generating peak memory

---

[9] The ranges of actual runtime over which the percentiles in Figure 20(a)-(c) are
computed are: 0-1 minute, 1-10 minutes, 10-100 minutes, 1.7-17 hours, 17-170 hours,
and above 170 hours.

as a fraction of memory requested after requested memory and actual runtime have been generated as described earlier in this paper.

5.4   Summary of Execution Characteristics

To generate actual runtime and peak memory usage to complete a synthetic workload that is representative of the O2K weekday peak arrival rate workloads, these characteristics are obtained from the distributions in Figure 16 and 21, respectively. Processor utilization can also be generated from the distribution in Figure 4(b). To create a synthetic workload for intermediate arrival rate periods, the peak memory usage might be adjusted slightly as shown in Figure 17(c). Low arrival rate periods have approximately the same distributions of actual runtime and peak memory usage as weekday peak arrival rate periods.

Note that, depending on the purpose of the synthetic workload, any of the characteristics that are not needed can be ignored.

6   The Largest Jobs Each Month

This section provides characteristics of the fifteen jobs that have the largest processor demand (i.e., the product of the number of requested processors and the actual runtime of the job) each month.

Table 6 summarizes the total processor and memory demand, and the average job size of these largest jobs for each month. Figure 22 provides more detailed characteristics of the largest jobs in December 2000, a recent month in which the average processor demand per largest job is high.

For most months, the 15 largest jobs account for 10-15% of the total processor and memory demand for the month. Also for most months, these largest jobs have an average of over 200 hours of actual runtime and and average demand of 7000-8000 processor hours, while the respective averages over all jobs in the monthly workload is at least an order of magnitude smaller.

As shown in Figure 22(b) and (d), the top three jobs in December 2000 had run times of 300-400 hours on 32-64 processors. Although two of the largest

Table 6. Fifteen Largest Jobs Each Month

| Month | Demand/Demand All | | Job Size | | | |
	Processor Demand	Memory Demand	Avg Processors Requested	Avg Memory Requested (GB)	Avg Actual Runtime (hours)	Avg Processor Demand (P×T hrs)
Jan 2000	17.1%	15.7%	27.7	6.1	311.0	7173
Feb 2000	16.5%	17.2%	36.1	7.7	254.5	7031
Mar 2000	15.6%	11.0%	36.1	6.6	209.5	6944
Oct 2000	9.1%	3.4%	41.7	3.8	102.9	3888
Nov 2000	11.1%	9.2%	39.8	5.1	168.4	4657
Dec 2000	16.6%	13.3%	40.5	8.0	222.0	8044

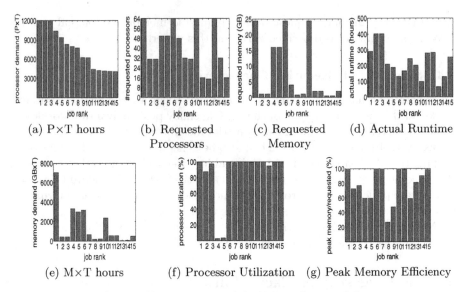

(a) P×T hours   (b) Requested   (c) Requested   (d) Actual Runtime
                Processors   Memory

(e) M×T hours   (f) Processor Utilization   (g) Peak Memory Efficiency

Fig. 22. Characteristics of the Fifteen Largest Jobs
(December 2000)

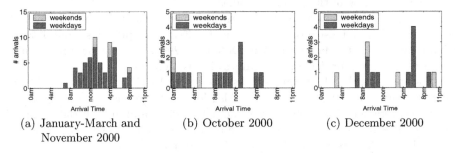

(a) January-March and   (b) October 2000   (c) December 2000
November 2000

Fig. 23. Job Arrival Times For the Fifteen Largest Jobs

jobs in December 2000 had very low processor utilization, Figure 22(f) shows that many of the largest jobs achieve nearly 100% utilization of their requested processors. For the other five months analyzed, (1) 2-7 jobs per month have approximately 100% processor utilization, and (2) 2-5 jobs per month have under 50% utilization, of which a total of three jobs have utilization under 10%.

As shown in Figure 22(c) the largest jobs request either the maximum memory (16-25 GB), or under 4 GB of memory. Peak memory usage divided by memory requested (Figure 22(g)) tends to be somewhat higher (i.e., 60-100% for most of the largest jobs) than for the workload as a whole. On the other hand, a few of the largest jobs have peak memory efficiency under 20%.

Figure 23 shows that most of the largest jobs of each month arrive during weekday peak arrival rate hours. However, during October 2000 a significant fraction of the top jobs were submitted during weekday low arrival rate hours (i.e., midnight to 4am).

7   Conclusions

This paper has provided a characterization of the large production parallel workload submitted to the NCSA O2K over two three month periods. This characterization is more complete than previous parallel workload characterizations in that new characteristics are provided (e.g., distributions of requested runtime, processor and memory utilizations, distribution of requested memory over more flexible range of possible requests), correlations among the characteristics are more fully explored, and conditional distributions are provided for generating synthetic workloads that include the observed correlations in the O2K workload. Another key difference in this analysis as compared with prior work is that job characteristics are provided for jobs that are submitted during periods of approximately stationary job arrival rate. From these characteristics we determined that the jobs submitted in different months or in different arrival rate periods are statistically very similar. The roadmaps for generating similar synthetic workloads are summarized in Sections 4.6 and 5.4.

Interesting characteristics of the O2K workload include: (a) the fifteen largest jobs in a typical month have average running time of over 200 hours and use an average of 4000-8000 processor hours, (b) most requested runtimes are default values (i.e., 5,50,200, or 400 hours), (c) whether or not a default runtime is requested, over half the jobs have actual runtime less than 20% of the requested value, and (d) overall utilization of allocated processors is approximately 80% whereas overall utilization of allocated memory is closer to 50%.

Some of the O2K workload characteristics that differ from previous workloads (e.g., the CV of job interarrival time equal to 1-2 instead of 2.5-6) are most likely due to measuring the O2K characteristics during periods of stationarity. Other differences (e.g., longer runtimes and larger memory requests) are most likely due to general trends in production parallel systems. Still other differences (e.g., lack of correlation between requested runtime and requested number of processors, or the large number of jobs with very inaccurate requested runtime) may either be due to the trend toward more widespread use of parallel/distributed computing, or may instead be reflective of the O2K usage and environment. Characterization of further modern production parallel/distributed computing workloads are needed to distinguish the trends from the environment-specific results.

Topics for future research include (1) analysis of the workload characteristics of the jobs submitted during the occasional high-load days (i.e., the days that have over 500 arrivals rather than the more typical 350 arrivals), to determine whether such jobs have different characteristics than the jobs submitted during typical weekday peak periods, (2) a more detailed analysis of whether statistical fluctuations in finite sample sizes accounts for the small fluctuations observed among daily and monthly workloads on the O2K, (3) analysis of the characteristics of the jobs that request dedicated time on the NCSA O2K hosts, (4) investigation of the feasibility of more accurate requested runtimes, and the impact of more accurate requested runtimes on the performance of the O2K scheduling policy, and (5) analysis of (future) production workloads on clusters of workstations and for more widely distributed computing resources.

Acknowledgments

This work was partially supported by the NSF PACI Program through a partnership grant from the NCSA. The authors thank the anonymous reviewers for comments that improved the quality of the paper.

References

1. Feitelson, D.G., Nitzberg, B.: Job characteristics of a production parallel scientific workload on the NASA Ames iPSC/860. In: Proc. 1st Workshop on Job Scheduling Strategies for Parallel Processing, Santa Barbara, Lecture Notes in Comp. Sci. Vol. 949, Springer-Verlag (1995) 337–360
2. Hotovy, S.: Workload evolution on the Cornell Theory Center IBM SP2. In: Proc. 2nd Workshop on Job Scheduling Strategies for Parallel Processing, Honolulu, Lecture Notes in Comp. Sci. Vol. 1162, Springer-Verlag (1996) 27–40
3. Feitelson, D.G.: Packing schemes for gang scheduling. In: Proc. 2nd Workshop on Job Scheduling Strategies for Parallel Processing, Honolulu, Lecture Notes in Comp. Sci. Vol. 1162, Springer-Verlag (1996) 89–110
4. Subhlok, J., Gross, T., Suzuoka, T.: Impact of job mix on optimizations for space sharing schedulers. In: Proc. 1996 ACM/IEEE Supercomputing Conf., Pittsburgh (1996)
5. Hotovy, S., Schneider, D., O'Donnell, T.: Analysis of the early workload on the Cornell Theory Center IBM SP2. Technical Report TR234, Cornell Theory Center (1996)
6. Downey, A.B.: Predicting queue times on space-sharing parallel computers. In: Proc. 3rd Workshop on Job Scheduling Strategies for Parallel Processing, Geneva, Lecture Notes in Comp. Sci. Vol. 1291, Springer-Verlag (1997)
7. Feitelson, D.G.: Memory usage in the LANL CM-5 workload. In: Proc. 3rd Workshop on Job Scheduling Strategies for Parallel Processing, Geneva, Lecture Notes in Comp. Sci. Vol. 1291, Springer-Verlag (1997) 78–94
8. Windisch, K., Lo, V., Feitelson, D., Nitzberg, B., Moore, R.: A comparison of workload traces from two production parallel machines. In: Proc. 6th Symp. on the Frontiers of Massively Parallel Computation. (1996) 319–326
9. Jann, J., Pattnaik, P., Franke, H., Wang, F., Skovira, J., Riodan, J.: Modeling of workload in MPPs. In: Proc. 3rd Workshop on Job Scheduling Strategies for Parallel Processing, Geneva, Lecture Notes in Comp. Sci. Vol. 1291, Springer-Verlag (1997)
10. Squillante, M.S., Yao, D.D., Zhang, L.: The impact of job arrival patterns on parallel scheduling. Performance Evaluation Review **26** (1999) 52–59
11. Setia, S.K., Squillante, M.S., Naik, V.K.: The impact of job memory requirements on gang-scheduling performance. Performance Evaluation Review **26** (1999) 30–39

12. Platform Computing Corporation, North York, Canada: LSF Scheduler, (http://www.platform.com/)
13. Maui High Performance Computing Center, Maui, Hawaii: Maui Scheduler, (http://www.mhpcc.edu/maui/)
14. Chiang, S.H., Vernon, M.K.: Production job scheduling for parallel shared memory systems. In: Proc. Int'l. Parallel and Distributed Processing Symp. (IPDPS) 2001, San Francisco (2001)
15. Wan, M., Moore, R., Kremenek, G., Steube, K.: A batch scheduler for the Intel Paragon MPP system with a non-contiguous node allocation algorithm. In: Proc. 2nd Workshop on Job Scheduling Strategies for Parallel Processing, Honolulu, Lecture Notes in Comp. Sci. Vol. 1162, Springer-Verlag (1996) 48–64
16. Downey, A.B., Feitelson, D.G.: The elusive goal of workload characterization. Performance Evaluation Review **26** (1999) 14–29
17. Feitelson, D.G., Mu'alem Weil, A.: Utilization and predictability in scheduling the IBM SP2 with backfilling. In: Proc. 12th Int'l. Parallel Processing Symp., Orlando (1998) 542–546
18. Gibbons, R.: A historical application profiler for use by parallel schedulers. Master's thesis, Univ. of Toronto, Ontario (1997)
19. Allen, A.O.: Probability, Statistics, and Queueing Theory with Computer Science Applications. 2nd edn. Academic Press (1990)
20. Johnson, N.L., Kotz, S., Kemp, A.W.: Univariate Discrete Distributions. 2nd edn. Wiley (1992)
21. MathWorks, Natick, MA.: Matlab, (http://www.mathworks.com/)
22. Gibbons, R.: A historical application profiler for use by parallel schedulers. In: Proc. 3rd Workshop on Job Scheduling Strategies for Parallel Processing, Geneva, Lecture Notes in Comp. Sci. Vol. 1291, Springer-Verlag (1997)
23. Harchol-Balter, M., Downey, A.B.: Exploiting process lifetime distributions for dynamic load balancing. ACM Trans. on Computer Systems **15** (1997) 253–285
24. Harchol-Balter, M.: Task assignment with unknown duration. In: Proc. Int'l. Conf. on Distributed Computing Systems, Taipei, Taiwan (2000)

Metrics for Parallel Job Scheduling
and Their Convergence

Dror G. Feitelson

School of Computer Science and Engineering
The Hebrew University, 91904 Jerusalem, Israel

Abstract. The arrival process of jobs submitted to a parallel system is
bursty, leading to fluctuations in the load at many time scales. In particular, rare events of extreme load may occur. Such events lead to an
increase in the standard deviation of performance metrics, and thus delay
the convergence of simulations used to evaluate the scheduling. Different performance metrics have been proposed in an effort to reduce this
variability, and indeed display different rates of convergence. However,
there is no single metric that outperforms the others under all conditions.
Rather, the convergence of different metrics depends on the system being
studied.

1   Introduction

It has long been recognized that the performance of computer systems depends
not only on their design and implementation, but also on the workload to which
they are subjected. But the results may also depend on the *metric* being used
for the evaluation. In some cases interactions may occur between the metric
and certain characteristics of the system, leading to results that actually depend
on the metric being used [21]. In this paper we concentrate on another effect,
whereby some metrics converge more rapidly than others.

The conventional methodology of simulating computer systems calls for con-
tinuing the simulation until the desired relative precision is achieved with the
desired level of confidence [22]. The relative precision reflects the size of the
confidence interval relative to the estimated value. The confidence level is a statistical statement regarding the probability that the actual value we are trying
to estimate actually resides within the confidence interval. Put together, the
calculation is based on the ratio of the standard deviation of the performance
metric to its mean, multiplied by some factor that takes the statistical properties
of the simulation into account.

The standard deviation measures the divergence of individual measurements
from the mean. Due to the averaging over multiple measurements, it tends to
shrink as the simulation is continued. This leads to the conventional wisdom
that any desired relative precision and level of confidence can be achieved by
running the simulation for long enough. This conventional wisdom has been
challenged lately with the realization that workloads that are characterized by

D.G. Feitelson and L. Rudolph (Eds.): JSSPP 2001, LNCS 2221, pp. 188–205, 2001.

heavy tailed distributions may prevent the simulation from reaching a steady state [4]. But even if the simulation does not diverge, it may take a long time to reach the desired relative precision. Moreover, the relative precision may not improve monotonically as the simulation is extended.

The conventional way to deal with these problems is to employ advanced statistical techniques for variance reduction. An alternative is to use performance metrics that are more robust in the face of a fluctuating workload. Indeed, several different performance metrics have been proposed for the evaluation of parallel job schedulers, with the goal of reducing the susceptibility to being affected by extreme workload conditions. We compare the convergence properties of these metrics, and evaluate the degree to which they achieve this goal.

2   Variability in Workloads

The root cause for convergence problems is variability in the workloads. We therefore start by characterizing the variability in the runtimes and arrivals of workloads observed on different systems, and in models based on them.

2.1   The Distribution of Job Runtimes

We begin by collecting some data about the runtime distributions of jobs executed on large scale parallel supercomputers. This is based on the following logs, which are available on-line from the Parallel Workloads Archive (www.cs.huji.ac.il/labs/parallel/workload/):

LANL-CM5: The Los Alamos National Lab 1024-node CM-5
(201387 jobs, 10/1994 to 9/1996)

SDSC-Par: The San-Diego Supercomputer Center 416-node Intel Paragon
(115595 jobs, 1/1995 to 12/1996)

CTC-SP2: The Cornell theory Center 512-node IBM SP2
(79296 jobs, 7/1996 to 5/1997)

KTH-SP2: The Swedish Royal Institute of Technology 100-node IBM SP2
(28490 jobs, 10/1996 to 8/1997)

SDSC-SP2: The San-Diego Supercomputer Center 128-node IBM SP2
(67665 jobs, 4/1998 to 4/2000)

LANL-O2K: The Los Alamos National Lab 2048-node Origin 2000 cluster
(122233 jobs, 12/1999 to 4/2000)

Whenever the logs contain data about jobs that did not complete execution successfully, this data was discarded.

Regrettably, it is not clear that this data accurately represents real distributions of job runtimes. One problem is that most sites have limits on the allowed length of jobs, and these limits can be pretty low during the working hours of weekdays (e.g. 4 hours or 12 hours). Users that need to run very long jobs therefore resort to making a checkpoint whenever they run out of time, and then

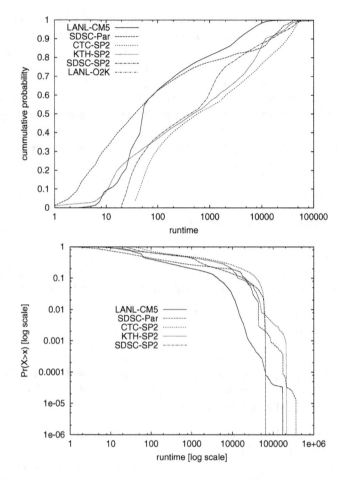

Fig. 1. Cumulative distribution of job runtimes for different systems, and log-log complementary distribution plots.

restarting the job. Such behavior appears as a sequence of short jobs in the data rather than a single long job.

The conjecture that this is the case is strengthened by observations of the cumulative distribution function of the job runtimes on the different systems: they all seem to have about the same upper bound, with little if any tail (Fig. 1). This bound, at about 50000 seconds (14 hours) looks like an administrative constraint based on daily work cycles. To verify the absence of a heavy tail we also create log-log complementary distribution plots (Fig. 1). Again, the evidence is against such tails as there are no linear regions that spans several orders of magnitude. Note that the limited and seemingly non-dispersive distributions we see are in stark contrast to data from interactive workstations, where the tail of the distribution is indeed heavy and follows a Pareto distribution [17,12].

There is no reason to expect such long jobs to be absent on supercomputers —
on the contrary, sans administrative restrictions, long jobs may be expected to
dominate the workload.

Table 1. Statistics of runtimes in different workloads.

system	mean	median	std dev	CV
LANL-CM5	1232.21	62.00	3268.29	2.65
SDSC-Par	4223.77	43.00	10545.10	2.50
CTC-SP2	9580.50	705.00	16388.91	1.71
KTH-SP2	6146.68	583.00	14483.63	2.36
SDSC-SP2	5481.20	521.00	12776.01	2.33
LANL-O2K	1965.26	23.20	7203.51	3.67

Finally, we note that even if the distribution of job runtimes does not conform
to the formal definition of having a heavy tail, it is nonetheless very skewed, and
its mean is much higher than its median (Table 1). As we show below, this
is enough to cause significant problems in the analysis and evaluation of job
scheduling algorithms.

2.2 Workload Models

Several models have been proposed in the literature for the distribution of job
runtimes.

Traditionally the observation that job runtimes have a coefficient of variation
larger than 1 motivated the use of a hyperexponential distribution rather than an
exponential distribution [23]. However, crafting a hyperexponential distribution
so as to match the first two moments of the target distribution may create a
distribution with the wrong shape, resulting in misleading evaluations [16].

Jann et al. have improved on this by using a hyper Erlang distribution and
matching the first three moments of the data in the CTC-SP2 log [15]. In addition, they divided the jobs submitted to a parallel machine according to their
degree of parallelism, and created a separate model for each range of degrees of
parallelism. The result was a model with a large number of parameters (about
40) that closely mimics the original data.

One problem with creating distributions based on moments is that with
skewed distributions the estimation of high-order moments (and even the second
moment) is very sensitive to the values of the few highest values sampled [6].
This has lead to the proposed use of distributions based on direct observations
of the CDF and goodness of fit metrics, in lieu of trying to match the moments.

Feitelson used a two-stage or three-stage hyperexponential distribution,
choosing the parameters so that the CDF "looked right" (that is, similar to that
in various logs) [8]. To accommodate the slight correlation observed between
runtime and the degree of parallelism, the probability of using each exponential
depends on the degree of parallelism.

Downey has proposed the log uniform distribution based on observation of the SDSC-Par log [5]. This uses the smallest number of parameters, unless multiple segments are used. Unlike the other distributions, it has an upper bound on the values it might produce.

Lublin proposed a hyper Gamma distribution, based on the CTC-SP2, KTH-SP2, and SDSC-Par logs [19]. This distribution requires 5 parameters: two for each Gamma distribution, and the probability of selecting one or the other. This probability is modified based on the degree of parallelism as was done by Feitelson. The parameters of the Gamma distributions were selected using an Expectation-Maximization algorithm and goodness of fit metrics.

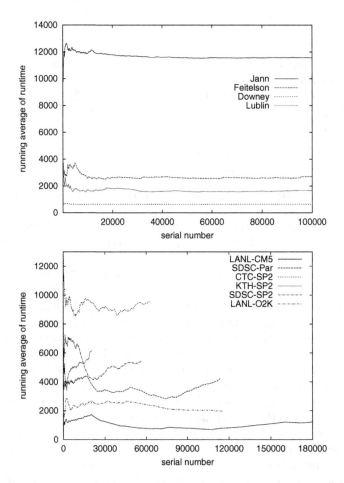

Fig. 2. Running average of mean job runtime from different models. Data for logs is shown for comparison.

Table 2. Statistics of runtimes in different models.

model	mean	median	std dev	CV
Jann	11547.19	794.12	18616.14	1.61
Feitelson	2700.89	81.11	8786.63	3.25
Downey	638.54	18.84	2107.36	3.30
Lublin	1668.34	18.00	6824.61	4.09

Programs for generating workloads according to these models are available on-line at the Parallel Workloads Archive. Generating such workloads and calculating their statistics and running average leads to the results shown in Fig. 2 and Table 2. The models are much more stable than any of the real workloads, and quickly converge to a stable average runtime. However, they are just as skewed as the original workloads.

2.3 Burstiness of Arrivals

The arrival process of parallel jobs has received much less analysis than the distribution of job runtimes. Most studies simply make the assumption of a Poisson process, with exponentially distributed interarrival times. A notable exception is the Jann model, which creates a model of interarrival times that parallels the model of run times [15].

Burstiness, or self-similarity, in the arrival process can lead to large fluctuations in load, just like fat-tailed runtime distributions. To check the degree of burstiness we first plot the arrival process of 5 logs, using aggregation in 10-minute buckets. The results are shown in Fig. 3, and are indeed bursty. Similar results are observed for the arrival of processes.

In order to test for self-similarity, we use the eyeball method of plotting the same data using different levels of aggregation. The righthand side of Fig. 3 shows results at 5 decimal orders of magnitude for the SDSC-Par log, and seems to indicate that self-similarity is present. Somewhat surprisingly, job arrivals even show some burstiness at the very low scale of 36 seconds. Daily cycles are barely discernible in the middle plot.

Rather than focusing on the phenomenon of self similarity, we are interested in the distributions describing the arrival process. Self similarity and burstiness seem to imply that there is a non-negligible probability that many jobs will arrive practically at once. In other words, we expect the distribution of the number of jobs (or processes) arriving per unit time to have a fat tail. To check this, we plot log-log complementary distribution plots of this distribution, at different levels of aggregation. This means, in essence, that different time units are used (e.g. jobs per 6 minutes, jobs per hour, and jobs per 10 hours). Crovella et al. have shown that with heavy-tailed distributions these plots should be linear with the same slope, whereas if the tail is not heavy (and the variance is finite) the slope should become steeper with higher levels of aggregation, and the plots will seem to converge [3]. Our results are mixed (Fig. 4). For some workloads the plots do indeed seem to be parallel (albeit over a smaller scale than for the web traffic

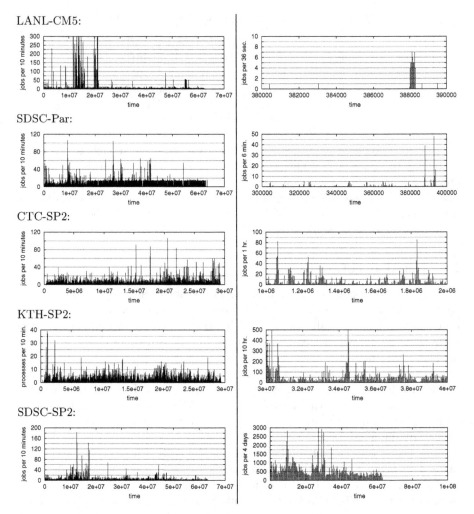

Fig. 3. Left: arrival pattern of jobs for five logs. Right: Burstiness of arrivals to SDSC-Par at different time scales.

data of [3]). For others they seem to converge. In conclusion, a heavy-tailed distribution cannot be postulated, despite the fact that the arrival process is bursty.

3   The Effect of Workload on Convergence

The skewed nature of dispersive distributions and the non-negligible probability of sampling very high values have significant implications on systems. For example, Harchol-Balter and Downey have shown that when the distribution of job runtimes has a heavy tail, migration for load balancing can be very beneficial

LANL-CM5:   SDSC-Par: CTC-SP2:

KTH-SP2:   SDSC-SP2

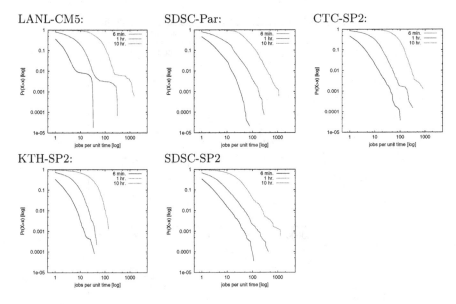

Fig. 4. Log-log complementary distribution plots of job arrivals with different aggregation levels.

[12]. This is based on the fact that a small number of jobs use more CPU time than all the others; the benefits come from identifying these jobs and migrating only them. This contradicts evaluations based on a more moderate distribution, in which migration did not lead to significant benefits [7]. In another work, Harchol-Balter et al. have shown that when job sizes are heavy tailed it is beneficial to distribute jobs among servers according to size, thus effectively serving the short jobs on a dedicated set of servers that are unaffected by the long jobs from the tail of the distribution [11]. But what happens with the bounded runtime distribution observed on parallel systems?

As an initial check of how simulations of parallel systems behave, we simulated two versions of backfilling when operating on the Jann workload[1]. The load was adjusted to 0.75 by modifying all interarrival times by a constant factor. The algorithms are EASY backfilling, in which short jobs are allowed to move ahead provided they do not delay the first job in the queue [18], and a more conservative version of backfilling, in which jobs move forward provided they do not delay any previously scheduled job [21]. The metric used was the mean response time. Confidence intervals are calculated using the batch means method [14], with a batch size of 5000 job completions (matching the recommendation of MacDougall for a CV larger than 1 and high load [20]).

---

[1] This model has a problem in that the program occasionally does not manage to solve the equations used for the distributions, and prints an error message. This happened 20 times when generating a workload of 1000000 jobs, and was ignored. in an additional 43 jobs the program created an infinite runtime. These jobs were simply replaced by a clone of the previous job.

196   D.G. Feitelson

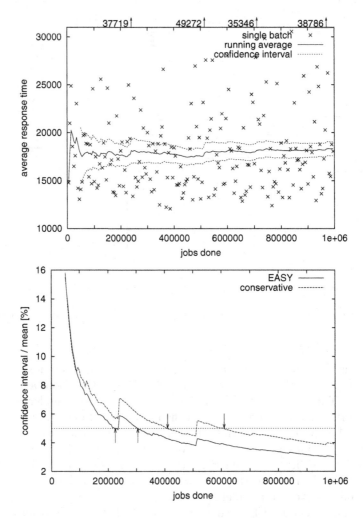

Fig. 5. Backfilling using the Jann model as the workload. Top: convergence of mean response time for conservative backfilling. Bottom: behavior of the confidence interval.

The results are shown in Fig. 5. While the mean response time does seem to converge, there are relatively big jerks even after half a million job terminations. And it is not clear that additional jerks will not occur even after a million jobs were simulated. Note that this represents more or less the whole lifetime of a large-scale parallel machine. Thus it is not clear what such simulation results mean with relation to the use of new machines.

The 95% confidence interval suffers from similar jerks. As a result the size of the confidence interval is not monotonically decreasing. Using the common methodology of terminating the simulation when the confidence interval becomes smaller than say 5% of the mean [22] would lead to different results for the first

Table 3. Mean response time selected by confidence interval criteria.

	1st 5% xing	2nd 5% xing	million
EASY	16427.23	16774.40	16865.80
cons	17727.68	18154.75	18313.90

and second times such a crossing is made, though the "final" result — after simulating 1000000 jobs — is within the confidence interval in both cases (Tab. 3). However, there are points in the simulation (e.g. after the termination of 475000 jobs) where the confidence interval is smaller than 5% of the mean, and does *not* contain the final value obtained after simulating a million jobs. A detailed coverage analysis is needed to determine whether this occurs more or less than 95% of the time, but it is troubling that it was so easy to find an example.

We note in passing that warmup is not a problem in our setting. The problem leading to the variable and jerky simulation results shown above is not one of initialization, but a problem of real variability and burstiness in the workload, due to its dispersive distributions. Indeed, Crovella and Lipsky have suggested that such situations be handled by explicitly noting the time horizon for which the results are valid [4]. Another approach is to use the techniques of rare event simulation [13]. We leave the detailed study of such optimizations in the context of scheduling with dispersive distributions for future research.

4 Performance Metrics for Job Scheduling

As we saw above, it may take the average response time a very long time to converge when the simulated job stream being scheduled is based on dispersive distributions. Do other metrics converge more quickly? And indeed, what is the most meaningful metric?

The first metric we deal with is the response time. We define "response time" to mean the total wallclock time from the instant at which the job is submitted to the system, until it finishes its run. This can be divided into two components: the running time T_r, during which the job is actually running in parallel on multiple processing nodes, and the waiting time T_w, in which it is waiting to be scheduled or for some event such as I/O. The waiting time itself can also be used as a metric, based on the assumption that T_r does not depend on the scheduling.

Obviously, a lower bound on the response time of a given job is its running time. As the runtimes of jobs have a very large variance, so must the response time. It has therefore been suggested that a better metric may be the slowdown (also called "expansion factor"), which is the response time normalized by the running time:

$$\text{slowdown} = \frac{T_w + T_r}{T_r}$$

Thus if a job takes twice as long to run due to system load, it suffers from a slowdown factor of 2, etc. This is expected to reduce the extreme values associated with very long jobs, because even if a week-long job is delayed for a whole year the slowdown is only a factor of 50. Moreover, slowdown is widely perceived as better matching user expectations that a job's response time will be proportional to its running time. Indeed, 30 years ago Brinch Hansen already suggested that slowdowns be used to prioritize jobs for scheduling [1].

The problem with the slowdown metric is that it over-emphasizes the importance of very short jobs. For example, a job taking 100 ms that is delayed for 10 minutes suffers from a slowdown of 6000, whereas a 10-second job delayed by the same 10 minutes has a slowdown of only 60. From a user's perspective, both are probably annoying to similar degrees, but the slowdown metric gives the shorter job an extremely high score, because the running time appears in the denominator.

To avoid such effects, Feitelson et al. have suggested the "bounded-slowdown" metric [9]. The difference is that for short jobs, this measures the slowdown relative to some "interactive threshold", rather than relative to the actual runtime. Denoting this threshold by τ, the definition is

$$\text{bounded-slowdown} = \max\left\{\frac{T_w + T_r}{\max\{T_r, \tau\}}, 1\right\}$$

The behavior of this metric obviously depends on the choice of τ. In the simulations below, we check three values: 10 seconds, one minute, and 10 minutes.

The fact that the definition of slowdown (and bounded slowdown) is based on a job's running time leads to new problems. On one hand, it makes practically equivalent jobs look different. On the other hand, it encourages the system to make the jobs run longer!

Zotkin and Keleher have noted that jobs that do the same amount of work with the same response time may lead to different slowdown results due to their shape (that is, ratio of processors to time). For example, a job that runs immediately on one processor for 100 seconds has a slowdown of 1, whereas a job that is delayed for 90 seconds and then runs for an additional 10 seconds on 10 processors (thus utilizing the same 100 processor-seconds as the first job, and finishing with the same 100 seconds response time) has a slowdown of 10. This lead them to suggest a new metric, which we shall call "per-processor slowdown" [24]:

$$\text{pp-slowdown} = \max\left\{\frac{T_w + T_r}{P \cdot \max\{T_r, \tau\}}, 1\right\}$$

where P is the number of processors used by the job. The name derives from the fact that this has the units of $1/P$, and divides the original bounded slowdown by the number of processors used; it can be understood as a further normalization of the slowdown metric, for the putative case where the job runs on a single processor. In terms of the above example, this normalizes the delayed 10-processor job to the undelayed single-processor job, so both now have a pp-slowdown of 1.

A possible counter argument is that if a user makes the effort to parallelize a program, and runs it on more processors, he actually expects it to finish faster. Therefore a parallel program that is delayed is not equivalent to a serial one that runs immediately. But what about cases in which the number of processors used is chosen automatically by the scheduler? Cirne and Berman observe that in this scenario the system can improve its slowdown metric by choosing to use fewer processors: the job will then probably start running sooner, and even if not, it will run for longer. As a result, the ratio of the response time to the running time will be smaller, even if the response time itself is larger [2].

Their solution to this problem is to do away with the use of slowdowns altogether, and stick with response times. They then go on to suggest the use of a geometric mean rather than an arithmetic mean to calculate the average response time, with the goal of reducing the effect of excessively long jobs. Notably, a similar argument is used to justify the use of a geometric mean in calculating the score of SPEC benchmarks. However, it has also been noted that the geometric mean may order results differently from the sum of the represented times [10]. In other words, given two sets of measurement A and B, it is possible that the sum of the measurements in A is smaller, but their geometric mean is larger. Obviously, the arithmetic mean does not suffer from such inversions.

5   Convergence Results for Different Metrics

To compare the behavior of the different metrics, we ran long simulations as in Section 3, and observe the way in which the different metrics converge. This simulation again uses EASY and conservative backfilling on one million jobs generated according to the Jann model.

The results are shown in Fig. 6. The most important observation from these graphs does not concern the convergence, but rather the ranking produced by the different metrics: the response time and wait time metrics give lower (better) scores to EASY, whereas slowdown-based metrics give lower (better) scores to conservative. Using a geometric mean of response times is in the middle: it asserts that they are both the same. The interactions between the scheduling algorithms and the workloads that lead to these divergent results are interesting in their own right [21], but lie beyond the scope of the current paper; here we are interested in the convergence properties.

To the naked eye, all the graphs seem to be jerky in similar degrees. The slowdown graph is distinguished by the fact that the jerks are in different places than in other graphs. For slowdown they result from short jobs that get delayed, whereas for bounded slowdown they result from long jobs (these jerks actually also appear in the slowdown curve, but are less prominent there). A somewhat surprising result is that the shape of the graphs for bounded slowdown are practically identical to that of the response time! The explanation is that as the value of τ grows larger, more and more jobs are covered — in the Jann model, specifically, about 48% of the jobs are shorter than 10 minutes. For these jobs, the definition of bounded slowdown is just the response time divided by a constant. As these are the higher values, they dominate the shape of the curve. Moreover, comparison with the graph for wait time shows that the wait time is indeed the dominant factor in these cases.

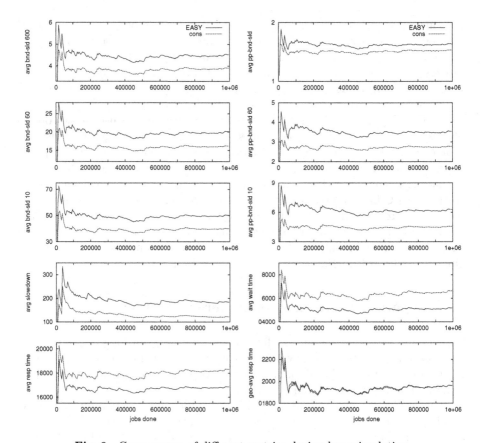

Fig. 6. Convergence of different metrics during long simulation.

To quantify the rate of convergence, we plot the size of the confidence intervals calculated using the batch means approach. The results for the SDSC-SP2 and CTC-SP2 logs are shown in Fig. 7. It seems that the slowest metrics to converge are either the slowdown or the geometric mean of response times. The arithmetic mean converges rather quickly. Bounded slowdown is in the middle, and is not very sensitive to the threshold value. Per-processor slowdown is much more sensitive, and provides better convergence as the threshold value is increased. It should be stressed that the differences are very significant: for some metrics, the confidence interval size is more than 10% of the mean even after the simulation of a million jobs. For many it would require unrealistically long simulations to get within 5% of the mean.

Finally, we note that there is another variable that may influence the convergence: the scheduling algorithm itself. Specifically, part of the problem with queue-based scheduling algorithms such as backfilling is that jobs get held up in the queue. They then tend to pile up, leading to jerks in the various metrics. But with time slicing, jobs don't affect each other as much, and as a result

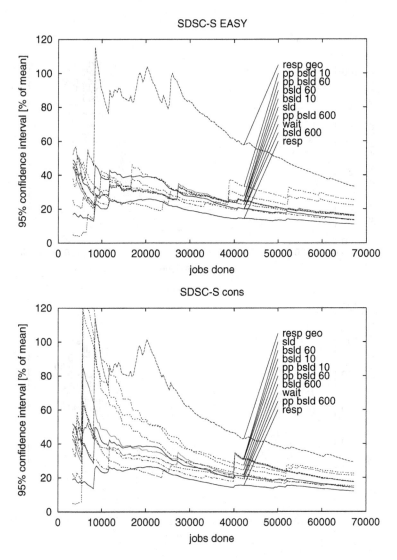

Fig. 7. Convergence of different metrics for real logs (a): SDSC-SP2.

smoother convergence can be expected. To check this conjecture, we used the
same SDSC-SP2 log as an input to a simulation of gang scheduling, with two
different time quanta: one minute and 10 minutes. The results are shown in
Fig. 8. With short time quanta, this is indeed similar to processor sharing, and
leads to smoother convergence. In addition, the normalization inherent in the
slowdown-based schemes causes them to converge significantly faster than the
un-normalized response-time based metrics. However, the absolute size of the

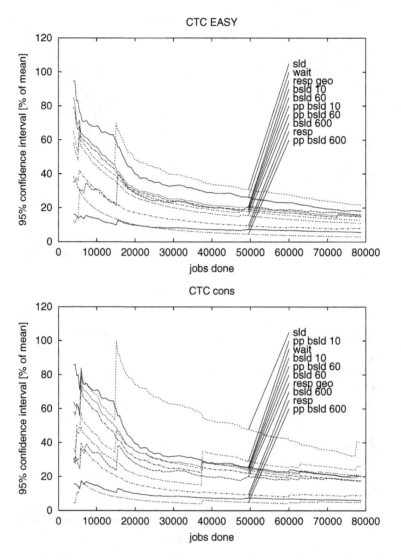

Fig. 7. (Cont.) Convergence of different metrics for real logs (b): CTC-SP2.

confidence interval is not any smaller than for the non-preemptive backfilling schemes. Things improve somewhat for the longer time quantum.

6 Conclusions

Contrary to common belief, the distribution of job runtimes on parallel super-computers is not fat tailed, possibly due to the widespread use of administrative limitations. However, the distribution of load on these machines is indeed fat-

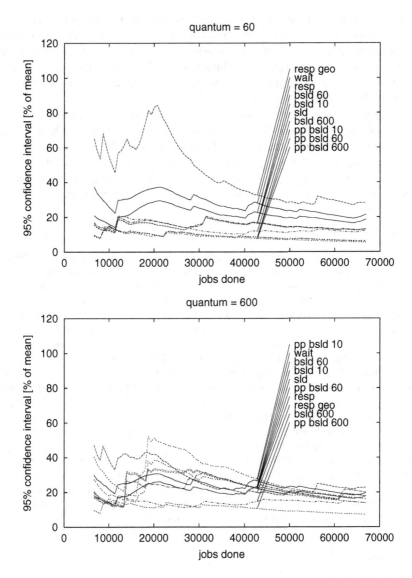

Fig. 8. Convergence of different metrics for gang scheduling of the SDSC-SP2 log.

tailed (and possibly even heavy tailed) due to the burstiness of arrivals. This means that occasionally the load becomes excessively high, enough to counterweigh the lower load between high-load events.

The existence of high-load events means that it is hard or impossible to converge to a stable result. The rate of convergence depends on the metrics being used, and on the nature of the system. For example, with non-preemptive scheduling it seems that using the well-known response-time metric leads to faster convergence, whereas with preemptive scheduling it seems that slowdown-based metrics converge faster. Plain slowdown displays very slow convergence in some cases, indicating that some version of bounded slowdown is preferable; within this family of metrics, high thresholds lead to faster convergence. As for using the geometric mean instead of the arithmetic mean of response times, this too suffers from slow convergence in some cases.

This paper has served to showcase the difficulties resulting from the complexities of real workloads. Much work remains to be done, both in terms of further characterization, analysis, and modeling of workloads, and in terms of understanding their effects on system performance. Of particular interest is the identification and characterization of cases in which the relative performance of different systems depends on the workloads and the metrics being used.

Acknowledgements

This research was supported by the Israel Science Foundation founded by the Israel Academy of Sciences and Humanities. This research could not be conducted without the wealth of data available on-line at the Parallel Workloads Archive. The following acknowledgements are from there. The workload log from the LANL CM-5 was graciously provided by Curt Canada, who also helped with background information and interpretation. The workload log from the SDSC Paragon was graciously provided by Reagan Moore and Allen Downey, who also helped with background information and interpretation. The workload log from the CTC SP2 was graciously provided by the Cornell Theory Center, a high-performance computing center at Cornell University, Ithaca, New York, USA. The workload log from the KTH SP2 was graciously provided by Lars Malinowsky, who also helped with background information and interpretation. The workload log from the SDSC SP2 was graciously provided by Victor Hazlewood of the HPC Systems group of the San Diego Supercomputer Center (SDSC), which is the leading-edge site of the National Partnership for Advanced Computational Infrastructure (NPACI), and is available from the NPACI JOBLOG repository at http://joblog.npaci.edu. The workload log from the LANL Origin 2000 was graciously provided by Fabrizio Petrini, who also helped with background information and interpretation. Thanks are also due to Joefon Jann, Allen Downey, and Uri Lublin for providing C programs that implement their models.

References

1. P. Brinch Hansen, "An analysis of response ratio scheduling". In IFIP Congress, Ljubljana, pp. TA-3 150–154, Aug 1971.
2. W. Cirne and F. Berman, "Adaptive selection of partition size for supercomputer requests". In Job Scheduling Strategies for Parallel Processing, D. G. Feitelson and L. Rudolph (eds.), pp. 187–207, Springer Verlag, 2000. Lect. Notes Comput. Sci. vol. 1911.
3. M. E. Crovella and A. Bestavros, "Self-similarity in world wide web traffic: evidence and possible causes". In SIGMETRICS Conf. Measurement & Modeling of Comput. Syst., pp. 160–169, May 1996.
4. M. E. Crovella and L. Lipsky, "Long-lasting transient conditions in simulations with heavy-tailed workloads". In Winter Simulation conf., Dec 1997.

5. A. B. Downey, "*A parallel workload model and its implications for processor allocation*". In 6th *Intl. Symp. High Performance Distributed Comput.*, Aug 1997.

6. A. B. Downey and D. G. Feitelson, "*The elusive goal of workload characterization*". *Performance Evaluation Rev.* **26(4)**, pp. 14–29, Mar 1999.

7. D. L. Eager, E. D. Lazowska, and J. Zahorjan, "*The limited performance benefits of migrating active processes for load sharing*". In *SIGMETRICS Conf. Measurement & Modeling of Comput. Syst.*, pp. 63–72, May 1988.

8. D. G. Feitelson, "*Packing schemes for gang scheduling*". In *Job Scheduling Strategies for Parallel Processing*, D. G. Feitelson and L. Rudolph (eds.), pp. 89–110, Springer-Verlag, 1996. Lect. Notes Comput. Sci. vol. 1162.

9. D. G. Feitelson, L. Rudolph, U. Schwiegelshohn, K. C. Sevcik, and P. Wong, "*Theory and practice in parallel job scheduling*". In *Job Scheduling Strategies for Parallel Processing*, D. G. Feitelson and L. Rudolph (eds.), pp. 1–34, Springer Verlag, 1997. Lect. Notes Comput. Sci. vol. 1291.

10. R. Giladi and N. Ahituv, "*SPEC as a performance evaluation measure*". *Computer* **28(8)**, pp. 33–42, Aug 1995.

11. M. Harchol-Balter, M. E. Crovella, and C. D. Murta, "*On choosing a task assignment policy for a distributed server system*". In *Computer Performance Evaluation*, R. Puigjaner, N. Savino, and B. Serra (eds.), pp. 231–242, Springer-Verlag, 1998.

12. M. Harchol-Balter and A. B. Downey, "*Exploiting process lifetime distributions for dynamic load balancing*". *ACM Trans. Comput. Syst.* **15(3)**, pp. 253–285, Aug 1997.

13. P. Heidelberger, "*Fast simulation of rare events in queueing and reliability models*". *ACM Trans. Modeling & Comput. Simulation* **5(1)**, pp. 43–85, Jan 1995.

14. R. Jain, *The Art of Computer Systems Performance Analysis*. John Wiley & Sons, 1991.

15. J. Jann, P. Pattnaik, H. Franke, F. Wang, J. Skovira, and J. Riodan, "*Modeling of workload in MPPs*". In *Job Scheduling Strategies for Parallel Processing*, D. G. Feitelson and L. Rudolph (eds.), pp. 95–116, Springer Verlag, 1997. Lect. Notes Comput. Sci. vol. 1291.

16. E. D. Lazowska, "*The use of percentiles in modeling CPU service time distributions*". In *Computer Performance*, K. M. Chandy and M. Reiser (eds.), pp. 53–66, North-Holland, 1977.

17. W. E. Leland and T. J. Ott, "*Load-balancing heuristics and process behavior*". In *SIGMETRICS Conf. Measurement & Modeling of Comput. Syst.*, pp. 54–69, 1986.

18. D. Lifka, "*The ANL/IBM SP scheduling system*". In *Job Scheduling Strategies for Parallel Processing*, D. G. Feitelson and L. Rudolph (eds.), pp. 295–303, Springer-Verlag, 1995. Lect. Notes Comput. Sci. vol. 949.

19. U. Lublin, *A Workload Model for Parallel Computer Systems*. Master's thesis, Hebrew University, 1999. (In Hebrew).

20. M. H. MacDougall, *Simulating Computer Systems: Techniques and Tools*. MIT Press, 1987.

21. A. W. Mu'alem and D. G. Feitelson, "*Utilization, predictability, workloads, and user runtime estimates in scheduling the IBM SP2 with backfilling*". *IEEE Trans. Parallel & Distributed Syst.* **12(6)**, pp. 529–543, Jun 2001.

22. K. Pawlikowski, "*Steady-state simulation of queueing processes: a survey of problems and solutions*". *ACM Comput. Surv.* **22(2)**, pp. 123–170, Jun 1990.

23. R. F. Rosin, "*Determining a computing center environment*". *Comm. ACM* **8(7)**, pp. 465–468, Jul 1965.

24. D. Zotkin and P. J. Keleher, "*Job-length estimation and performance in backfilling schedulers*". In 8th *Intl. Symp. High Performance Distributed Comput.*, Aug 1999.

Author Index

Agrawal, M., 11

Bansal, N., 11
Brent, R.P., 103
Bucur, A.I.D., 66

Chiang, S.H., 159
Clement, M., 87
Crovella, M.E., 1

Devadas, S., 116

Epema, D.H.J., 66

Feitelson, D.G., 188
Franke, H., 133

Giné, F., 41

Harchol-Balter, M., 11
Hernández, P., 41

Jackson, D., 87
Jette, M.A., 21

Luque, E., 41

Moreira, J.E., 133

Rudolph, L., 116

Schroeder, B., 11
Sivasubramaniam, A., 133
Snell, Q., 87
Solsona, F., 41
Suh, G.E., 116

Vernon, M.K., 159

Yoo, A.B., 21

Zhang, Y., 133
Zhou, B.B., 103

Lecture Notes in Computer Science

For information about Vols. 1–2135
please contact your bookseller or Springer-Verlag

Vol. 2067: F. Cassez, C. Jard, B. Rozoy, M.D. Ryan (Eds.), Modeling and Verification of Parallel Processes. Proceedings, 2000. X, 223 pages. 2001.

Vol. 2136: J. Sgall, A. Pultr, P. Kolman (Eds.), Mathematical Foundations of Computer Science 2001. Proceedings, 2001. XII, 716 pages. 2001.

Vol. 2138: R. Freivalds (Ed.), Fundamentals of Computation Theory. Proceedings, 2001. XIII, 542 pages. 2001.

Vol. 2139: J. Kilian (Ed.), Advances in Cryptology – CRYPTO 2001. Proceedings, 2001. XI, 599 pages. 2001.

Vol. 2140: I. Attali, T. Jensen (Eds.), Java on Smart Cards: Programming and Security. Proceedings, 2001. VIII, 255 pages. 2001.

Vol. 2141: G.S. Brodal, D. Frigioni, A. Marchetti-Spaccamela (Eds.), Algorithm Engineering. Proceedings, 2001. X, 199 pages. 2001.

Vol. 2142: L. Fribourg (Ed.), Computer Science Logic. Proceedings, 2001. XII, 615 pages. 2001.

Vol. 2143: S. Benferhat, P. Besnard (Eds.), Symbolic and Quantitative Approaches to Reasoning with Uncertainty. Proceedings, 2001. XIV, 818 pages. 2001. (Subseries LNAI).

Vol. 2144: T. Margaria, T. Melham (Eds.), Correct Hardware Design and Verification Methods. Proceedings, 2001. XII, 482 pages. 2001.

Vol. 2145: M. Leyton, A Generative Theory of Shape. XVI, 554 pages. 2001.

Vol. 2146: J.H. Silverman (Eds.), Cryptography and Lattices. Proceedings, 2001. VII, 219 pages. 2001.

Vol. 2147: G. Brebner, R. Woods (Eds.), Field-Programmable Logic and Applications. Proceedings, 2001. XV, 665 pages. 2001.

Vol. 2149: O. Gascuel, B.M.E. Moret (Eds.), Algorithms in Bioinformatics. Proceedings, 2001. X, 307 pages. 2001.

Vol. 2150: R. Sakellariou, J. Keane, J. Gurd, L. Freeman (Eds.), Euro-Par 2001 Parallel Processing. Proceedings, 2001. XXX, 943 pages. 2001.

Vol. 2151: A. Caplinskas, J. Eder (Eds.), Advances in Databases and Information Systems. Proceedings, 2001. XIII, 381 pages. 2001.

Vol. 2152: R.J. Boulton, P.B. Jackson (Eds.), Theorem Proving in Higher Order Logics. Proceedings, 2001. X, 395 pages. 2001.

Vol. 2153: A.L. Buchsbaum, J. Snoeyink (Eds.), Algorithm Engineering and Experimentation. Proceedings, 2001. VIII, 231 pages. 2001.

Vol. 2154: K.G. Larsen, M. Nielsen (Eds.), CONCUR 2001 – Concurrency Theory. Proceedings, 2001. XI, 583 pages. 2001.

Vol. 2155: H. Bunt, R.-J. Beun (Eds.), Cooperative Multimodal Communication. Proceedings, 1998. VIII, 251 pages. 2001. (Subseries LNAI).

Vol. 2156: M.I. Smirnov, J. Crowcroft, J. Roberts, F.Boavida (Eds.), Quality of Future Internet Services. Proceedings, 2001. XI, 333 pages. 2001.

Vol. 2157: C. Rouveirol, M. Sebag (Eds.), Inductive Logic Programming. Proceedings, 2001. X, 261 pages. 2001. (Subseries LNAI).

Vol. 2158: D. Shepherd, J. Finney, L. Mathy, N. Race (Eds.), Interactive Distributed Multimedia Systems. Proceedings, 2001. XIII, 258 pages. 2001.

Vol. 2159: J. Kelemen, P. Sosík (Eds.), Advances in Artificial Life. Proceedings, 2001. XIX, 724 pages. 2001. (Subseries LNAI).

Vol. 2161: F. Meyer auf der Heide (Ed.), Algorithms – ESA 2001. Proceedings, 2001. XII, 538 pages. 2001.

Vol. 2162: Ç. K. Koç, D. Naccache, C. Paar (Eds.), Cryptographic Hardware and Embedded Systems – CHES 2001. Proceedings, 2001. XIV, 411 pages. 2001.

Vol. 2163: P. Constantopoulos, I.T. Sølvberg (Eds.), Research and Advanced Technology for Digital Libraries. Proceedings, 2001. XII, 462 pages. 2001.

Vol. 2164: S. Pierre, R. Glitho (Eds.), Mobile Agents for Telecommunication Applications. Proceedings, 2001. XI, 292 pages. 2001.

Vol. 2165: L. de Alfaro, S. Gilmore (Eds.), Process Algebra and Probabilistic Methods. Proceedings, 2001. XII, 217 pages. 2001.

Vol. 2166: V. Matoušek, P. Mautner, R. Mouček, K. Taušer (Eds.), Text, Speech and Dialogue. Proceedings, 2001. XIII, 452 pages. 2001. (Subseries LNAI).

Vol. 2167: L. De Raedt, P. Flach (Eds.), Machine Learning: ECML 2001. Proceedings, 2001. XVII, 618 pages. 2001. (Subseries LNAI).

Vol. 2168: L. De Raedt, A. Siebes (Eds.), Principles of Data Mining and Knowledge Discovery. Proceedings, 2001. XVII, 510 pages. 2001. (Subseries LNAI).

Vol. 2169: M. Jaedicke, New Concepts for Parallel Object-Relational Query Processing. XI, 161 pages. 2001.

Vol. 2170: S. Palazzo (Ed.), Evolutionary Trends of the Internet. Proceedings, 2001. XIII, 722 pages. 2001.

Vol. 2172: C. Batini, F. Giunchiglia, P. Giorgini, M. Mecella (Eds.), Cooperative Information Systems. Proceedings, 2001. XI, 450 pages. 2001.

Vol. 2173: T. Eiter, W. Faber, M. Truszczynski (Eds.), Logic Programming and Nonmonotonic Reasoning. Proceedings, 2001. XI, 444 pages. 2001. (Subseries LNAI).

Vol. 2174: F. Baader, G. Brewka, T. Eiter (Eds.), KI 2001: Advances in Artificial Intelligence. Proceedings, 2001. XIII, 471 pages. 2001. (Subseries LNAI).

Vol. 2175: F. Esposito (Ed.), AI*IA 2001: Advances in Artificial Intelligence. Proceedings, 2001. XII, 396 pages. 2001. (Subseries LNAI).

Vol. 2176: K.-D. Althoff, R.L. Feldmann, W. Müller (Eds.), Advances in Learning Software Organizations. Proceedings, 2001. XI, 241 pages. 2001.

Vol. 2177: G. Butler, S. Jarzabek (Eds.), Generative and Component-Based Software Engineering. Proceedings, 2001. X, 203 pages. 2001.

Vol. 2180: J. Welch (Ed.), Distributed Computing. Proceedings, 2001. X, 343 pages. 2001.

Vol. 2181: C. Y. Westort (Ed.), Digital Earth Moving. Proceedings, 2001. XII, 117 pages. 2001.

Vol. 2182: M. Klusch, F. Zambonelli (Eds.), Cooperative Information Agents V. Proceedings, 2001. XII, 288 pages. 2001. (Subseries LNAI).

Vol. 2183: R. Kahle, P. Schroeder-Heister, R. Stärk (Eds.), Proof Theory in Computer Science. Proceedings, 2001. IX, 239 pages. 2001.

Vol. 2184: M. Tucci (Ed.), Multimedia Databases and Image Communication. Proceedings, 2001. X, 225 pages. 2001.

Vol. 2185: M. Gogolla, C. Kobryn (Eds.), «UML» 2001 – The Unified Modeling Language. Proceedings, 2001. XIV, 510 pages. 2001.

Vol. 2186: J. Bosch (Ed.), Generative and Component-Based Software Engineering. Proceedings, 2001. VIII, 177 pages. 2001.

Vol. 2187: U. Voges (Ed.), Computer Safety, Reliability and Security. Proceedings, 2001. XVI, 249 pages. 2001.

Vol. 2188: F. Bomarius, S. Komi-Sirviö (Eds.), Product Focused Software Process Improvement. Proceedings, 2001. XI, 382 pages. 2001.

Vol. 2189: F. Hoffmann, D.J. Hand, N. Adams, D. Fisher, G. Guimaraes (Eds.), Advances in Intelligent Data Analysis. Proceedings, 2001. XII, 384 pages. 2001.

Vol. 2190: A. de Antonio, R. Aylett, D. Ballin (Eds.), Intelligent Virtual Agents. Proceedings, 2001. VIII, 245 pages. 2001. (Subseries LNAI).

Vol. 2191: B. Radig, S. Florczyk (Eds.), Pattern Recognition. Proceedings, 2001. XVI, 452 pages. 2001.

Vol. 2192: A. Yonezawa, S. Matsuoka (Eds.), Metalevel Architectures and Separation of Crosscutting Concerns. Proceedings, 2001. XI, 283 pages. 2001.

Vol. 2193: F. Casati, D. Georgakopoulos, M.-C. Shan (Eds.), Technologies for E-Services. Proceedings, 2001. X, 213 pages. 2001.

Vol. 2194: A.K. Datta, T. Herman (Eds.), Self-Stabilizing Systems. Proceedings, 2001. VII, 229 pages. 2001.

Vol. 2195: H.-Y. Shum, M. Liao, S.-F. Chang (Eds.), Advances in Multimedia Information Processing – PCM 2001. Proceedings, 2001. XX, 1149 pages. 2001.

Vol. 2196: W. Taha (Ed.), Semantics, Applications, and Implementation of Program Generation. Proceedings, 2001. X, 219 pages. 2001.

Vol. 2197: O. Balet, G. Subsol, P. Torguet (Eds.), Virtual Storytelling. Proceedings, 2001. XI, 213 pages. 2001.

Vol. 2198: N. Zhong, Y. Yao, J. Liu, S. Ohsuga (Eds.), Web Intelligence: Research and Development. Proceedings, 2001. XVI, 615 pages. 2001. (Subseries LNAI).

Vol. 2199: J. Crespo, V. Maojo, F. Martin (Eds.), Medical Data Analysis. Proceedings, 2001. X, 311 pages. 2001.

Vol. 2200: G.I. Davida, Y. Frankel (Eds.), Information Security. Proceedings, 2001. XIII, 554 pages. 2001.

Vol. 2201: G.D. Abowd, B. Brumitt, S. Shafer (Eds.), Ubicomp 2001: Ubiquitous Computing. Proceedings, 2001. XIII, 372 pages. 2001.

Vol. 2202: A. Restivo, S. Ronchi Della Rocca, L. Roversi (Eds.), Theoretical Computer Science. Proceedings, 2001. XI, 440 pages. 2001.

Vol. 2204: A. Brandstädt, V.B. Le (Eds.), Graph-Theoretic Concepts in Computer Science. Proceedings, 2001. X, 329 pages. 2001.

Vol. 2205: D.R. Montello (Ed.), Spatial Information Theory. Proceedings, 2001. XIV, 503 pages. 2001.

Vol. 2206: B. Reusch (Ed.), Computational Intelligence. Proceedings, 2001. XVII, 1003 pages. 2001.

Vol. 2207: I.W. Marshall, S. Nettles, N. Wakamiya (Eds.), Active Networks. Proceedings, 2001. IX, 165 pages. 2001.

Vol. 2208: W.J. Niessen, M.A. Viergever (Eds.), Medical Image Computing and Computer-Assisted Intervention – MICCAI 2001. Proceedings, 2001. XXXV, 1446 pages. 2001.

Vol. 2209: W. Jonker (Ed.), Databases in Telecommunications II. Proceedings, 2001. VII, 179 pages. 2001.

Vol. 2210: Y. Liu, K. Tanaka, M. Iwata, T. Higuchi, M. Yasunaga (Eds.), Evolvable Systems: From Biology to Hardware. Proceedings, 2001. XI, 341 pages. 2001.

Vol. 2211: T.A. Henzinger, C.M. Kirsch (Eds.), Embedded Software. Proceedings, 2001. IX, 504 pages. 2001.

Vol. 2212: W. Lee, L. Mé, A. Wespi (Eds.), Recent Advances in Intrusion Detection. Proceedings, 2001. X, 205 pages. 2001.

Vol. 2213: M.J. van Sinderen, L.J.M. Nieuwenhuis (Eds.), Protocols for Multimedia Systems. Proceedings, 2001. XII, 239 pages. 2001.

Vol. 2214: O. Boldt, H. Jürgensen (Eds.), Automata Implementation. Proceedings, 1999. VIII, 183 pages. 2001.

Vol. 2215: N. Kobayashi, B.C. Pierce (Eds.), Theoretical Aspects of Computer Software. Proceedings, 2001. XV, 561 pages. 2001.

Vol. 2216: E.S. Al-Shaer, G. Pacifici (Eds.), Management of Multimedia on the Internet. Proceedings, 2001. XIV, 373 pages. 2001.

Vol. 2217: T. Gomi (Ed.), Evolutionary Robotics. Proceedings, 2001. XI, 139 pages. 2001.

Vol. 2218: R. Guerraoui (Ed.), Middleware 2001. Proceedings, 2001. XIII, 395 pages. 2001.

Vol. 2220: C. Johnson (Ed.), Interactive Systems. Proceedings, 2001. XII, 219 pages. 2001.

Vol. 2221: D.G. Feitelson, L. Rudolph (Eds.), Job Scheduling Strategies for Parallel Processing. Proceedings, 2001. VII, 207 pages. 2001.

Vol. 2233: J. Crowcroft, M. Hofmann (Eds.), Networked Group Communication. Proceedings, 2001. X, 205 pages. 2001.